West German
Poets
on Society
and Politics

West German Poets on Society and Politics

Interviews with an Introduction by
Karl H. Van D'Elden
Hamline University

Wayne State University Press   Detroit   1979

Copyright © 1979 by Wayne State University Press,
Detroit, Michigan 48202. All rights are reserved.
No part of this book may be reproduced without formal permission.

Library of Congress Cataloging in Publication Data

Main entry under title:

West German poets on society and politics

Bibliography: p.
Includes index.
1. Authors, German—20th century—Political and
social views—Addresses, essays, lectures. 2. Authors,
German—20th century—Interviews. 3. German literature
—20th century—History and criticism—Addresses,
essays, lectures. 4. Social problems in literatures.
5. Literature and society—Addresses, essays, lectures.
I. Van D'Elden, Karl H., 1923–
PT405.W38   831'.9'140931   78–20793
ISBN 0–8143–1628–X

In Memoriam
Philip Allison Shelley

contents

preface

Why a book on the political and social involvement—the *engagement*—of contemporary West German poets?

The publication of journals such as *Dimension* has made modern German poetry far more accessible to the English speaking reading public than it has been heretofore. Poetry currently being written in the Federal Republic of Germany can now be read, side by side with English translations, by individuals whose acquaintance with the literary scene in Germany had previously been severely limited. With this increased visibility of modern German poetry, questions may be raised regarding the position of the German poet in society and his sense of responsibility in a troubled world.

It is evident to scholars in the field of German literature that poets have been able to cope with the past and its sometimes sinister implications more effectively than have politicians. Many German poets have shed the shackles of provincialism and have become involved in the process of seeking solutions to the problems that affect not only their society but mankind as a whole, problems that are both social and political.

It is the purpose of this book to make contemporary German poetry available not only to students of German literature, but also to the general reading public. A selected bibliography is provided for those who may wish to examine in greater detail the works of specific poets or engagement in West German poetry.

The term *engaged* (German *engagiert*) is used throughout the text in the same sense as the French term *littérature engagée,* meaning literature which, in contrast to the *l'art pour l'art* approach, concerns itself with the dialectic relationship between mankind and society, literature which is critical of social and political conditions. I use

9

"engaged" for want of a clearer word to describe a poet's commitment and involvement in contemporary political and social affairs.

In selecting the poets to be considered I limited myself to living poets of the Federal Republic of Germany (FRG), and thus deliberately excluded Austrian poets, Swiss poets, and poets from the German Democratic Republic (GDR), as well as poets living in exile. Even though the poets included vary greatly in age (the oldest, Friedrich Georg Jünger, was born in 1898; the youngest, Jürgen Theobaldy, was born in 1944) they share a common heritage: that of the post-World War II years in the FRG, a nation closely allied politically and economically to Western Europe and to the United States. Had the sampling not thus been limited, a common denominator would have been lost. Since I am interested in the relationship between lyric poetry and social and political realities I had to be as rigorous as one experimenting in the natural sciences in establishing criteria. I even eliminated the prominent Peter Handke because, though now a resident of the FRG, he was raised as an Austrian and not as a German.

I invited some twenty-five poets, including three women, to participate in the project—sixteen accepted, including some of the best known poets of our day as well as others whose reputations (perhaps undeservedly) are limited to their home country. They disagree markedly on the role of the poet in today's society. I believe that the spectrum they represent is indeed a fair sampling, though I realize that another writer might well have selected different poets.

A number of the poems included in the book have been previously translated. But many of the translations, though poetically attractive, do not convey the poets' ideas as accurately as they might, chiefly because they were intuitively created rather than the result of a detailed discussion with the poets themselves. Where, in my judgment, adequate translations were available these have been used and credit is given in each instance. In some cases I prepared my own translations before I became aware of the existence of a previously published translation. All translations not specifically attributed to someone else are my own and reflect the insights gained during the interviews.

Poetry usually suffers by translation, but it is better to read a poet in translation than not at all. I hope, of course, that these translations will inspire some readers to learn the language to enable them to read German poetry in the original. I promise them an experience as worthwhile as that of reading Auden, Spender, and Allen Ginsberg in the original.

I have often wondered what great poets of the past would say if they could comment on the interpretations inflicted upon their poems by literature professors. I am convinced that their reactions to what is read into their words would range from approval to horror. The analyses in Hilde Domin's controversial anthology *Doppelinterpretationen* [Double interpretations] prove my point: critics often see in a poem ideas and motifs that were far from the poet's mind during the creative process—as Domin notes in my interview with her. For this reason, only the best evidence—the voice of the author—is used in this book. I must hasten to add, however, that while many of the poets I interviewed are happy to explicate their own poetry (a comment frequently found in their writings), others do not like to do so.

I reached the conclusion that a separate chapter on each poet would be the best solution to the problem of how to arrange the material. The format I followed is patterned after Serge Gavronsky's *Poems & Texts* (New York: October House, 1969). I considered grouping poets according to their degree of involvement but discarded the idea because no natural groupings became apparent. Instead, they are arranged chronologically, the oldest first, the youngest last. This order has the advantage that adjacently placed poets share approximately the same years of experience, were exposed to many of the same historical events of this century—events that affected their lives and attitudes, and thus helped shape the thoughts they express in their poems.

A series of standard questions was sent to the participating poets prior to the actual interviews, not to serve as a limiting factor, but to afford them an insight into my concerns (see Appendix). An accompanying letter emphasized that these questions were merely suggestions for discussion and, as the contents of the various chapters show, this list was used in varying degrees. In addition, I suggested discussion of certain poems and also invited the introduction of other poems considered relevant by the poets. In this manner there was some structure to facilitate comparisons, but this structure was sufficiently loose to allow for the personality differences that exist in as talented and as creative a group as these poets represent.

Most of the interviews were conducted entirely in German, some in both English and German (Hilde Domin and Friedrich

Georg Jünger). Except for Friedrich Georg Jünger, Ernst Meister, Peter Jokostra, and Walter Helmut Fritz, the interviews were tape-recorded in their entirety. All interview transcripts were prepared immediately after the interviews. Several poets requested to see the transcriptions before publication, a request that was honored in each case, and an appropriate notation accompanies each chapter.

In the interviews that follow, my interpolations (translations, comments, and clarifications) within the poets' responses appear in brackets; any interpolations by the poets are in parentheses. At the express request of my publisher, I have provided translations for all foreign titles cited in the text. Generally, the translations parenthetically follow the original titles, with poetry titles enclosed in quotation marks, and book titles set in italics. But, in instances where works are known principally by their German titles only, I have furnished literal word-for-word translations to aid readers unfamiliar with the language; these are set in brackets following the title, with only their first word capitalized.

A biographical listing of all names mentioned in the text is included in the subject index at the back of the book.

acknowledgments

I express my sincere appreciation to the following authors, their translators, and their publishers for permission to reprint certain works in this book:

Bender, Hans—"Der junge Soldat," "Der tote Gefangene," and "Heimkehr" from *Lyrische Biografie*, Wuppertal, n.p., 1957, by permission of the author.

Born, Nicolas—"Das Verschwinden aller im Tod eines einzelnen," and "Naturgedicht" from *Das Auge des Entdeckers*, das neue buch 21, Hamburg: Rowohlt, 1972, by permission of the author, of the Rowohlt Verlag, Reinbeck bei Hamburg, and of Sanford J. Greenburger Associates, New York (Foreign Publishers' Representatives).

Domin, Hilde—"Lied zur Ermutigung II," "Schneide das Augenlid ab," and "Postulat" by permission of the author. Translations were prepared by Tudor Morris in collaboration with the author, and are reprinted with the permission of both.

Fritz, Walter Helmut—"Vorwände," "Bald ohne Namen," and "Dezember 1944" by permission of the author and Hoffmann und Campe Verlag. Hoffmann und Campe published "Vorwände" and "Bald ohne Namen" in *Die Zuverlässigkeit der Unruhe* and "Dezember 1944" in *Aus der Nähe*. The translation of "Bald ohne Namen" ("Soon Without Name") will be included in a forthcoming anthology of new German poetry, translated by Ewald Osers, with whose permission it is reprinted here. "Das Wort Friede" by permission of the author.

13

Grass, Günter—"Pünktlich" from *Glasdreieck* (1960). "Irgendetwas machen" and "Neue Mystik" from *Ausgefragt* (1967), by permission of the author and of Luchterhand Verlag, Darmstadt and Neuwied. The translations "Do Something" and "New Mysticism" by Michael Hamburger are contained in the volume *New Poems* and are published here with the permission of Harcourt Brace Jovanovich.

Heise, Hans-Jürgen—"Quer" from *Uhrenvergleich* (Claassen, 1971). "Dich" from *Vorboten einer neuen Steppe* (Limes, 1961). "Aktennotiz" from *Besitzungen in Untersee* (Claassen, 1973), by permission of the author, of Limes Verlag, Munich, and of Claassen Verlag, GmbH Hamburg and Düsseldorf, (1973). The translation of "Dich" ("You") was first published in *Underseas Possessions*, Selected Poems by Hans-Jürgen Heise, Translated by Ewald Osers, The Oleander Press, Stoughton (Wisconsin) and Harrow (England), 1972. It also appears in *Stand*, Vol. 13, No. 2, 1972, and was broadcast on the BBC in 1974. It will be included in a forthcoming anthology of new German poetry, translated by Ewald Osers, with whose permission it is reprinted here.

Höllerer, Walter—"Der lag besonders mühelos am Rand," "Wie die hohe Mauer auch heißt," "Kinderlied für Florian gegen Wut zu singen," and "Der hat die Koffer getragen," all by permission of the author. The translation of "Der hat die Koffer getragen" ("He Carried the Suitcase") by A. Leslie Willson was first published in *Dimension* 3/1 (1970), and is reprinted here by permission of the translator.

Jokostra, Peter—"Ode an Lorca" by permission of the author. "Mururoa" by permission of the author and of Claassen Verlag, GmbH Hamburg and Düsseldorf.

Jünger, Friedrich Georg—"Vaterland" and "Abschiedslied" by permission of the author and of Hanseatische Verlagsanstalt, Hamburg. "Chimären" from *Schwarzer Fluß und windweißer Wald*, Frankfurt a.M.: Vittorio Klostermann, 1955, by permission of the author and of Vittorio Klostermann.

Keller, Hans Peter—"Kurzgeschichten aus der Geschichte," "Stacheldraht," and "Zeitzünder," all by permission of the author and of Limes Verlag, Wiesbaden and Munich.

ACKNOWLEDGMENTS

Krolow, Karl—"Die Macht" from *Alltägliche Gedichte* (1968); "Angesichte einer Landschaft" from *Gesammelte Gedichte* (1965); "Gar nicht lustig" from *Nichts weiter als Leben* (1970); all by permission of the author and of Suhrkamp Verlag, Frankfurt a.M.

Meckel, Christoph—"Was dieses Land betrifft" from *Wen es angeht. Gedichte* (1974), by permission of the author and Verlag Eremiten-Presse, Düsseldorf, West Germany. "Hymne" and "Flaschenpost für eine Sintflut" by permission of the author. "Der Pfau" from *Wildnisse. Gedichte*, S. Fischer Verlag, GmbH, Frankfurt a.M, 1962, by permission of the author and of S. Fischer Verlag. The translation by Christopher Middleton was first published in *German Writing Today*, ed. Christopher Middleton, Baltimore: Penguin Books, 1967, and is reprinted here with the permission of the translator.

Meister, Ernst—"Totenreich, darin Lebendiges sich träumt" from *Sage vom Ganzen den Satz* (1972). "Im Stalle zu B." and "Nahkampf auf einem Rosenfeld" from *Gedichte 1932/1964* (1964), all by permission of the author and of Hermann Luchterhand Verlag, Darmstadt and Neuwied.

Schnurre, Wolfdietrich—"Strophe," "Kassiber" ("Eine Staubwolke kam"), "Geschäftsmann," "Wohnzimmer," and "Wahrheit," all by permission of the author.

Theobaldy, Jürgen—"Bilder aus Amerika" by permission of the author. "Auf ein Foto des toten 'Che' Guevara" and "Ein Bier, bitte" from *Blaue Flecken*, Rowohlt, 1974, by permission of the author, of the Rowohlt Verlag, Reinbeck bei Hamburg, and of Sanford J. Greenburger Associates, New York (Foreign Publishers' Representatives).

Weyrauch, Wolfgang—"Das Vaterland," "Ezra Pound," "Einmaleins" (from *Die Spur*), and "Einmaleins" (from *Gesang um nicht zu Sterben*), all by permission of the author.

In addition, I am indebted to the German Academic Exchange Service (*Deutscher Akademischer Austauschdienst*) whose financial assistance supplemented my sabbatical income from Hamline University to enable me to prepare this study; to the library of the University of Vienna where I did most of my preliminary research under optimal conditions; and, of course, to the participating poets who gave generously of their time and were most hospitable during the interview phase. Special recognition is also due my wife Stephanie Cain Van D'Elden, who patiently read my manuscript and made many helpful suggestions. Finally, my thanks to Hamline University for providing clerical support for the preparation of most of the final manuscript.

introduction

Literature must be critical; it must evaluate unless it wants to renounce truth entirely. This is an often quoted pronouncement of Hans G Helms,[1] which expresses the task-oriented approach that distinguishes most of contemporary literature from the *l'art pour l'art* approach that denies to all art (and thus also to all literature) didactic functions.

But who assigns literature its tasks?[2] If we disregard the poets themselves, each of whom has his own conception of the motivating forces that compel the creative process, it is primarily the events of the times which, acting as a social or intellectual environment, consciously or unconsciously influence what a poet will write. Contemporary society will then pass judgment on his efforts. If a poet is particularly original or innovative he will initially meet with resistance and will have to struggle to establish himself, for the reading public is uncomfortable when suddenly confronted with a work that does not fall into conventional patterns, whether of form or of content.

One may well ask why literature is relevant in this commercialized and technological age. The answer may be found in Bertolt Brecht's concept that the world can be changed, indeed needs to be changed, but can only be changed by changing mankind—which is the province of the writer. But therewith a conflict between the traditional aesthetic expectations of literature and the frequently

---

[1]Cf. Martin Doehlemann, "Zur gesellschaftlichen Rolle des heutigen Schriftstellers," in *Poesie und Politik. Zur Situation der Literatur in Deutschland*, ed. Wolfgang Kuttenkeuler (Stuttgart: W. Kohlhammer, 1973), pp. 32–42.

[2]Cf. Peter Suhrkamp, "Die Aufgabe der Literatur," *Welt und Wort* 15 (1960): 175–76.

17

tendentious nature of engaged poetry immediately comes into focus.

Politically and socially involved poetry is activist by nature. It wants to intervene, advance causes, topple systems and replace them with something better. It is practical and conscious of a mission. Yet, when read by later generations it often loses its impact, unlike the great classics which transcend specific times and convey a message of lasting value generations later. But engaged poetry need not be limited in its effectiveness to the time of its conception. As Benno von Wiese[3] noted a generation ago: Is not all great literature tendentious? Does it not seek new values?

There are many arguments pro and con as to the significance of engaged poetry and the role of the poet. Peter Handke, for example, states that he cannot be an engaged author because he knows of no alternatives, except for anarchism, to existing conditions.[4] A number of poets consider engagement to be beneath the lofty purposes to which a poet should dedicate his efforts. Some challenge the poet to exemplify his engagement by his attitude. Others question whether the poem is the best vehicle for the expression of engagement. Still others cite Pablo Neruda's success in reading in football stadiums as the ultimate in engagement. The ensuing interviews reflect the diversity of opinion.

Our concern is with lyric poetry only. Such poetry expresses direct and usually intense personal emotion, as distinguished from epic or dramatic works which are primarily narrative in nature. Therefore, the present status of politically and socially involved poetry in the Federal Republic of Germany is best revealed, first of all, by an understanding of the basic scope of lyric poetry.

Martin Pfeifer, for example, asserts that lyric poetry enables us to experience that which cannot be expressed verbally. Of the three genres (dramatic, epic, and lyric poetry) only lyric poetry offers almost unlimited possibilities of expression. It alone permits myriad imaginary excursions without fixing, by means of specific facts, locale and time. It thus gains in universal validity, which is especially true when the reader finds an apparent reinforcement or

---

[3]Benno von Wiese, *Politische Dichtung Deutschlands* (Berlin: Junker und Dünnhaupt, 1931), p. 17.
[4]Peter Handke, *Prosa Gedichte Theaterstücke Hörspiele Aufsätze* (Frankfurt a.M.: Suhrkamp, 1969), p. 270.

confirmation of his existing notions. Yet such truth is more difficult to convey in the case of modern poetry which may initially appear to be the mere playing of word games.[5]

Hilde Domin believes that the lyric poet's activities never change, regardless of the age in which he lives, that lyric poetry primarily offers a pause in which time stands still.[6] The poet praises, even when he condemns. Lyric poetry is no longer a flight from reality but has become a prerequisite for progress, because it contributes so materially to human communication and understanding, even if it is not politically oriented; in any case, it acts as a seismograph of its time which, by reporting disquieting disturbances, enhances consciousness. Domin uses the term "unspecific accuracy" with respect to poetry and contrasts it with the "specific accuracy" of the natural sciences: the latter describes and analyzes individual or single occurrences, categorizes them and fits them into an overall pattern; the former does not want to dominate or arrange reality, but wishes to create a superior potential reality. It is important, she asserts, that "unspecific accuracy" not be confused with "inaccuracy," an accusation that has at times been leveled against poetry.

Anyone who attempts to analyze an art form such as lyric poetry from a scientific perspective runs the danger of "labeling" that which should be taken at face value, of applying inappropriately impersonal criteria to one of the most delicate products of creative minds. It is not our purpose to use poetry to demonstrate political and sociological theories. Rather, it is our intent to add to the understanding and appreciation of poetry by calling attention to two of its many facets: its political and social functions. Poetry not only describes emotions shared by all or most of its readers; it also, in many instances, reflects the concerns of its author, who, after all, is a member of the society for which and in which he writes, and who has a stake in its progress toward an ever elusive but nonetheless enticing ideal.[7]

Victor Hugo expressed a conception of the poet as seer:

[5]Martin Pfeifer, "Unsagbarkeit-Erlebbarkeit," *Blätter für den Deutschlehrer* 12 (1968): 14–16.

[6]Hilde Domin, *Wozu Lyrik heute. Dichtung und Leser in der gesteuerten Gesellschaft* (Munich: R. Piper, 1968), esp. pp. 13, 23.

[7]Cf. Theodor W. Adorno, "Rede über Lyrik und Gesellschaft," in *Noten zur Literatur* 1 (Frankfurt a.M.: Suhrkamp, 1963): 73–104.

In ungodly days the poet
Comes to prepare better ones.
He represents utopia
With his feet here, his eyes elsewhere. . . .

Max Rychner added that the poet must, like a prophet, regardless of criticism, proudly carry a torch that will illuminate the future.[8]

But engaged poetry does more than simply record the present or presage the future of a changing society. It also illustrates changing ideological trends, both political and sociological. As the following chapters illustrate, neither critics nor poets agree on the precise scope of either the "political" or the "social" aspects of engagement. Frequently such concerns overlap. Generally, however, politically involved poetry deals with contemporary political problems, most frequently in the poet's own country, but often beyond this narrow sphere of interest. By contrast, socially involved poetry concerns itself with the more general problems of mankind in modern society, be they economic, the results of various kinds of discrimination, or the product of the arbitrary and unjust stratifications that pervade most societies.

To be engaged it is not necessary that a poem name places, names, or events, as long as its message is clearly understandable to discerning contemporaries. To take an example from English literature: Shelley's "Ode to the West Wind" (1819) clearly contains both a political and a social message even though his concerns about the widening gap between wealth and poverty in England are not specifically expressed in it.

The political function of engaged poetry is not limited to concentration on specific internal affairs of a particular state or nation but includes any aspect of politics which evokes a poet's comments. The world-wide reaction of poets to the recent involvement of the United States in Southeast Asia is a convincing example of engaged poetry's political concern, demonstrating that such poetry encompasses the moral and the ethical elements of politics and not just those secular affairs which immediately affect the political lives of both the poet and his reading public.

Poetry that is strictly political presents a problem of quality, however. Banal verses that might be classified as propagandistic, such as the "Horst-Wessel-Lied"[Horst-Wessel song] which Hitler

---

[8]Hans Holthusen, *Plädoyer für den Einzelnen* (Munich: R. Piper, 1967), p. 17.

elevated to the status of a second national anthem, or the *Agitprop* ("agitation and propaganda") poetry that serves similar purposes of the extreme left today, are excluded from our examination of contemporary West German poetry. This exclusion is not based on an ideological judgment, but on a qualitative one. Most products of Nazi poets, for example, simply do not measure up to the aesthetic standards implied for "lyric poetry" as a genre.

While there is by no means unanimity among poets and critics regarding the proper political role of the poet in society, Karl August Horst[9] suggests that a distinction should be made between the ideal of personal leadership as exemplified in Hermann Hesse's *Glasperlenspiel* [*The Glass Bead Game*, best known in English as *Magister Ludi*], which summarizes Hesse's artistic and spiritual aspirations, and the ideal of engagement, which Horst considers to be more narrowly directed toward a specific situation, as in Saint-Exupéry's conception that flying offers man the supreme opportunity to test his mettle and to transcend his limitations. For the contemporary poet, Horst cautions that engagement which lacks idealism runs the risk of becoming an empty gesture.

Peter Handke claims that it is the task of literature to effect changes in the personalities of its readers. He bases his theory on the recognition that literature changed him, that literature enabled him to live at an enhanced level of consciousness. By extension, he argues that he is convinced that he can change others through his literary works.[10] Yet, Handke contradicts himself when he asserts that he can use literature to effect changes in mankind but later denounces engaged writers by denying them their status as "writers" and then redefining them as politicians who "write" what they mean to "say."

The originator of the term *littérature engagée*, Jean-Paul Sartre, distinguishes between "authors" who use prose as their medium and "poets" who write lyric poetry. He demands that authors become engaged, that is, endeavor to expose and thereby change existing conditions, while granting that poets have no such duty—a position that Handke considers untenable.[11]

---

[9]Karl-August Horst, "Der Schriftsteller und seine Öffentlichkeit," *Studium Generale* 23 (1970): 698–709, esp. 701.

[10]Handke, esp. pp. 264, 269.

[11]Handke, pp. 278–81.

Martin Walser,[12] in a radio address of May 7, 1967, subsequently published and amended by four postscripts, attacks the
grandstanding of authors who claim to be politically and socially
concerned and challenges them to be positively engaged rather than
meaninglessly occupied in endorsing political candidates, primarily
on the left of the political spectrum.

Dieter Wellershoff[13] rather boldly compares the function of
literature with that of a space capsule simulator: the author may
transcend practical experience without risk in his search for new
models. The reader of the literary work thus created can safely leave
his established patterns and vicariously gain new experiences which
he would otherwise avoid at any cost. Literature, a simulation of life,
may include innovative or even alien ideas and activities; it need not
conform to the rules of society. It does not imitate society but is
juxtaposed to it. But if the author has the right to create his own
alternative world he must also be permitted to promulgate the laws
that govern this world. To do this, an author must be able to lock his
door and isolate himself, a practice which, to Wellerhoff's regret,
society no longer condones.

Brecht stated that poetry could no longer exist in modern
society if its production and consumption were dependent upon the
exclusion of rational criteria, because human feelings (instincts,
emotions) are in constant conflict with basic economic interests.
Walter Hinderer[14] sees evidence for this conflict in the prevalence of
pragmatic rhetoric in contemporary political poetry, which he distinguishes from the political song that uses deliberate emotionalism
and music to convey its message.

When Brecht's criteria are applied to literature in general,
ideas such as those of Peter Weiss[15] are their logical extension. Weiss
deliberately addresses himself to the largest possible audience in
order to achieve a maximum effect of his words, which are designed
to convey a specific political message to the "consumers" of his
literary production. He considers utmost precision of expression

[12]Martin Walser, "Engagement als Pflichtfach für Schriftsteller," in *Heimatkunde. Aufsätze und Reden*, ed. Martin Walser (Frankfurt a.M.: Suhrkamp, 1968).

[13]Dieter Wellershoff, *Literatur und Veränderung. Versuche zu einer Metakritik der
Literatur* (Cologne, Berlin: Kiepenheuer und Witsch, 1969).

[14]Walter Hinderer, "Probleme politischer Lyrik heute," in *Poesie und Politik*,
ed. Wolfgang Kuttenkeuler (Stuttgart: Kohlhammer, 1973), pp. 91–136.

[15]*Materialien zu Peter Weiss' "Marat/Sade"*, compiled by Karlheinz Braun
(Frankfurt a.M.: Suhrkamp, 1967).

paramount to ensure the greatest possible impact of his opinions. Aware that he is read in both East and West, he carefully takes into consideration that the Western reader expects an aesthetic or spiritual experience while his audience "on the opposite side" looks for a practical (that is, rational) function in any work of art, recognizing the dichotomy which, if ignored, could render him ineffective with either or both potential audiences. His decision: to write for the "world," to depict the truths which he seeks to represent.

As early as 1950 Wolfgang Weyrauch[16] called poets "physicians" and claimed that what they write constitutes the handwriting on the wall. Hans Holthusen[17] equates the problem of the writer with the famous "Gretchenfrage" ("Gretchen's question") from Goethe's *Faust*, transposing Gretchen's "Tell me what religion means to you!" ("Wie hast du's mit der Religion?"), a question which Faust had answered evasively, to read "Tell me what politics mean to you!" ("Wie hast du's mit der Politik?"). Holthusen recalls that political poetry in the Germany of the thirties was beyond discussion, that intellectuals regarded it as tendentious and thus inferior. This attitude which demanded that all poetry be beyond and above politics was in effect an admission of a lost battle for political freedom in Germany. He continues that this apolitical attitude, which resulted in a flight to Rilke, Hölderlin, and Stifter, could, on the one hand, be condemned as an admission of failure, and, on the other hand, be recognized as a form of political nonconformity, a form of passive resistance.

For the reader as well as the literary critic, socially engaged poetry presents difficulties similar to those encountered with politically engaged poetry. Peter Demetz expresses the dilemma in confronting a contemporary text as follows:

> By training and, often, by personal inclination, the literary scholar feels tempted to consider himself a stranger, if not a displaced person, among sociologists concerned with the future of society. He usually keeps his eyes close to texts that always belong to the past (even if he reads a story written two weeks ago . . .).[18]

[16]Ernst Nef, "Wolfgang Weyrauch," in *Schriftsteller der Gegenwart*, ed. Klaus Nonnenmann (Olten and Freiburg i.B.: Walter, 1963), p. 313.

[17]Holthusen, pp. 11, 42–45.

[18]Peter Demetz, "Literary Scholarship: Past and Future," *Comparative Literature Studies* (Urbana) 10 (1973): 364.

Hans Norbert Fügen[19] probably comes closest to a working definition of socially involved literature. He hypothesizes that, if sociology is the science which deals with the processes and structures of interhuman behavior, and if literature depicts a series of events which makes no claim to empirically provable factuality yet is based on truthfulness in principle, then the sociology of literature is that branch of sociology which examines literary works for their objectivity of treatment of social behavior. It further concerns itself with the interpersonal behavior from which the production, tradition, diffusion, and reception of fictional works emanates. He calls this interhuman activity "literary behavior" (*literarisches Verhalten*).

Engaged poetry has a long and distinguished history in Germany going back to the Middle Ages. Although little evidence of German poetry survives from the tenth century, there is a poem entitled "De Heinrico," half in German and half in Latin, by an unknown poet, which apparently tells of the reconciliation of an Emperor Otto and a Duke Henry, though its implications are impossible to reconcile with available historical data. Walther von der Vogelweide, the greatest poet of medieval Germany (ca. 1170–ca. 1228), is generally considered the creator of politically and socially concerned poetry in Germany; he achieved considerable poetic heights in this new genre. Walther adopted the simple form of the *Spruch* (in its oldest form a one-strophe poem of satiric or didactic content) for his political poetry. After the death of Emperor Henry VI he was deeply troubled by the rivalry for the vacant throne of the Holy Roman Empire, which brought the Empire (and thus Germany) to the brink of civil war. He also observed and commented on the ever increasing political ambitions of Pope Innocent III. Walther's example was followed by many other poets throughout succeeding centuries. It would lead too far afield to mention more than a few highlights: Hans Sachs (1494–1576), perhaps the greatest of the Meistersingers, wrote partisan poetry on the side of Martin Luther at another very troubled time in German history and German politics. The Thirty Years' War, most of which was fought on German soil, prompted an outpouring of politically inspired poetry and antiwar poetry. Much of it has been lost; much of what survives is of questionable literary merit. One name must be mentioned, that

[19]Hans Norbert Fügen, ed., *Wege der Literatursoziologie*, Soziologische Texte, Vol. 46 (Neuwied and Berlin: Luchterhand, 1968), pp. 18–19.

24

of Friedrich von Logau (1604–55), Germany's finest epigrammatist, an astute observer of his time and one of the few who saw things clearly in a time of bloody religious strife.

A century later, Johann Wilhelm Ludwig Gleim (1719–1803), otherwise chiefly known for his mediocre Anacreontic imitations, became famous through his *Preußische Kriegslieder von einem Grenadier (Prussian War Songs of a Grenadier)*, of 1758, inspired by the Seven Years' War (even though Gleim himself had never been exposed to the smell of gunpowder). The patriotic enthusiasm of these poems recommended them to his contemporaries, who were not disconcerted by their chilling classical imagery.[20] In a way, he might be considered the somewhat inferior precursor of the political and patriotic lyric inspired by the fervid patriotism of the Napoleonic era. The Wars of Liberation (1812–15) inspired a lyric outburst which is astounding in sheer quantity. Three of the poets of this era cannot be omitted from even a brief discussion: Ernst Moritz Arndt (1769–1860), Max von Schenkendorf (1783–1817), and Karl Theodor Körner (1791–1813), who kindled the imagination of the German people through his heroic death in combat. Arndt, the oldest and most influential of the three, is stylistically a descendant of the political *Volkslieder* ("folksongs") of the Thirty Years' War. He wrote in an earnestly spiritual vein, using an almost Biblical language, to inspire sacrifice and total devotion in what he considered to be a holy war. The opening words of his "Vaterlandslied" [Song of the fatherland] suffice as an example: "Der Gott, der Eisen wachsen ließ,/Der wollte keine Knechte . . ." ("The God who created iron ore / does not approve of slavery . . ."). While his poetry witnesses fervent patriotism, his prose envisions a united Germany and new politics. Where Arndt looked toward a brighter and more just future, Schenkendorf, perhaps the most gifted poet of the three, sought his inspiration in the glory of the Middle Ages and dreamed of a revival of the old German empire. Körner gained his poetic fame posthumously: his father, in 1814, published his political and patriotic poetry in the volume *Leyer und Schwerdt (Lyre and Sword)*.[21]

As previously stated, the poem that is closely tied to the events of its time almost never becomes a classic. Yet there are two exceptions in the literary history of Germany, the political *Sprüche* of

[20]Cf. J. G. Robertson, *A History of German Literature*, 6th ed. (New York: London House and Maxwell, 1970), p. 231.
[21]Robertson, pp. 392–95.

Walther von der Vogelweide and the lyric poetry of the Napoleonic era, both of which were the products of great national emergencies. The poets of the Romantic era "discovered" the Middle High German literary past and drew inspiration from it. There is a traceable connection between Hoffmann von Fallersleben's interest in Middle High German poetry and the song that made him immortal and was destined to become the national anthem of Germany: "Deutschland, Deutschland über alles."[22]

The German poetry of the Napoleonic era was inspired by a threat from abroad, and it was not too great a step from a cry for freedom from foreign domination to a demand for freedom from internal oppression. Feudalism was rapidly approaching the moment of truth. Poets like Johann Ludwig Uhland (1787–1862), Adalbert von Chamisso (1781–1838), and Heinrich Heine (1791–1856) called upon the consciences of their fellow Germans to demand an end of feudalism. Uhland's *Vaterländische Gedichte* (*Patriotic Poems*) of 1816 were the forerunners of the political poetry of the forties. Chamisso, a French nobleman who at one time in his life was seriously torn between French and German as a medium of expression, imitated Béranger's political lyric, and his poems in turn proved a significant influence on later political poets. And Heine, as he himself expressed it in *Deutschland, ein Wintermärchen* (*Germany, A Winter's Tale*), had in his political poetry written much that was punishable by execution by firing squad. Political poetry was beginning to move away from the low esteem expressed in the often quoted line from Goethe's *Faust*: "Ein garstig Lied, pfui, ein politisch Lied" ("A nasty song! Fie! A political song!").

The political ferment that had begun in the Napoleonic era erupted in the Revolution of 1848, which transcended political boundaries in Europe and signalled the beginning of the end of feudalism. With the revolution came the revolutionary lyric, which, as early as 1840 with the Rhine poems of Becker, Schneckenburger, and Prutz, had cried out against the forces of reaction. Heinrich Hoffmann von Fallersleben was dismissed from his university teaching position in 1842 because of two volumes of *Unpolitische Gedichte* (*Nonpolitical Poems*). When called upon to explain his poetry, he defended himself in words which are of special significance here:

[22]Cf. Johannes Klein, *Geschichte der deutschen Lyrik*, 2nd ed. (Wiesbaden: Franz Steiner, 1960), p. 554.

26

> I cannot and will not interpret my poems, and I believe that a poet
> should never be requested to do this, nor should he be held responsi-
> ble for his state of mind [*Stimmung*]. Poets depict the state of mind of
> the time in which they live. That has always been the case . . .[23]

His poetry combined protest against feudalism with a deep conviction that the German people were destined to fulfill an important
mission in Europe and the world. Ferdinand Freiligrath (1810–1876)
suffered greatly for his convictions, was forced to live in exile on
several occasions, published revolutionary poems as early as 1844,
and saw in the national victories of 1870–71 an opportunity for a
united Germany in which social justice could finally be established.
His two little volumes of poetry, published in 1849 and 1851, which
contain the best poetry of the revolutionary age, bore the title *Neuere
politische und soziale Gedichte (More Recent Political and Social Poems)*,
thus combining the social concept with the political one for the first
time in the title of a literary work.

Georg Herwegh (1817–75), a socialist, led the stormiest life of
the major political poets of the 1840s. Exiled several times, he led a
group of some eight hundred freedom fighters into Germany during
the Revolution of 1848 with the intention of establishing a republic,
an idea whose time had not yet come. His effort met with total
disaster. He fled once again and did not return until after the
amnesty of 1866. In his political poetry he called for involvement in
party politics, a considerably different perspective of that of his
fellow poets, who generally shunned the practical aspects of social
and political change and preferred to limit themselves to loftier,
though perhaps less practical, discussions of ideas and ideals. Herwegh's poem "Die Partei" ("The Party") maintains in stirring
rhetoric that only he who joins the shock troops of a party can hope
to achieve his goals for humanity in general. Generalities will not
produce results, he felt, and his poetry contains language reminiscent of stirring speeches of the French Revolution. Both Heine and
Emanuel Geibel (1815–84) wrote poems entitled "An Georg Herwegh" ("To Georg Herwegh") Heine predicting sarcastically that
Herwegh's visions would fail, and Geibel expressing disapproval of
Herwegh's radicalism.

The nineteenth century was characterized by a liberal
bourgeoisie in whose breasts stirred the desire to break the shackles

[23]Klein, p. 556.

of a monarchy that was quickly becoming anachronistic. But after the founding of the Second Reich in 1871 a wave of nationalism swept Germany. Dreams of imperial grandeur saw her acquire colonies and it appeared almost as though the clock of progress had been turned back successfully. However, the defeat in World War I and the disastrous and reckless adventures of National Socialism, culminating in the almost total destruction and subsequent partition of Germany, established democracy in two stages: a fitful, timid start in the Weimar Republic, and, after the traumatic interruption by the Third Reich, the Federal Republic of Germany, a nation with a young but strong tradition of implementing the dreams of earlier generations, though not without a multitude of problems. Since this book is exclusively concerned with the poets of the FRG, the in many ways quite different developments in the GDR will not be discussed.

One cannot escape noticing semantic changes in the German vocabulary when examining political and social poetry historically. There is, for example, no recognizable similarity between the *Vaterland* ("fatherland") concept of Arndt or Friedrich Georg Jünger and that of the Nazi propagandist Alfred Rosenberg (1893–1946). Much of the political poetry that inspired National Socialism was written years before 1933; literary histories published in both East and West Germany are remarkably silent with respect to the writers of National Socialism, while others, like Wedekind, Kraus, Tucholsky, and Brecht, whose ideologies are acceptable, receive their fair share of coverage. Not that they do not deserve it. Karl Kraus (1874–1936), born in Bohemia to wealthy Jewish parents, but a resident of Vienna for most of his life, characterized himself with the words: "Where they subjugated life to a lie I was a revolutionary . . . Where they used freedom as an empty word I was a reactionary."[24] He prophesied the disasters that lay ahead for Europe in his journal *Die Fackel (The Torch)*, which appeared from 1899 until his death and which, from 1911 on, contained exclusively his own poetry, aphorisms, and essays. He condemned mediocrity, demanded that language be treated with respect, and, during the 1930s, aroused the ire of the National Socialists by efforts such as his parody of Joseph Goebbels's pompous tirades. Frank Wedekind (1864–1918), a dramatist and satirist, rejected middle-class morality, immersing

[24]Wilhelm Duwe, *Deutsche Dichtung des 20. Jahrhunderts* (Zurich: Orell Füssli, 1962), 1: 413.

himself in a world of criminals, prostitutes, and bohemians. His poems, less well known than his plays, show a keen political awareness and an almost prophetic gift. Even before Germany decided to expand her navy in 1898, he warned against the consequences in the poem "Von der deutschen Flotte" ("About the German Navy"), which begins with the lines:

O Deutschland, Deutschland, wird sie niemals enden
des alten Irrwahns mörderische Lust!

Germany, oh Germany. Won't the murderous lust
of the old insanity ever come to an end!

Other poems written around the turn of the century similarly reflect voices in the wilderness. Erich Kästner once described Kurt Tucholsky (1895–1935) as a "little, fat Berliner, who wanted to stem a catastrophe with his typewriter." A passionate enemy of militarism and fascism, Tucholsky sensed the rise of National Socialism in the 1920s when many other Germans deluded themselves with the hope that the Weimar Republic would eventually bring a true democracy to Germany. His keen wit and humor were appreciated by his contemporaries, but he made his real contribution as a political satirist, who recognized that martial folly had not stopped with the demise of the Second Reich: it lived on in the goose-stepping *Reichswehr*, the 100,000 man army which the Treaty of Versailles permitted a defeated Germany to maintain. In his poems he recognized the interplay between economic despair and political brinksmanship. And when, after he was forced to leave Germany in 1935, he recognized that his worst fears were coming true, he took his own life while in exile in Sweden.

Bertolt Brecht (1898–1956) has been the subject of so many books and articles that it would be redundant to discuss him at length here. Suffice it to say that this product of a middle-class family, a former medical student, developed such an intense hatred for war and all of its horrors during his stint as an orderly in a military hospital in the First World War that he devoted the rest of his life to political and social reform. Although he embraced Marxism, it should never be forgotten that he was far from popular in the GDR after he criticized the brutal suppression of the abortive revolt of June 17, 1953.

As Werner Neuse pointed out in his article "Poetry in the

Third Reich,"[25] German commentators of the Nazi era liked to divide their "poets" into two categories, the *Rufer* ("hailers") and the *Dichter* ("poets"). The former served as inspiring heralds during the political struggles that led to the takeover in 1933 and continued in that role as unashamed mouthpieces of the "movement," while the latter were lyricists, sometimes of considerable poetic talent, who actively participated in the national life of their country and thus prostituted their art to a regime which they should have despised. Among the latter, at least for a time, was Gottfried Benn (1886–1956), who, in a eulogy honoring Stefan George (1868–1933), insisted that he could hear the spirit of an "imperative world order" reminiscent of the marching columns of the "brown battalions" in George's art. George, however, wanted no part of National Socialism, despite Nazi attempts to court him; when Propaganda Minister Joseph Goebbels tried to force upon him an award from his government, George went into exile in Switzerland where he died later in the same year. How deeply George resented National Socialism can be deduced from his testamentary refusal to be buried on German soil.

Gerhard Schumann (1911–   ) was perhaps the most gifted of the Nazi poets, a member of the *Reichskultursenat* (Senate for Arts and Culture), of the board of directors of the *Reichskulturkammer* (Chamber for Arts and Culture), and an officer in the "SA" (*Sturmabteilung*, the Nazi "Storm Troopers"). He wrote occasional poetry and even "cantatas" praising Nazi ideas. Also among the best known Nazi poets were Hans Baumann (1914–   ) and Erwin Guido Kolbenheyer (1878–1962). Baumann became famous through the song "Es zittern die morschen Knochen" ("The Crumbling Bones are Trembling"), which he wrote as an eighteen-year-old student in 1932, and which contains the infamous refrain:

Wir werden weitermarschieren
wenn alles in Scherben fällt,
denn heute gehört uns Deutschland
und morgen die ganze Welt.

We shall march onward and onward
though everything crumbles into shambles,
for today Germany is ours
and tomorrow all of the world.

[25]Werner Neuse, "Poetry in the Third Reich," *Books Abroad* 12 (1933): 14–16.

Although many of Baumann's songs were heavily tainted by Nazi ideology, his other songs survive on their merits and are found in many German songbooks today: "Gute Nacht, Kameraden" ("Good Night, Comrades"), "In die Welt will ich reiten" ("I Want to Ride into the World"), "Wollt im Winter ein Brieflein schreiben" ("I Wanted to Write a Letter Last Winter"), to cite but a few examples. Kolbenheyer's work, which preached the racist doctrine that the decadent peoples of Mediterranean Europe were destined to be dominated by the Germanic peoples from the north, has mercifully sunk into oblivion, although he gained new notoriety at a celebration in his honor in Munich in 1954 where he greeted his ideological comrades by thrice raising his arm in a Nazi salute.

It is difficult to decide who should be included in a brief survey, but a fourth Nazi poet surely deserves mentioning, chiefly because he had shown so much early promise. Hanns Johst (1890–   ) began his career as a gifted expressionist. He turned away from pacifism as early as 1919, rose to the rank of brigade commander in the "SS" (*Schutz-Staffel*, the Nazi "Blackshirts"), and was convicted as a war criminal in 1949. Political zealotry induced him to write the panegyric "Dem Führer," which might well be dubbed the most ridiculous and despicable poem of that era for its equating the reaction to Hitler's smile with the joy of a believer at the sight of the monstrance.

The defeat of Germany in 1945 brought with it strongly apolitical reaction. But all wounds heal, and at this writing two politically, economically, and socially different Germanies face one another across minefields. Both countries have mounted incredible efforts toward rehabilitation, and in both there are new voices among the poets that concern themselves with the past, the present, and the future. The following chapters present some of the most prominent and most significant poetic reactions to political and social concerns in the Federal Republic of Germany.

While the poets I interviewed speak clearly enough for themselves, their positions can be briefly outlined.

Friedrich Georg Jünger (1898–1977) rejects social engagement as a matter of principle because he harbors a deep distrust of sociology as a discipline. He maintains that sociology can feed only upon the carcass of a decaying society. Nor does he advocate political engagement; instead he demands that a poet focus all his efforts on his primary mission: the creation of good poetry. Although some of Jünger's poems caused problems for him in the Third Reich and thus, at least in my opinion, recognizably demonstrated his concerns for what was happening in Germany under National Socialism, he insists that engagement smacks of subordination to someone else's ideas and should be beneath the dignity of a true poet.

Wolfgang Weyrauch (b. 1907) focuses on the individual as a part of society. He demands that the writer—unlike the effete poet of the past—concern himself with conditions in the world in general and in his country in particular. The writer must be humane and, therefore, must discuss everything that is inhumane. A humane attitude begins with the apparently insignificant details of interpersonal relationships; only if this attitude exists there can it pervade all of society. While Weyrauch considers himself engaged, he also cautions that literary-political engagement cannot occur incessantly: occasional detachment is necessary.

Ernst Meister (b. 1911) has given much thought to an analysis of the creative process. He considers the professional polemicists suspect and believes that poets who occasionally, and only when acting under a genuine compulsion, become politically involved are far more effective. His own engagement reached an apex after World War II. He remains horrified by the violent death that is inflicted upon so many human beings even today, for he believes that death should instead be an aesthetic act.

Peter Jokostra (b. 1912) considers conscious engagement ahumane and tendentious, particularly when it occurs in response to a tide in which poets join for materialistic reasons. Politicians should not write poetry and poets should eschew politics. Jokostra is neither prepared to die for the fiction of the fatherland nor for the fiction of poetry. He rejects any and all prosodic theories, claiming that the form of his poems is never the result of a conscious process; he demands total spontaneity. But if an event compels a poet to deal with it poetically the resulting poem can have artistic validity.

The poem is a "guarantor of freedom," Hilde Domin (b. 1912) asserts. The poet writes when he receives a "secret order" to express his crucial experiences by formulating them as "model experiences." This requires the courage to speak out and faith in the responsiveness of the reader. According to Domin, each reader, in turn, because of what he has gained by exposure to a poem, exerts his influence on others. A poem cannot be programmed to effect a political or social result—it is a spontaneous creation. If it helps to improve mankind, the poem has fulfilled its noblest purpose, she believes.

Hans Peter Keller (b. 1915) wants to influence individuals, not masses. He sees a process of germination, which then results in radiation of ideas to the reader's neighbors and in ultimate transfer to society as a whole. For him engagement is a matter of attitude rather than of content. He rejects high sounding slogans, but wants to promote skepticism which, in turn, will promote progress.

A subtle unveiling of disproportions in human society is needed, asserts Karl Krolow (b. 1915). Poems cannot change the world, but they do influence people who, depending upon their readiness to do so, may contribute to a positive evolution of society. Some poets, like the Russian Yevgeny Yevtuchenko, can move the masses, but they tread on dangerous ground, as did the poets of the Nazi era. Krolow views the politicizing of literature with great reservations. Even if a poem is written in response to a current event, it must clearly transcend the situation that occasioned it. The poet should not expect immediate effectiveness, nor would this be desirable. If only one reader's perspective is changed, the effect will have been worthwhile.

How dangerous political poetry can be is illustrated by Hans Bender (b. 1919) as follows: a couple of days *before* Rosa Luxemberg's assassination a Berlin newspaper published a poem advocating such an act. Did the assassin see this poem? We will never know, but the inference is frightening. Nevertheless, says Bender, there should no longer be a poem without a message that communicates the subjective engagement of its author. He demands that the poet use simple (as opposed to "academic") language to express experiences that strike reponsive chords in others.

Contrary to his much publicized statement of 1961, Wolfdietrich Schnurre (b. 1920) no longer asserts that poets must be the conscience of the nation. They should rather act as seismographs who can, at times, give an early warning of impending disaster. When Schnurre writes, he claims to be totally asocial: he does not think socially, nor does he care who his ultimate reader may be. He does, however, classify his work into purely literary poems and utilitarian poems, the former limited in their appeal to an elitist audience, the latter designed to reach a larger reading public. The quintessence of his message is: If you put your money on the

33

powerless and the nonviolent, you can accomplish something great.

Walter Höllerer (b. 1922) has lost some of the faith he used to have in the efficacy of the poem to inspire social and political change. He now places his emphasis on an attempt to create the feeling of being touched *(Betroffenheit)*, which in turn leads to a cognitive process in the reader. This he considers to be his engagement. He tries to be understandable by avoiding, if possible, post-surrealistic metaphors. While he consciously disassociates himself from concrete poetry, he does acknowledge that some of his most recent poems create the first impression of being concrete because of their unusual arrangement of lines. But his lines, like those of Charles Olson, are designed to alert the reader to breathing intervals and thus to facilitate comprehension of the poems.

Günter Grass (b. 1927), like Schnurre, defines the writing of a poem as an asocial process, and he too rejects the concept of the writer as the "conscience of the nation." But as a "citizen with special abilities" the writer should participate in the political process. He considers engagement to be inevitable and even describes determined nonengagement as a form of engagement. But he does not mean that a poet should use the lyric as a vehicle for expressing ideas better suited for inclusion in an editorial or a political speech: the message must be suitable for the medium selected, he asserts. To him poetry is the most elementary and existential of all modes of expression and the only literary form sure to survive.

Grass's premise meets with the approval of Walter Helmut Fritz (b. 1929), who also considers all literature to be engaged: because it is devoid of practical utility it creates freedom, and while it cannot change reality, it can affect concepts of reality. Fritz attempts to influence reality by using language as economically as possible, often fragmentary sentences designed to create in the reader a feeling for what the poet wants to express, by forcing the reader to participate in the creative process.

Any artist who totally consigns himself to politics will ultimately become a politician in the view of Hans-Jürgen Heise (b. 1930). Politics is not the function of the writer, who should instead lead his reader into the almost lost catacombs of the psychic elements within man. When the reader has been induced by the writer to recognize the interior of the social creature called man, the writer has fulfilled his engagement. The beautiful in art is a psychic and spiritual necessity, Heise believes. Among his own concerns, ecology occupies a prominent position. Heise suggests that the reader of poetry will often discover implicit interpretative possibilities that never occurred to the writer. Like Grass, Heise is convinced that the poem has the greatest prospect for survival of all existing literary genres.

In the opinion of Christoph Meckel (b. 1935), there is no such phenomenon as a purely political poem, since a living poem by its very nature has an infinite number of foregrounds and backgrounds. He tries to make his poems as complex, inclusive, opulent, and extensive as possible. Contrary to the elitist perspective regarding poetry, which is embraced by many scholars and some poets, Meckel considers the general reading public to be far more gifted than it realizes itself. He rejects the term *engagement* because it has been overused. A poet should embrace any and all poetic forms, as long as he feels comfortable with them. Meckel's chief concern: The poet must do forthrightly that which he considers correct. Rather than dealing in his poetry with specific social or political grievances on a case by case basis, the poet must irrevocably and irrefutably personify his protest by his life. Poetry is necessary, Meckel states, and an era in which it might be superfluous cannot even be imagined.

The poem, despite its former effectiveness as a conduit for political ideas from poet to public, is no longer viable for that purpose, according to Nicolas Born (b. 1937). The mass media are far better suited for such endeavors. But the poem, because of its inherent subtlety, can support the cognitive process by fine tuning the sensibilities of its readers. Even though his own early poems were written with a didactic purpose in mind Born no longer believes in the manifest usefulness of the engaged poem.

Jürgen Theobaldy (b. 1944), a product of the student movement of the 1960s and 1970s, feels that poetry is anticipatory, that it has an uncanny ability to forecast. He considers it to be a suitable mass medium, citing Pablo Neruda's success in reading in football stadiums as evidence for the general public's receptiveness to engaged poetry. He demands, at least of himself, a poetic production that is free of obscurities and accessible to all those willing to read or to hear. All poets are engaged, because only engaged human beings can write poetry. Any attempt to distinguish engaged poets from those who are not engaged is merely an attempt to suppress free speech, he believes, since the sensitization of the general public is not necessarily in the best interest of the ruling classes. It is Theobaldy's ambition to write poems that help restore the faith of his readers in a better life.

If these poets are representative of the poetic scene in the FRG today, their views illustrate that there is, at least theoretically, no unanimity among them regarding the function of the poet in contemporary society. It is evident that engagement has been carefully considered by each of these poets, whether they reject or embrace it as a personal attitude. However, the reader of this book will discover that there often is a substantial difference between what these poets preach and what they practice; their poems do not always conform to the theories to which they subscribe.

West German Poets on Society and Politics

the interviews

Friedrich Georg Jünger

Born 1898 in Hannover

After serving as an officer in World War I, Friedrich Georg Jünger studied law at the universities of Leipzig and Halle and was awarded a J.D. degree. He practiced law until 1926, then turned to the writing of poetry and essays. Because of anti-Nazi writings, he was interrogated by the Gestapo and placed under surveillance. In 1936 he left Berlin and moved to Überlingen on Lake Constance, where he lived in an old mansion overlooking the lake until his death on July 20, 1977.

Jünger's poetry and essays show a pronounced classical bent: he was influenced by the writers of ancient Greece, by Goethe, and by Hölderlin. He considered technology as dehumanizing and demanded that man control the machines he creates, rather than permit them to control him.

He was interviewed on March 17, 1975, in his study, before a large picture window overlooking Lake Constance. Not surprisingly, he declined to be taped, but suggested that I take notes and requested that I forward to him my English draft for possible corrections and emendations. This I did—the draft was returned without changes.

41

You have been a publishing poet for over forty years and thus have an unusually extensive overview of German poetry over the years. Has it changed? If so, how?

Yes, it has, just as, for example, Goethe's poetry changed during his decades of poetic productivity. As a young man he wrote in the style of the rococo period, ultimately as a classicist. Similarly, poetry is undergoing a constant evolution in our century.

What is the poet's responsibility toward his reader?

It is really quite unimportant, for the poet's chief responsibility is toward the language. Your question should include the following inquiry: What is the reader's responsibility toward the poet? I answer by demanding that he must make a sincere effort to understand, that he must be capable of coping with the sensitive aspects of language which the poet employs. These two responsibilities cancel one another. In most instances the reader is anonymous as far as the poet is concerned, which is especially true if you consider that the reader, as do I, often reads poets long since deceased, not just those who are his contemporaries.

Do you write for a specific reading public?

Neither do I know my readers, nor do I want to know them while I am involved in the creative process of writing. But you must not misunderstand me: If a reader comes to see me to discuss something which I have published I will be glad to talk to him.

In other words, you subscribe to the principle: l'art pour l'art.

I have given this much thought. I believe that adherence to this principle ends in isolation. Do you follow me? *L'art pour l'art* says, in effect, that the poem exists solely for itself—an artificial concept to which symbolists subscribed. When they carry this principle to its extreme, the result is incomprehensible and thus unproductive, as in the case of Mallarmé. In contrast to Baudelaire, these poets created artificial symbols resulting in artificial poems. But a poem should relate an experience which transcends it.

Do you believe that a poet has both an aesthetic and a social responsibility?

If I understand you correctly you are referring to a responsibility toward contemporary society. In my letter to you of January 29,

1975, and with specific reference to the discussion topics which you proposed, I said the following:

> I will not respond to the questionnaire which you enclosed in your letter. I do not like questionnaires, whether they come from the police or from anyone else. Judging from the quotation marks, some of these questions have been asked by people I do not know, others have probably been formulated by you. It seems to me that many of the calamities in this world are caused by people who concern themselves with matters which are none of their business.
>
> In elaboration I would like to state the following: All of these questions are either openly or by implication sociological in origin. I am a lyric poet, and when I write poems they are not sociological treatises. For me the difference between a good society and bad society is sufficient: A good society can not be defined sociologically. There are many types of sociologists, and they all try, each in his own way, to inflict terror—this I despise.
>
> I do not know whether it has ever occurred to you that sociology can establish itself as a science only where a living society no longer exists, in other words, where an attempt is undertaken to control the masses. Whoever writes poems for this purpose must bear the responsibility for the results.

Ultimately we should ask ourselves what we mean by the term *social responsibility*. Naturally the poet as a citizen has the same responsibilities as anyone else.

Does not the poet often act as the conscience of his fellow-man?

It could easily lead to presumptuousness, if he were to set himself up as the conscience of others. What is conscience? To what does it pertain? The poet's responsibility is toward the language, not toward political or social movements, or toward the state. Even if he were to become involved in a movement (I suppose there was a valid situation of this type during the Napoleonic Wars), he must guard against the danger of neglecting his responsibility toward the language. It is a matter of conscientiousness, a virtue which can rightfully be demanded of everyone regardless of his position in society or his particular duties. Everyone has the obligation to work to the best of his ability. Just as a baker must bake good bread a poet must write good poetry.

Today's confusion is caused by the fact that everyone minds everyone else's business. The press, radio, and television give us more information than we can digest—just think of Vietnam, Portugal, and the Congo. We do not have the knowledge to evaluate and digest all of this information. As a result we become involved in things which we should avoid.

I once talked to Fjodor Stepun, who was the Minister of Culture under Kerensky. Stepun told me: "He who enters politics must be prepared to do evil!" This is a regrettable reality in political life. While I cannot condone evil I have to accept this, unfortunately. But there is never an excuse for vulgarity on the part of a public figure.

I have read that you too were drawn into a political dilemma. Because of your poem "Der Mohn" ("The Poppy") the Nazis prohibited publication of your writings.

As you know, I was a contributor to Ernst Niekisch's journal *Widerstand*. The Nazis knew this too, and when "Der Mohn" was published it was apparent to everyone what I was driving at, that this poem was strongly anti-Nazi. But the Gestapo agents who came to interview me were incapable of understanding my poem. They simply could not comprehend the concept of irony. It is interesting that they always came in pairs: one asked questions, the other one listened. (This may also have been so because they were afraid that some of the people they were questioning might become sufficiently agitated to do physical harm to them, had they appeared singly.) In any case, I played dumb—and I stayed out of jail. You must also remember that there were a few anti-Nazis in the party who merely joined to prevent even more injustice from being done. And these people were occasionally able to exert sufficient influence to keep someone like me out of trouble. Today I do not consider "Der Mohn" to be one of my best poems because it is too involved in contemporary affairs. At the time when I wrote it, it was an intellectual act of self-defense. This poem is now well more than thirty years old and I am no longer involved with it, which brings me to the interesting topic of the survival of poems. *L'art pour l'art* poems soon become incomprehensible. Conversely, some somewhat tendentious poems survive because they contain a recognizable germ of lasting value.

Strangely enough, agents from both French and American intelligence organizations questioned me. I seem to have had a proclivity for winding up "between two chairs" time and again.

Despite my contempt for National Socialism I would never have served a foreign power as Ezra Pound did.

The prefatory poem to your poetry volume Der Taurus *[The Taurus] (1937) expresses an intense sense of loyalty to your country on a universal and aesthetic basis:*

Vaterland ist mir das Lied, ist der offne helle Gesang mir.
Vaterland ist mir das Licht und die Luft und die Liebe zur Erde,
Vaterland Flamme und Flut, Vaterland Wolke und Strom.
Vaterland, Sprache, du bist's, dein Wuchs, dein Gedeihen im
    Licht ist's.
Vaterland bin ich mir selbst, indem ich die Guten verehre.
Genius, wo du dich regst, tanzender sei mir gegrüßt.

Fatherland—it is a song, an open bright chant within me.
Fatherland—it is light and air and love of the earth,
Fatherland flame and flood, Fatherland cloud and stream.
Fatherland, the German language, it is you, your growth,
    your prosperity in the light.
Fatherland I am myself, when I honor those who are good.
Dancing genius, wherever you stir, I greet you.

Yes, this political poem did nothing to increase my popularity with the Nazis because of the ideals I expressed in it. My readers recognized at once that I was addressing myself against Adolf Hitler.

I am surprised that you did not wind up in a concentration camp when you published poems such as "Abschiedslied" ("Farewell Song") in which your disgust with the tendentious poets of the Nazi era was, or better, is, only thinly disguised. I am especially thinking of the last three stanzas:

Ich verlache eure Schliche, eure Tücken,
Plumpe Schlangenfänger.
Eure Weise kann mich nicht berücken,
Dumpfe, dunkle Sänger.

Laßt die abgegriffnen Leiern
Selbst im Lied sich preisen.
Besser ist, du fliehst die Feiern,
Fliehst die hohen Weisen.

Ruhm nicht bringt es, eure Schlachten
Mitzuschlagen.
Eure Siege sind verächtlich
Wie die Niederlagen.

I deride your artifices, your malice,
Rude snakecharmers,
Your ways cannot beguile me,
You dull, dark singers.

Let the worn-out lyres
Praise themselves in song.
It is better if you flee from celebrations,
Flee from lofty ways.

It brings no glory to partake
In your battles.
Your victories are despicable
Like defeats.

I did get away with this. I did not join the *Reichsschrifttumskammer* (National Socialist Writers Organization), but I had my silent fans in the governmental hierarchy who looked out for me.

Yours was an early voice raised against the perils of the machine age. Your essay "Maschine und Eigentum" ("Machine and Property") seems to be reflected in the poem "Chimären," ("Chimeras") where you predict man's enslavement by technology:

Ernst, sehr ernst ist der Maschinenmensch.
Späht er mit langer Nase ins All,
Sinnt er genaue Formeln sich aus
Für sein eigenes Zuchthaus.

Somber, very somber is the machine age man.
When he reconnoiters the universe with his long nose
He devises for himself
Formulas for his own prison.

Mankind now finds itself in a jail, constructed by an economy which has entrapped us by demanding constant increases in productivity and consumption to the point where it all becomes absurd. Our present and ever increasing problems are a logical result of such a nonsensical policy. Constant escalation must necessarily lead to disaster.

Like certain atomic reactions, history also consists of chains of events which, once they have been set into motion, cannot be stopped.

The concept of engagement is not only suspicious but also very dangerous. As you know, the German verb *engagieren* also means "to employ," to give a job to someone. Thus, someone who engages himself becomes an employee, a subordinate, whether it be of a firm, a political party, or of a government. A true poet would never permit himself to be put in such a miserable state.

Photograph by Karin Voight

Wolfgang Weyrauch

Born 1907 in Königsberg

A former actor, Wolfgang Weyrauch studied literature and history at the University of Berlin, worked as an editor for a publishing house, and then served in the German Army from 1940–45. After spending a brief period as a prisoner of war of the USSR, he edited the satirical journal Ulenspiegel for a couple of years, served as an editor for the Rowohlt publishing house for eight years, and has been living in Darmstadt as a freelance writer since 1959.

Weyrauch wrote his first radio plays and short stories before 1945 (his first radio play appeared as early as 1931), and has been widely published since 1946. His publications include poetry, prose, legends, and anthologies. His experiences during the war are reflected in a strongly pacifistic and antimilitaristic attitude.

He was interviewed in his home on March 12, 1975, and the entire interview was taped. It is reprinted in an unedited translation from the original German.

48

In the epilogue of your book Expeditionen [Expeditions] *you called poets surrogates for prophets. Do you still see the poet in this light, now that we are in the last third of the twentieth century?*

No, not any longer. This expression, which dates back to 1959, if I remember correctly, now seems too solemn. If we stick to the term *surrogate*, I would not call the writer the surrogate of his neighbor, because, in contrast to my opinion back then, I am now rather inclined to believe that the writer is an everyday person, like his neighbor, like anyone he might meet in the street or who might live in the same house with him. That the writer then segregates himself, isolates himself from his neighbors, is a part of his craft, necessary for his inspirations and his language.

Surrogate of his neighbor! When you first said this I thought about it in terms of the poet representing his neighbor's cause, fighting for his neighbor, concerning himself with his problems.

That is naturally included in this concept.

Fine. This leads to my second question. I began with the word Dichter *("poet"), you answered using the word* Schriftsteller *("writer"). I am always especially interested in hearing from a poet-writer his interpretation of these two terms.*

I do not know how it is in other countries and in other languages, but among us Germans the distinction between a poet [*Dichter*] and writer [*Schriftsteller*] is awkward indeed. In the recent past our *Dichter* have been mystics, poets, who renounce reality, and who, because of this renunciation, can manufacture word complexes—I am deliberately using the term *manufacture*—which hide, mask, embellish, hush up reality. The French have an expression *homme de lettres* which I consider superior, because it summarizes everything. It includes the so-called *Dichter*, *Schriftsteller*, journalists, and *Publizisten* ("political writers"—a somewhat more elegant term now used here to describe journalists). I do not think much of *Dichter*; I have a high opinion of *Schriftsteller*.

Poets who forgo reality would include "concrete" poets (those who convey their intent by graphic patterns of letters, words, or symbols, rather than by the conventional arrangement of words)?

49

I did not think of them in this connection. Let me instead mention a great name of the past: Stefan George. No matter what one's attitude toward him may be, he was a *Dichter*, not a *Schriftsteller*. I think that the concrete poets are a quite different matter altogether. I have a theory—I don't know whether it is original with me, but in any case it seems new to me—I am not sufficiently educated to make an authoritative judgment here. In the fall of this year (1975) my new poetry anthology also entitled *Expeditionen* will be published, and I am naturally writing an epilogue for it. In this epilogue, as in the entire book, I attempt to divide current German lyric poetry into three parts. One chapter of the book will contain the authors who are interested in the "I"; a second chapter will contain the authors interested in the "we"; and the authors in the third chapter focus upon the "it." I consider those interested in the "it" to be the concrete writers.

And I suppose that those focusing on the "we" are engaged. Since engagement is my topic I would like to hear your response to the statement that poets have both an aesthetic and a social responsibility to fulfill. If your answer is in the affirmative, what is your reasoning?

My answer may sound a little "cute." Alfred Andersch, in a review of my poetry volume *An die Wand geschrieben (Written on the Wall)*, wrote the following statement: "At last poems written by a human and not an aesthete." The publisher subsequently, and also in what might be described a "cute" manner, printed this on a strip of paper that was folded around the outside of the dustcover.

The humane in your work is even more important to you than the production of something that is aesthetically pleasing!

I would like to pick up the word *pleasing* by saying: better displeasing than pleasing. That is the way it is. I also do not think too much of the contrast which my former friend Andersch—we are not enemies now, only separated by a far greater geographical distance— formulated: "At last poems written by a human being and not an aesthete!" That is wrong. There really is no contrast. It is self-evident that a writer, and this includes someone producing lyric poetry whom I also include in the term *writer*, pays attention to form (how else could he write?); and it is just as self-evident that humaneness is a prerequisite.

The humane. The writer who concerns himself with the problems of his fellow man. There seem to be different trends in the Federal Republic of Germany: poets who occupy themselves exclusively with problems of the Federal Republic; others whose engagement embraces the entire world, Vietnam, Chile, the fate of the Jews in the Soviet Union, etc. What should be the concern of German poets today? What direction does your engagement take?

Everything inhumane should be discussed in these decades, also by German authors. They should treat what happens in America, in the Soviet Union, the cockeyed tottering between war and peace among Israel and the Arabs—I need not elaborate on this, everyone is familiar with it. But of primary significance, and no one can doubt this, are German conditions. There are East German conditions, West German conditions, those in Switzerland, Austria, and Berlin. Since we are in the Federal Republic we should focus primarily on West German conditions, all that is inhumane or could become so. And I am not just talking about major issues. Not just that this republic, in which we live, must remain a republic characterized by freedom, and how and by what this could be endangered. We should stand up against the fascism within us in everyday life. I think that before writing about what could lead to the dissolution of our republic, we should begin with such matters as whether a father, out of anger or for moral reasons, with "moral" in quotation marks, is justified in beating up his son who has stolen a motor-scooter. We must start with the apparently least significant matters, and then proceed from them to larger issues. But because of minor matters the big ones should not be forgotten, and vice versa.

What you are saying is that society is a compositum of small matters, all of which must ideally be right to ensure that the big picture lives up to our ideals. I would like to refer to one of your poems from the volume Die Spur *(The Clue), "Das Vaterland" ("The Fatherland"):*

> Da lag es, ganz entzwei,
> ein Aas, weil es geschändet hatte,
> mich dauerts, denn der Hölderlin,
> ein Irgendwer in Salzderhelden,
> verrieten's nicht, sie waren gut,
> wie andre anderswo, vielleicht in Birmingham,
> und wie's so lag, dacht' ich,

51

was liegt, wird stehn, jedoch, wie stehts,
wie gehts, wohin, zu neuen Schatten,
zum Recht für Dich, das heißt, Du bist
im guten Recht wie alle andern,
falls Du nur keinen kränkst.
Ists anders, Vaterland: geh, leg Dich hin,
und steh nie wieder auf.

There it lay, totally asunder,
a carcass, because it had desecrated,
I regret this, because Hölderlin
and a somebody in Salzderhelden
did not betray it, they were good people,
like others somewhere else, perhaps in Birmingham,
and as it lay there I thought,
what lies now will stand again, however, what's up,
how goes it, whereto, to new shadows,
to justice for you, which means, you have
as much right as anyone else,
as long as you injure no one.
If it is otherwise, fatherland: go and lie down
and never arise again.

I wrote this poem in 1961 or 1962, but it could have been written earlier, just as it could be written in this month or next month. It could also bear the title "Das Stiefvaterland" ("The Stepfather-land"). This refers to the following: In the second line I call the fatherland *carrion*, "a carcass, because it had desecrated, I regret this. . . ." This means that I feel sorry for the fatherland in its broken condition, in its carrion-like state, which it brought upon itself. I too am responsible, because I was here when it happened. On the other hand, there are here, there were here and everywhere, people like a Hölderlin who denounced his fatherland, which he did indeed. And there is always, everywhere, a somebody, some unknown citizen, characterized here by the individual in Salzderhelden. Salzderhel-den is a town on the main line between Frankfurt and Hamburg. It dates back to the Thirty Years' War, 1618–48. The place-name did not exist prior to that time, and this is probably historically accurate. The term *Salzderhelden* refers to a large cemetery, where thousands of soldiers are buried, both Swedes and members of Wallenstein's army. These unknown soldiers did not betray their fatherlands. Others did, but they did not. They were faithful like other people, "perhaps in Birmingham," though I could just as well have said Stockholm or Buenos Aires. And now the fatherland is prostrate; and then the poem continues "and as it lay there I thought, what lies . . ." meaning that what has been flung to the ground will rise once again. Our country, the Federal Republic of Germany, in which we are conducting this conversation, will rise again and has risen. Then the next question: "What's up, how goes it, whereto. . . ." Is it headed toward new shadows? To shadows like Salzderhelden? To shadows of desecration? Or, as the poem says, "to justice for you . . . you have as much right . . ."? The citizen, the human being, has rights, as long as he does not injure others. This repeats a brief statement by Matthias Claudius where he says, with more adequate words than I am using now, that you can lie down on the lawn, perform somersaults, stretch your legs, sleep, do anything, as long as you do not harm anyone else. As I put it in the poem, ". . . as long as you injure no one"; and then comes a period. The last two lines of the poem state: "If it is otherwise, fatherland: go and lie down and never arise again." This means that, under other conditions, I do not want to have anything to do with the fatherland but will emigrate, because it has not found the right direction, the direction toward the humane.

And this concept of the "stepfatherland" runs through your work like a leitmotif. I am thinking of the poem "Muster" ("Example") which I just read in the anthology Deutsche Teilung (A Partitioned Germany).
One of your poems concerns itself with one of the most famous and, in the eyes of some, infamous, American poets, Ezra Pound. Since this book will be published in the United States a discussion of the poem "Ezra Pound" will be of greatest interest.

Ezra Pound,
in der Mitte der italienischen Stadt,
in einem Käfig, ausgestellt,
stinkenden Stein unter sich,
stinkende Pferdedecke über sich,
frierend, weil Winter ist,
bebend, vor Gleichgültigkeit
über die amerikanischen Soldaten,
die ihn beschimpfen, bespucken,
durch das Gitter nach ihm treten,
betrachtend den Tausendfüßler
aus Stiefel, Pistole, Uniform,
US-Tausendfüßler, UdSSR-Tausendfüßler,

NS-Tausendfüßler, Nasser-Tausendfüßler,
Tausendfüßler ohne Ursache, Wirkung,
ohne Voraussetzung, Erkenntnis,
Irrtum, Verwerfung des Irrtums,
stinkend, frierend, bebend,
denkend: wohl Euch,
daß ich kein Gedicht mache,
denn schreibe ich ein Gedicht,
und einer stört mich dabei,
töte ich ihn,
aber ich mache kein Gedicht,
ich kann kein Gedicht machen,
denn ich überlege mir,
ob ich mich geirrt habe,
im Gehege des Tausendfüßlers,
im Gehäuse der Anfechtung.

Ezra Pound,
in the middle of an Italian city
exhibited in a cage,
stinking stones under him,
a stinking horse blanket over him,
freezing, because it is winter,
trembling, because of indifference
toward the American soldiers
who curse him, spit at him,
try to kick him through the bars,
contemplating the centipede
of boots, pistol, uniform,
US-centipede, USSR-centipede,
Nazi-centipede, Nasser-centipede,
centipedes without a cause, effect
without rationale, understanding,
error, repudiation of error,
stinking, freezing, trembling,
thinking: Good for you
that I am not writing a poem,
for when I write a poem
and someone disturbs me
I kill him,
but I am not writing a poem,
I cannot write a poem,
for I am wondering
whether I was wrong
in the preserve of the centipede,
in the shell of the opposition.

Ezra Pound—I barely dare to say anything about this great lyric poet. One of his most beautiful poems—I do not know it by heart—is called "In a Station of the Metro." It consists of just two lines. He is talking about Paris, and in this poem he succeeds in doing what I demanded earlier, without myself being able to do so. Just as I demand that a poem about the moon should also deal with the docking of American and Russian astronauts, Ezra Pound succeeded in coupling together the Paris metro and the spirit of the city. And he does this in just two lines!

I must preface my further remarks by stating that I have the greatest respect for Ezra Pound as a writer of lyric poetry, but by no means approve of his political behavior, although there may be many rumors extant about him which make him worse than he actually was. To be perhaps too blunt, I consider him a political fool [*Spinner*].

My poem is likewise an attempt at coupling—I, a German writer, am for Ezra Pound (and I have told you why), and I am against Ezra Pound (and I have told you why). I do not know whether it is based on invented anecdotes, but time and again it was reported that Pound who had made anti-Semitic statements and statements against Wall Street, was picked up in or near Rome by your soldiers, and that he was then locked into some sort of a cage and insulted, even spat upon, as I describe it in my poem. One might argue that he had it coming to him, when looking at the matter from a political perspective. But these people who kicked the cage with their boots were soldiers, awful military types, who did not have the right to punish him with such kicks. It was unjust politically and poetically. My disgust with the military is expressed in this poem when I call the American soldiers "centipedes." But I do not limit myself to them, I also mention Soviet centipedes, Nazi centipedes, Nasser centipedes (i.e., Egyptian centipedes: Nasser's name comes up because this poem was written some years ago, before his death). I am thus attacking military centipedes no matter what their nationality.

And then the author of this Ezra Pound poem turns to something positive, to the poet Ezra Pound, identifies with him, at least, tries to do so, even dares to express thoughts which Pound has, or might have, in this situation, by saying:

> . . . Good for you
> that I am not writing a poem,
> for when I write a poem
> and someone disturbs me (as you are doing now)
> I kill him. . . .

But I am not writing a poem, I am unable to do so, I have to think. I was probably, possibly, perhaps, wrong in expressing pro-Hitler and pro-Mussolini political views, and this thought occurs to me in this enclosure, "in the preserve of the centipede/in the shell of the opposition."

Balancing the books, as it were, reminds me of the poem "Einmaleins" ("Multiplication Table") from Die Spur. *It seems quite simple, and yet I am not sure that I understand it as you intended it, despite several readings. As a professor of German I was naturally tempted to compare it with Goethe's famous Multiplication Table of the Witches from* Faust.

I suppose you are referring to the poem "Multiplication Table" from *Die Spur*. I am a little confused because there is another poem with the same title, written years earlier, and published in *Gesang um nicht zu Sterben* [*Song to Prevent Death*]. But you referred to the one that reminds you of our forefather (*Urvater*), Goethe.

Eins	One
ist keins,	is none,
zwei	two
ist vorbei,	is past,
drei	three
ist entzwei,	is asunder,
vier	four
ist nicht hier,	is not here,
fünf	five
fällt in die Sümpf,	falls into swamps,
sechs	six
hat ein Gewächs,	has a growth,
sieben	seven
kann keinen lieben,	can love no one,

acht	eight
rennt in die Nacht,	runs into the night,
neun	nine
wirds bereun,	will regret it,
zehn	ten
wird vergehn.	will vanish.

You know, and now I sound like Willy Brandt, if one is time and again tagged an engaged lyric poet, which is the natural consequence of continued attempts to be involved, which I consider obviously to be the only attitude I could take, then there arise moments or hours or days of self-doubt, of despair. Thus, this "Multiplication Table" is a poem of renunciation, of melancholy, of resignation. You can determine this simply by looking at the second line of each of these small stanzas. They read (and I am adding them now): is none, is past, is asunder, is not here, falls into swamps, has a growth, can love no one, runs into the night, will regret it, will vanish. This enumeration really has nothing to do with the Multiplication Table of the Witches, but it manifests fear, this listing from one to ten—a fear, doubt, despair, which I try to systematize by affixing to it the recitation of the numbers from one to ten.

By the way, the same is true of my earlier "Multiplication Table" which also includes the numbers from one to ten, but is not rhymed:

Eins.	*One.*
Zieh die Schuhe aus,	Take off your shoes,
zieh das älteste Hemd	put on your oldest shirt
und die älteste Hose an.	and your oldest trousers.
Zwei.	*Two.*
Schenk alles weg,	Give everything away
was Du hast,	that you own,
oder laß es einfach liegen.	or simply leave it behind.
Drei.	*Three.*
Geh am frühsten Morgen	At the crack of dawn
von zuhaus fort,	leave home,
in den Wald,	go into the woods,
der am weitesten	farthest away
von Dir entfernt ist.	from you.

Vier. Aber groß muß er sein, dunkel und dicht, keiner darf darin wohnen.	*Four.* They have to be huge, dark and thick, and no one may live there.
Fünf. Geh dorthin, wo Du Glaubst daß die Mitte ist.	*Five.* Go there, where you believe the center to be.
Sechs. In der Mitte bleib stehn, setz Dich, leg Dich, deck dich mit Blättern zu.	*Six.* Stop in the middle, sit down, lie down, cover yourself with leaves.
Sieben. Wart, bis die Tiere kommen, dann atme ein, atme aus, atme ein, hör auf zu atmen.	*Seven.* Wait for the animals, then breathe in, breathe out, breathe in, stop breathing.
Acht. Dann werden die Tiere singen, und Du wirst auch singen, obwohl Du nicht atmest.	*Eight.* Then the animals will sing, and you too will sing, although you are not breathing.
Neun. Schließlich hörst Du nichts mehr, und Du wirst Farn sein, Pilz oder Beere.	*Nine.* Finally you hear nothing more, and you will be a fern, a mushroom or a berry.
Zehn. Schweigendstes Schweigen.	*Ten.* Most silent silence.

Here the author, naked and poor, like St. Francis of Assisi (do pardon the comparison), goes into the woods and lives only with leaves and animals and mushrooms and berries. The last stanza, though I may be using the word *stanza* here incorrectly, states "Most silent silence." This is not just doubt and despair, this is destruction and the end. As in the case of many other poems, I have often read this poem in public. But after hearing this particular poem young Germans have abusively asked me: "What is the matter with you? Why are you suddenly chickening out? Stand in the marketplace where you usually are!"

Thus even a poet well known for his strong engagement has to balance the books occasionally in a quiet hour and distance himself from himself.

The political-literary, or perhaps I should reverse the two: the literary-political engagement cannot occur incessantly. It is like making love. If you loved a girl very intensively and are all torn up because of some problems you are having with her, there have to be periods, whether they be one minute or one week in duration, when you get away and at least outwardly separate yourself from her, read a detective story or Grimmelshausen's *Simplizius Simplicissimus*, go on a hike—do something! But then—and I have experienced this— you return to the girl, and you likewise return to your engagement.

And this statement reminds me of your famous lines: "Writers are physicians, and what they write is the handwriting on the wall."

Photograph by Isolde Ohlbaum

Ernst Meister
Born 1911 in Hagen/Haspe

Ernst Meister returned after his student days (he studied theology, German literature, and art history) to the city of his birth and, with an interruption for military service, mostly in Italy, during the Second World War, has lived there since 1940. Until 1960 he worked in a spike machine factory owned by his father and his brother. He has been publishing poetry since 1932; he is also active as an artist.

He was interviewed in his home on May 8, 1975, and did not permit the use of a tape recorder. What follows is a reconstruction of the highlights of this interview, prepared from my notes and the recollections of my wife, Stephanie Cain Van D'Elden, who was present at the interview. At Meister's request I orally summarized my notes at the end of the interview—he approved of what I intended to publish.

Do you agree with the thesis that literature has both an aesthetic and a social function?

Literature often deals artistically with matters of mediocre significance. If the facts are horrifying it would be wrong to veil them aesthetically (cf. Adorno and Auschwitz). Some people have to cope by writing. By the use of artistic sensitivity matters are incorporated into a work as though they were facts. As long as a human being with artistic sensibility takes an interest in something, this something receives form through a process of cerebration. Two points: 1) perception is a prerequisite, and 2) the object described is given individualistic form. If an artistically gifted person discusses social conditions, a part of society is described with virtuosity. How should social and sociological facts be communicated: purely pragmatically—free of any aesthesis; or, reshaped—characteristic features made conspicuous, more abstracted. Many believe that an aesthetic rendition blunts social facts. According to this school of thought, aesthetics disguise, veil, put matters at a distance. What is at a distance is no longer as accessible, and more or less becomes a neutral object. The aesthetic has more charm than a sober fact, but aesthetic treatment must not serve a decorative purpose.

Let me give you an example: Erich Fried had an idea and wanted to get it published. His editor suggested that the idea would be of greater interest to the public if it were cast as a poem rather than presented in prose. Some people are of the opinion that an aesthethically treated topic loses seriousness. If that is so, if a text without aesthetic elements is more credible, then engaged poems should vanish. Then a cut-and-dried report would be preferable. But an aesthetic treatment actually has the faculty of bringing out the true nature of a thing—and I am not using the word *thing* [*Ding*] in the Rilkean sense. The talent of a virtuoso can penetrate its essence, make it more vivid.

Apparently the fate of an individual, depicted movingly in literary form, is much more likely to arouse empathy than the fate of large numbers portrayed in mass statistics.

Whatever does not pay attention to sociology is often judged as nothing but aesthesis, as lacking in value. True aesthetics are directed toward a faithful perception of the subject matter.

The poet has thus the responsibility of communicating "understandably?"

Although one may assume that a sensitive reader will absorb even a dry report corresponding to its content, it may be assumed that an aesthetically intensive text can present the subject matter more effectively.

61

I thus assume that the poem serves as a model?

Although I am not particularly enthusiastic about the *terminus technicus Modellcharakter* ["function as a model"] I must answer affirmatively.

If then the poem does depict a model situation from which the reader is expected to draw certain consequences, the poet should attempt to write comprehensible poetry and not to express himself by means of a coded secret language.

That is correct, but the poet *must* have the freedom to express himself as his inner needs dictate. If an idea is expressed well, hits the target, and if I am convincing I must hope to be understood. I do not believe that a poet should try to obtain outside opinions regarding his style—verbatim quotations are possible. Furthermore, I know that the spiritual needs of the reader are often quite different from mine. There are many readers whose needs are not nearly as lofty as mine. But this is no reason to let my language perish.

In other words, you are not writing with one eye on your potential reading public.

Ideally a writer should do justice to every person and above all to every person's misery. But much depends on the reader's willingness to read and hear what the poet has to say. It is naturally impossible to do justice to every misfortune. Horrors occur daily. This would lead to repetition. There should be an office—an office of polemics, where language must be used spontaneously; it otherwise cannot promote evolution. Authors who write polemic books on an assembly line basis are technically suspect. They are opportunists. Those who have written on such a subject on a few occasions, but because of a profound involvement or sense of indignation, are doing much better than the professional polemicists. Good discourses seem more effective than repeated effusions. We know from classical experiences how precise discourses can be.

Critics have described your lyrical work as being meditative, religiously motivated, and difficult to understand.

Religiously motivated—that was probably a phase. Whether it is accessible only with difficulty depends upon the reader. It is possible that readers have not undergone the same thought processes as I. The reader must try to find access. When my work is described as being hermetic I suppose the critics mean that I know what I am talking about but make it more difficult to follow. How strong the prejudices of critics are can be demonstrated by the fact that they quote incorrectly. Thus, for example, one critic misquoted my phrase "Unsinn und Sinn der Sinne" ["absurdity and consciousness of the senses"] to read "Unsinn und Sinn der Dinge" ["absurdity and sense of things or objects"]. The former, of course, is correct—but the latter was printed by a critic!

When I speak of patience it is assumed that I am writing with great effort. What actually happens is that ideas are considered and then described, and this I call patience. Patience means deliberate meditation, not effort.

Did you write "Nahkampf auf einem Rosenfeld" ("Hand-to-Hand Combat in a Rose Bed") as the result of a personal observation during the war?

No, it was a vision, not an actual happening:

Das Ding in der Kehle
war nicht aus Schmelzschokolade,
auch kein Mandelsplitter,
vom Munde der Liebsten
zwischen die Lippen geküßt.

Das Weiße im Auge des Gegners
hatte die Schenkel der Mädchen vergessen,
war Todeshimmel, in dem schwarze Eier zerkrachten,
und die Blätter der Teerosen stoben.

Immerhin
wurde der Mann in die Rosen geblutet,
an denen,
das sah der Gefallene unten,
feldgraue Läuse
wimmelnd nach oben stiegen,
um saugend
im gelben Rosenbette zu siegen

Und der hohe Himmel ward grau wie die Läuse.

The object in the throat
was not of glazed chocolate,
nor was it an almond sliver

transported between the lips
by a kiss from the beloved.

The white in the eyes of the enemy
had forgotten the thighs of girls,
was a sky foreboding death, in which black eggs burst,
and the leaves of the tea-roses dispersed.

After all
a man was bleeding to death among the roses,
on which,
this the dying man saw from below,
field grey lice
swarmed upwards,
sucking
to be victorious in the yellow rose bed.

And the sky above turned grey like the lice.

It seemed to me that the cruelties of war were symbolized by hand-to-hand combat on such a well-groomed piece of earth as a rose bed, whereby naturally soldiers are killed. The "object in the throat" is a grenade fragment in the throat of this soldier; the black eggs do not merely refer to exploding grenades but could also be interpreted sexually, and black is used here symbolically as the color of death. The relationship between lice and roses is exactly the same as that among the soldiers, a matter of victory versus defeat. The field grey lice remind one of the uniforms of the soldiers. When these swarms of lice climb up and finally reach the blossom, this beautiful flower is defeated, conquered, destroyed—a parallel action to that which is occurring among human beings on the field of battle.

When a poem is interpreted, the reader should be able to recreate the thoughts of the author, if the author was indeed thinking and did not merely contrive or hypercritically invent something. But even though the horizon may be wide open an author may be considered an encipherer by some. Oh, I suppose that the god Hermes would be the ideal reader!

We each live in a very small segment of time. The time which is granted an individual is asymmetrical. What we see happens only once. I jokingly call this the "aesthesis of disappearance." People have spoken of a thoughtful death. To experience this, one would have to have the good fortune of dying in bed. Dying is an aesthetic act. Man has lived in the contemplation of things, and this opportunity to observe is then darkly blanketed out through death. To be for a moment—and then again not to be.

At this point a discussion of your poem "Totenreich, darin Lebendiges sich träumt" ("Kingdom of death, in which the living dream") seems appropriate.

Totenreich, darin
Lebendiges sich träumt
Es scheint, ich sehe,
ich sehe Schein,
Kadaverspur dazwischen.

Ist jetzt ein Nachmittag,
ist Sommer, das
Schwitzen von Geschlecht?
In Schwebe der Geruch
der täglichen Geschichten.
So viel Mord.

Ohne Vernehmen ihrer selbst und
ohne unser Gespür
drehn sich die Sterne.
O fürchterliche Macht
der großen Körper.

Kingdom of death, in which
the living dream.
It seems, I see,
I see a glow,
the trail of a corpse in between..

Is this an afternoon,
is it summer, is it
the sweat of a loving embrace?
In suspension the aroma
of everyday stories.
So much murder.

Without perceiving themselves and
without our scent
the stars revolve.
O frightful power
of heavenly bodies.

A real world is here thought of as the realm of the dead. This poem deals with a repetition of that which leads to death. That which is alive drifts farther and farther away. In short, it is a realm of the dead. I frequently speak after the fact. If, for example, I use the phrase "trail of a corpse," then this means that death is an ever present phenomenon. The first three lines of the second stanza speak of facts which take place beyond this horizon. "So much murder"—the most upsetting fact of our world is violent death: one reads about it in the papers, it is shown on television. The poem ends with the thought that we are insignificant beings subjected to the functions of heavenly bodies: "O frightful power/of heavenly bodies."

Did you ever take up the problems of Vietnam or Cambodia in poems of which I may not be aware?

No, because today I do not consider political problems to be of paramount importance. But after World War II, I was deeply involved, engaged. I thought that the United States would take charge, restore order, that an age of morality lay ahead. On the other hand, there was the terrifying experience of the atomic bombs that were used in Japan. The reports from Hiroshima inspired a Christmas poem with the title "Im Stalle zu B." ["In the Stable at B."]:

Bei dir im Stalle ist's warm.
Auf dem Felde schlug uns mit Geißeln der Winter.
Heiliges Kind, entsprungen der schneeigen Rose,
leuchtend auf Stroh,
benetzt vom Seime der Kälber,
dich zu sehen sind wir gekommen,
nicht um aufzubürden dir
unsere dornige Angst.

Und wir stehen
im Hauch der milchsanften Tiere
wie unter dem milden Süd.
Goldenes Öl rinnt vom Berg der Oliven. . .

Auch sind Davids Harfentöne
zu dir gekommen wie Paten,
und ist es nicht, als weile Uria hier,
der treu einfältige Hauptmann,
dem der König das Weib nahm, Bathseba,
und es schwängerte auf Wolken Jehovas,

Uria, salomonische Weisheiten murmelnd?
Wie fern unsere stechende Angst,
da wir sehen, wie deine rosige Hand
aus dem Krippenstroh greift
nach des Mondes silbernem Horn . . .

Unter Mariens prophetischem Himmel
wandern noch immer gute Gäste zu dir
über des Schnees Leichentuch.
Und kürzlich ist zu dir eingekehrt
Tonoko, das Kind, mit tödlichen Wunden geboren,
das Mädchen, unter dem giftigen Pilz
in Hiroshima zur Sekunde des Blitzes,
Tonoko, an der Hand des verschwiegensten Schweigens
aus dem Schweigelager von W.

Next to you in the stable it's warm.
On the field winter lashed us with whips.
Holy Infant, arisen from the snow-white rose,
radiant on the straw,
moistened by the juices of calves,
we have come to see You,
not to burden You with
our thorny fears.

And we stand
in the tinge of the animals mild with milk
as under the mild southern sky.
Golden oil flows from the Mount of Olives . . .

The sounds of David's harp
have come to you like godparents,
and is it not as though Uria were here,
the faithful trusting soldier,
whose wife, Bathsheba, was taken by the king
who made her pregnant on the clouds of Jehova,
Uria, murmuring Salomonic wisdom?

How remote is our piercing fear
when we see, how Your rosy hand
reaches from the straw of the manger
to the silvery horn of the moon . . .

Under Mary's prophetic sky
more good guests are wandering toward you
across the shroud of snow.
And recently Tonoko, the child,

born with deadly wounds, came to you,
the child, under the poisonous mushroom
of Hiroshima at the second of the flash,
Tonoko, on the hand of the most silenced silence
from the camp of silence at W.

I believe that this poem is readily understandable and would only like to add that the phrase *Schweigelager von W.* ["camp of silence at W."] arbitrarily contains the letter *W* because it rhymes with *B* in German; furthermore, the interrogatives "where" and "why" could be read into it.

Photograph by Karin Voight

Peter Jokostra

Born 1912 in Dresden

Of Slavic parentage, Peter Jokostra was raised in a Slavic enclave in what is now the German Democratic Republic. He studied philosophy, psychology, and sociology at the University of Berlin, was drafted into the German Army. He deserted after the winter battle along the Volga and joined the resistance movement against National Socialism. After a brief period as a prisoner of war, he became a District School Supervisor and a lecturer in literature in a community evening college in the GDR. In 1958 he moved to Southern France, and since 1960 he has been living in the Federal Republic of Germany. He is now a freelance writer, publisher, and critic, and lives in Kasbach on the Rhine.

His first volume of poetry appeared in 1956, and since then he has published essays, novels and anthologies in addition to lyric poetry.

He was interviewed in his home on April 1, 1975, and did not consent to be taped. At his request a transcript of our consolidated notes (my wife was present for the interview and took notes simultaneously) was

69

forwarded to him for corrections. This resulted in a number of minor changes in the original German text.

In your story "Begegnung in Knokke" ("Encounter in Knokke") the poet says:

> "People keep insisting that poetry is dead, that poems can no longer be written, that poetry has lost its right to exist. And they have asserted this for more than twenty years, since the end of the war. If this is true I have no right to exist. I object! I am alive, and he who wants to live, who wants to survive, must protest. And what is so crazy is that more poems are being written now than before the war. Everybody talks about poetry. Here every taxi driver and every typist seems to be writing poems . . . a romantic generation."

Does this quote express your current opinion regarding modern German poetry?

No, this was the opinion of a colleague. This happens to be a true story—it is not Peter Jokostra's opinion, who is basically pessimistic with respect to the situation and future of lyric poetry. Perhaps because of this attitude I have published relatively few poems, although a new volume is in preparation at the present time. You know, I am, because of my experiences, schizophrenic to the bone. I am often asked whether I would like to contribute to volumes of Saxon poetry or prose since I was born in Dresden. But I do not feel like a Saxon. I am, because of my ethnic background which can be discerned from my name, more Slav than Saxon. I grew up in the so-called *Sorbenland*, a Slavic enclave near Berlin, in an area where the Prussians provided the upper social classes while the workers, who were usually exploited, were of Slavic descent. This is why I am without illusions and do not profess any faith in the usual sense. My pessimism is so well known among my friends that Paul Celan, years ago in Paris, invited me to join him in a suicide pact.

Does this pessimism also color your attitude toward lyric poetry? Would you subscribe to the statement that "literature intends to act and agitate but, in effect, all it does is react"?

I can subscribe to that sentence—but reaction is precisely what gives literature its purpose, while agitation is a matter for politicians and political ideologists. The question whether literature influences social change presupposes an exaggerated goal. Bobrowski once wrote: "Art is not suited to induce mass movements—it should be suited to question and to question urgently." We artists must ask questions, for this is our mission. We do not have any answers. As Bobrowski put it: "It [art] must identify, but must also avoid the short circuit of demanding an immediate result, the short circuit 'identified=exorcised.'" What is identified can be eliminated.

We now live in the seventies and have put confessional poetry behind us. My poems, except for a few early ones, do not point toward a specific situation. There remains an engagement, the function of a placard, but this is not the poet's business—it is the business of the politicians. But whenever politicians get involved in literature or men of letters in politics it turns out to be unfortunate for both, as Karl Krolow once formulated it when I visited him in his home on the Rosenhöhe in Darmstadt. And this is also my opinion regarding this well-worn topic.

Wolfdietrich Schnurre once asked: "What does it mean to be *engaged*? Ideally it means to participate, to sympathize, to feel touched. Touched by what? By everything that violates human dignity." This is how a poet should take sides. I am of the opinion that it violates human dignity if a poet is diverted from his real purpose, if one demands that he become politically engaged, if one demands, even drives him to the point where his poems represent a political trend. This involvement is where the ahumane begins, and it does not matter whether we are talking about a theory from the political right or the political left.

You talk about coercion. But what about the poet who voluntarily becomes politically engaged?

That does not exist here in the Federal Republic, because here it is a matter of *materialistic* necessity, for economic or political reasons, to take sides conspicuously. Schnurre calls the engaged poet a Don Quixote. Of himself he says that he writes "in order to confront transitoriness and death in all its incarnations known to me with the image of mankind," and I share this position. The German poet, who has accumulated his basic experiences in the Eastern regions which are Polish today and used to be German, or in the German Democratic Republic, has the task of paying off the debt which has been pressing heavily upon German shoulders since the extermination of the Old Prussians by the Teutonic Knights in the thirteenth century and above all of the Jews by the Nazis. This is his trauma with which he has to live and which he has to master. This probably created my schizophrenic situation, and because of this guilt, the consequences of which I experienced centuries later in the Sorbenland, as I mentioned earlier, I do not feel much like a German, even though my fellow-men generally consider me to be a German of Slavic descent. My home is wherever I can gain a footing, where I can develop literarily and linguistically. The interesting events of my life took place, though geographically in Germany, in a Slavic area. You might say that I live in exile. Here people have been generous and I have been published. In the German Democratic Republic I am on the blacklist. I have my homeland within me, as the Jews carry theirs around in a pouch. From the Provence I have brought the seeds of trees, which I had collected from the ground and carried here in a pouch, and then I have buried them in my garden and they have grown into trees. This is the only way I plant anything in my garden, starting with a seed.

That says a lot about you . . .

Yes, this archaism. But please do not look for *Blut und Boden* ["blood and soil," a Nazi catchword] in this, because I hate that, as I hate all ideologies, be they religious, political, or philosophic.

To live for me means to plant trees, to plant bushes. I feel at home among trees and bushes, which is why I write more prose than poetry—because I can describe forests and smells and forest fires better in this less compressed genre. In the East there are large pine forests and large forest fires. With them I associate unforgettable experiences from my youth; for example, how burned pine needles, carried by the wind, came down like a curtain ten or twenty kilometers from the fire, and with them an unforgettable aroma. For many years I was a passionate hunter. These experiences remain in my memory. I write about these things because they should be preserved. They do not happen anymore, and for this reason the younger generation does not understand them. The younger generation works from a different basis. Younger poets work from an aesthetic basis, not from the elementary feelings which I know. This is not intended to be critical—they are simply a different generation. On September 23, 1972, I wrote to Dagmar Deskau:

> For whom is Hannes' [Bobrowski's] image of nature obscure? Surely only for people who come from a different country, a different lan-

guage, a different sum total of experiences. Only for such readers must his nature images . . . be incomprehensible, strange and even "dark." Dark is a matter of location. For the participant these images are not "dark" and thus also not coded.

When I read these sentences again (quoted in Dagmar Deskau's book *Der aufgelöste Widerspruch, "Engagement" und "Dunkelheit" in der Lyrik Johannes Bobrowskis* [Stuttgart: Ernst Klett Verlag, 1975]), I was quite surprised that I had managed to write such literary-aesthetical sentences. Surrealism was my university. It was my point of departure. The manifestos of André Breton, Louis Aragon, Tristan Tzara, and other leading spokesmen of French Surrealism molded my literary education for life.

Your first literary work, the poetry volume An der besonnten Mauer (On the Sun Drenched Wall), *appeared in 1956 when you were thirty-four years old. Why did your literary activities begin so late?*

In the German Democratic Republic my art was considered *entartet* ("degenerate"), using that term similarly as the Nazis once did. Nevertheless, you will not get anywhere if you try to extract a weltanschauung from my poems. I absorb the impulses of whatever is close to me. There are two possible reactions to such stimuli, political action or poetic meditation.

The poet is the court fool of the throwaway society, especially the lyric poet, unless he writes political poems. But political lyrics are not worth discussing—they really are not lyrics.

I have been variously described as a radical leftwinger and a radical rightwinger. Johann Matthei, the central figure in several of my prose works, most recently in the autobiographical novel *Das große Gelächter* [*The Uproarious Laughter*], says at one time: "I am not prepared to die for the fiction of the fatherland." This sentence is quoted time and again in the press. But I continue, "neither for the fiction of poetry." This is why I have compromised in my life and written for newspapers and publishers whose political views I cannot accept. I suppose I am basically an anarchist, but one who uses paper bombs instead of explosive bombs. The poet is always considered to be a political being because he is an outsider. As soon as you write a poem you become suspect. The poet as a phenomenon is dangerous for society, especially in a dictatorship. A poem is a *Kassiber* ["Thieves' Latin," i.e., a clandestine communication between prisoners]. I once wrote a poem with the title "Kassiber." If you read a poem you necessarily have to read between the lines; only then will you know what a poet really is, that he cannot be either an orthodox Communist or a Nazi if he really is a poet.

P. O. Chotjewitz expresses his opinion regarding the now so popular utilitarianism as follows: "Two of the worst inheritances from bourgeois society . . . are the constraint to have to justify each thought and each action, and really not to be permitted to do anything that isn't of some utilitarian value."

Well put and entirely correct! Here anyone who does not submit to a compulsive performance standard [*Leistungszwang*] is excluded like poison. Industrial expansion robs us of the time for reflection, of the ability to contemplate. There is no time to relax. But a poem has a long incubation period. Anyone who is constantly forced to think of his material survival cannot write poems. I need time. Sometimes a poem occurs to me as I am taking a walk in the wood behind my house. While walking I memorize it, and then I write it down.

Is the form of a poem related to its content?

I abhor theories, I consider myself a subconscious, perhaps even reluctant poet, who follows no single method. Form is of secondary importance to me. It is as though I were writing into a tunnel. Lightning strikes, and then the question arises: What can I add to that. I never know how long or how short a poem will turn out. It simply continues to take form until it ends. I am naive, I only write about my own experiences. Rhythm is important, rhyme I reject. I write quickly, but then I look a poem over very deliberately and correct the rhythm.

Your topic is political engagement in modern poetry, to which I would like to comment that every poem is in effect a political act. An example would be Federico Garcia Lorca's ballad about the Guardia Civil, which led to his murder. My "Ode an Lorca" [Ode to Lorca] concerns itself with this tragic event.

Guardia civil:
wirf ihnen dein gelbes Auge hin.
Schwarzhaar, Pfefferminz, Zigeuneralchimie.
Sie sind umlagert von Dunst,
ein Klippenteppich, den Mördern hingebreitet,
ein Klippenteppich, taub der Erinnerung,

den Flüchen taub:
kretisch, gleißend, feist.

Komm, Lorca,
vergeblich getöteter Fürst des Gedichts.
Sieh, diese Hand, die dich sucht,
eine gefesselte Hand,
vagabundierend noch immer.
Als sie sich schloß,
blickte rückwärts dein Auge,
die Jahre zurück, an den Klippen empor,
die uns trennten von der Majestät deines Tods.

Ein schwarzes Vorgebirge:
hart, steil, verkarstet.
Die Legende des andalusischen Morgens,
die Legende, mit dem Echo der Schüsse begonnen,
wo aus den Helmen rot der Sommer troff.

Ach, Lorca, komm.
Tritt aus dem Schatten, deinem Tau, hervor.
Nenn uns noch einmal
den abendschweren Sitz des Windes,
dem Stein zu Häupten, Meer-Balkon.
Steck den Gewehren deine Rose auf,
die sanften Blitze deines schnellen Tods,
des Wortes sanfte Auferstehungsblitze.

Im Morgengrauen, sagten sie,
wird Theseus landen im Staub der Eselskarren,
wo die zertretene Frucht, der Sterbepfirsich, glänzt.
Wenn aus den Mörderhelmen
Andalusiens schwarzer Zigeunersommer schäumt,
webst du den Namen in ihr blutiges Tuch
mit den Pagodenhänden leicht,
mit dieses Widersinns Gehorsam,
schaudernd den Namen:
Guardia civil.

Guardia civil:
cast on them your jaundiced eye,
Black hair, peppermint, gypsy alchemy.
They are encompassed by an evil aura,
a carpet of crags, prepared by murderers,
a carpet of crags, deaf to memory,
deaf to curses:
Cretian, shiny, plump.

Come, Lorça,
Prince of Poetry killed in vain.
Behold, this hand, that seeks you,
a fettered hand,
still tramping about.
When it closed
you cast your eye backward,
years backward, high upon the crags
which separated us from the majesty of your death.

A black promontory:
hard, steep, stony.
The legend of an Andalusian morning,
The legend which began with the echo of shots
when red the summer dripped from the helmets.

Oh, Lorca, come.
Step forward from the shadow, from your dew.
Name once again for us
the home of the wind grave with evening,
atop the stone, ocean-balcony.
Decorate their rifles with your rose,
the gentle flashes of your quick death,
the gentle resurrection-flashes of the word.

In the grey of the morning, they said,
Theseus will land in the dust of the donkey carts
where the mangled fruit, the peach of death is glittering.
When from the helmets of the murderers
the black gypsy summer of Andalusia foams
you weave the name into their bloody cloth
with graceful pagoda hands,
with this absurd obedience,
shuddering the name:
Guardia civil.

There is much fear in this poem. I do not want to interpret it. Self-interpretations are not my thing. But I would be glad to help you with any possible difficulties since you plan to translate the poem into English for your readers.

I would appreciate this especially since the poem contains a number of original terms, such as Klippenteppich *and* Meer-Balkon.

The *Klippenteppich* ["carpet of crags"] is merely a vision of the country which Gracia Lorca symbolizes. "This hand, that seeks you" refers to the gypsies; it closes when it can reach Lorca no longer. The word *Meer-Balkon* ["balcony overlooking the ocean"] was coined by Lorca. With it he described the "lemon-yellow Malaga." Günter W. Lorenz, in his book *Federico Garcia Lorca*, describes Lorca's images as Arabic in inspiration, characterized by a "vehement joy" in "colorful arabesques."

I also would like to comment on the death of Garcia Lorca since there are many misunderstandings regarding it. He was killed by the Escuadra Negra ["Black Squadron"], a fascist elite organization that specialized in tracking down and liquidating enemies of Franco. His murder was ordered by General Valdes, the Governor of Granada, who assigned to a certain Captain Fonseca the task of liquidating 120 suspicious persons, among them a "certain Lorca." When they reached the spot where the murder was slated to happen in the Viznar gulley near Granada, Lorca was told to start running away. He was then shot in the back but did not die at once. Fonseca noticed that he was still alive and delivered the *coup de grace*. But because Lorca was a pederast he shot him in the anus, remarking: "This is how pederasts are killed!" The bullet traveled through his body and he died. Fonseca's daughter was so upset by this event that she entered a nunnery.

When you say: "Decorate their rifles with your rose," does this refer to a custom similar to that of the American flower children who, for example, put flowers into the bores of the guns of the National Guard during the unrest in the sixties?

No. The rifles of soldiers leaving for war were customarily decorated with flowers. Perhaps I should say something about the "gentle flashes." This is a surrealistic image. It need not be understood but must be felt. The sense of this poem is in its entirety, not in its individual images. The poem is a vision. I find it regrettable that today we want to explain everything and make everything easy to understand, because this hampers the imagination and the creation of new images. It was the purpose of this poem to erect a warning sign against the dangers of blind obedience—here represented by the Guardia Civil.

Lorca was a man with sinister premonitions, but he did not consider himself to be part of the revolution. He became the "mangled fruit," killed because of the hatred primitive people harbor toward intellectuals.

And I suppose that, in contrast, "pagoda hands" represent suppleness.

77

Indeed they do. They symbolize agility, something that floats, in contrast to the blind obedience of the Guardia Civil which is an absurdity. Then there are several antitheses:

helmets of the murderers	= mangled fruit
absurd obedience	= Lorca
bloody cloth	= peach of death

You wrote to me that you are currently particularly concerned about the environment.

Yes, and I have discussed this burning problem in a debate on the topic "Literatur und Politik" with the German Secretary of the Interior (*Bundesinnenminister*), Professor Maihofer.[1] This somewhat surprised the organizers of the meeting of the literary society "Die Kogge" in Minden in Westphalia, because from the title they had expected something other than what I said. Let me summarize it for you.

I am very dissatisfied with the state of literature in a time where our very existence is at stake, when there is the imminent danger of collective death, where—roughly estimated—90 percent of all printed pages should be left blank. Hermann Broch once said, in some more detail, that he who produces kitsch is a swine. I share this opinion. I maintain that every type of literature is political literature, for the written word reveals transparently the social structures to which the writer belongs. But one may not reverse this idea and assert that every act of politics is literature, as marvelous as it would be if literature would divest politics of its sterility and invest it with the so much needed imagination. This could lead to a larger engagement. As I pointed out in this address: Zola's *J'accuse* is and remains the pattern for the identity of literature and politics.

Today we are at the brink of a global ecological crisis which offers the conscientious writer inexhaustible material for novels and poems. Some German authors, among them Hans Magnus Enzensberger (in *Kursbuch 33*, "Ökologie und Politik oder Die Zukunft der Industrialisierung") and Wolfgang Hädecke (in "Das ökologische Dilemma," *Neue Rundschau*, 2 [1975]), understand that this is more than just one of many equally significant literary topics,

[1]Peter Jokostra, "Literatur und Politik," *Literatur und Kritik* 91 (Vienna, February 1975), 13–20.

but that the survival of mankind and all living creatures is at stake and that this problem can only be solved on a global basis. Before us lies the terrifying possibility of a future without man. Japan, a country whose population understands more, or should understand more, about the problem of depopulation, is a case in point. One only need remember Hiroshima and Nagasaki, as well as the mercury poisoning catastrophe of Minamata!

Let me close with my poem "Mururoa—Tod einer Insel" ["Mururoa—Death of an Island"]:

Heute um Mitternacht,
wenn die Blutorange aufsteigt
von deinen Hüften, mein Archipel,
wird dein Name gelöscht
aus der Geschichte des Lebens.

Mit allen deinen Fischen,
deinem Glanz, deiner Nacktheit,
mit allen deinen unbeweinten Steinen
stirbst du den Tod des Atom.

Deine Jahrtausende Schlaf
haben dir nichts genützt,
sie sind nun zu Ende,
heute um Mitternacht,
und ich sag, daß es
endgültig ist.

At midnight tonight,
when the bloodorange rises
from your hips, my archipelago,
your name will be extinguished
from the history of life.

With all your fish,
your glitter, your nakedness,
with all your stones for which no tears are shed
you die the atomic death.

Your millennia of sleep
are of no avail,
they now will end,
at midnight tonight,
and I assert, that this
is final.

Photograph by Scharowski Heidelberg

Hilde Domin

Born 1912 in Cologne

Hilde Domin studied law, political science, sociology, and philosophy at the universities of Heidelberg, Berlin, Florence, and Rome; she was granted a Ph.D. by the University of Florence. She has worked as a teacher, university lecturer, translator, photographer, and collaborated in the scholarly work of her husband, Professor Erwin W. Palm. An emigrant from Nazi Germany, she lived for years in Italy and the Dominican Republic, then returned to the FRG in 1954 after twenty-two years of exile, where she now lives in Heidelberg as a freelance writer and lecturer.

Her publications include poetry, prose, essays, anthologies. She has been writing poetry since 1951.

Domin was interviewed on December 8, 1974, in Vienna and the entire interview was taped. A transcript was forwarded to her and, on March 16, 1975, this transcript was edited jointly by Domin and myself while I visited her in her home overlooking Heidelberg. The revisions consist of a few cuts in length and a number of clarifications. Since she speaks

English fluently, she took a great personal interest in the translation of a number of terms.

All translations of poems contained in this chapter were prepared by Tudor Morris in collaboration with Domin.

You assert that it has been proved that the poem is a "guarantor of freedom." What is your evidence for this?

A poem cannot be created upon demand, but, on the contrary, it presupposes the requisite excitement. This means that the creation of a poem is more an act of "doing" than one of "making," and this "doing" is only set in motion when you are spiritually and emotionally excited. Then the poem appears. This is why the poem is by nature free—otherwise it would have to be a political poem, a party poem, or no poem at all. It is inherent in the poem that man is alone with his experiences (though these may well be experiences gained in the outside world), and that what comes forth is within him. And for this freedom the necessary distance is needed. Nothing poetic can be the product of a command. Just as you cannot make love on command you cannot write a poem on command. This is what Pablo Neruda called a "guided directness," and which I call the "secret order." You can give yourself a secret order. You can demand of yourself, for example, that you write more economically, but you cannot demand of yourself that you become emotionally involved in the death of so-and-so if you are not affected by it. The poem is a guarantor of freedom. You have to be yourself and yourself alone in order to be able to convince others, this I believe. Do you follow me?

Would you explain to me how you view the task of a poet in the Federal Republic of Germany in the last third of our century? What are his political and social obligations?

I do not believe that the poet in the FRG or in the last third of our century has different tasks from those which he had in other countries and in other times. I consider such an assumption almost presumptuous. I believe that the poet does what he always does, what he always has done. He objectifies the crucial experiences of his time, since he is a contemporary, and he puts into words that which happens to him and his contemporaries. And by this process of identification, he transforms himself and his reader (who, as Virginia Woolf put it, is merely a twin of the writer) into the subjects, instead of the objects, of what happens to them. That is his task. He enhances the conscience by this act of verbalization, and he sharpens the responsibility of each individual (if he happens to be one to whom responsibility matters, as it does to me). But he will do this, as he has always done it, if the century does not go to pieces and if we do not become robots. He will be a human being and do nothing else than what he already did in the days of the ancients. But he will do it in the new ways of his contemporary period, and this cannot be foreseen in detail.

Please discuss the term model situation *which you often use in your critical writings.*

I believe that the primary difference between a poem and a letter lies in the fact that in a letter all details of a private experience are communicated. But the lyric poet reduces this experience to its value as an example, to a behavioral model. The behavioral model is the core of what we experience in, let us say, an act of love, in political resistance, or in the feeling of outrage at injustice. And this core experience is then expanded by the detailed experience of the reader. In a chapter dealing with "nonspecific accuracy" I have discussed this technique. The poet should not be vague. The poet is precise, but he depicts what is exemplary in any given experience. Otherwise he would be writing letters. Thus he only mentions details when such details are exemplary. Otherwise we would not be able to appreciate in the light of our own experiences poems of distant times and distant countries. Naturally not everyone can use all model experiences. I have written somewhere that someone who has not been forced from his homeland is not afraid of exile. When I speak with children about the danger of being exiled they simply do not understand me. Then I say to them: "You are exiled and lose your home when your parents get a divorce," which they understand at once. Now that we are on the topic of exile: this is a very important subject, one of the main subjects of our century (although it was a central theme already as far back as Dante), and I believe that it exerted a decisive influence upon my own work. This is why refugees from the East and refugees in general have so often identified themselves with me.

In contrast to Nellie Sachs or Paul Celan, who focused upon the specific exile experience of one ethnic or religious group, the Jews in Central Europe, I consider the Jews merely to be an example, a special example of the tragedy of homelessness here on earth. The

82

church often states that God needs an example, and that the Jews are well suited for that purpose—this is not what I mean. I mean that the Jews have often been used as an example for the fragility of man, for the fact that he really does not have what he believes he has, and that man is at home nowhere on this earth. This is why I have called my apartments "stops," in the tradition of St. Theresa. They are my resting places, which implies my nonresting places.

When you talk about the tasks of a poet, I am of the opinion that poetry was never possible without courage, and that people make the achievement of courage more difficult today. Courage has become more expensive, because it has become rarer, because a great conformity is spreading as a result of the media. A poet needs at least three kinds of courage—the courage to *identify* concisely, which means not to change things by lies, not to identify incorrectly but to identify accurately; then the courage to *speak out*, because he must be able to relate that which has happened to him without consideration for himself, as though he were a third person, although he is himself. Finally, he must also be able to say something precise about himself—he may not think: "Does this reveal something intimate about me, or does it not?" On the contrary, he must have the courage of total candor even when it concerns himself, which is not easy. But one learns with experience that one is only one of many, meaning that, when one speaks out candidly, one does so also for those others. A person who really believes that his fellow-man is totally bad or deaf could not write. It takes a whole lot of courage to *believe in the responsiveness* of others. To sum it up: there is no writing without courage.

Culture has often been considered to be the privilege of the elite. Lyric poets are mostly read by the educated, by a relatively exclusive and small public. How can they make their influence felt as broadly as possible?

It seems to me that elites are changing. Today the children of the proletarian and bourgeois classes of society have the possibility of attending universities. Attendance is still somewhat difficult because they do not have as much encouragement at home as do the children of the educated. But if you think ahead to the end of the century, you can anticipate a change in the elites; it will depend upon the structure of society what elites will exist then. A person such as I hopes that there will not be an elite of functionaries, but that there will be an intellectual elite.

But I believe that if you reach one person, and then another, and still another, then this is quite a lot. Therein lies the difference among authors: some want to reach as many individuals as possible, because each individual who is *conscious* of his responsibility and *willing* to accept his responsibility will get through to other individuals. Others want to reach a mass of people, want to move a mass, but wind up being moved along by the mass. They do not remain masters of the situation but wind up being herded. And they then become the enemies of those who want to mobilize responsibility and humanitarian instincts through individuals, no matter what society will look like at that time.

How do you react to the assertion that literature has two functions—an aesthetic and a social function?

The aesthetic and social functions of literature cannot be separated from one another. A poem is either good—then it is effective; it is, as I would put it, contagious. Or it has no quality as a poem, in which case it will die at once. Thus I see no distinction there. I would say with Pablo Neruda who said "Canto porque canto"—he was in a position to talk big: "I sing because I sing" or "I write poetry because I write poetry"; I write because I write, to put it into the more modest nomenclature of the FRG. And what I have written, since I am a contemporary and talk about things which happen not only to me but also to others, subsequently acquires a function.

But the most important aspect is not for whom one writes— one must focus upon the experience which one wants to express, nothing more! The poet who does this as a trustee of his craft and of his own sensibility can speak also for others, which would otherwise be impossible. He should not permit himself to be influenced by slogans, be they literary in origin or anything else, nor by any sort of models—the "long" poem or the "short" poem, or whatever is popular or "in" at the time—solely by his own conscience. A conscience is both ethical and aesthetic, both rational and humane. These elements cannot be separated from one another.

P. O. Chotjewitz comments on the currently popular utilitarianism as follows: "Two of the worst inheritances from bourgeois society . . . are the constraint to have to justify each thought and each action, and really not to be permitted to do anything that isn't of some utilitarian value."

To this I would like to make the following comment: Things which

84

are really important in life are never useful in the sense of a prima facie profitableness or useability. Things which really matter are superfluous and, at the same time, cannot be relinquished: such as love—babies can be made without it; poetry—people can exist without it. To reiterate: They are superfluous but cannot be relinquished; they have a "usefulness" in a higher sense.

Can literature and especially lyric poetry change reality?

I believe that literature can merely change the individual, and it is the individual who changes reality or has the possibility of doing so. It can be said that literature (and thus also lyric poetry), which does not change reality, makes itself felt by tearing the individual away from his indifference of the heart. By taking from the individual— how shall I put it?—this indifference, it removes his inhumanity. Indifference is the chief inhumanity in fascism and in any system. By activating man as a human being—that is what a lyric poet really does—the poet changes reality, as this human being, this individual who is so very human, helps to improve reality. I discussed this matter in Budapest during the Petöfy Festival last year. Many poets read there, many Russians and poets from the GDR. Only Enzensberger and I were there from West Germany. They all talked about whether or not poetry changes the world. I asked for the microphone—I was not as well known then—I was not on the rostrum, and I said during this "live" taping that God would have been satisfied if there had been only one righteous person in Sodom and Gomorrah, and that I could not see for the life of me why we should be more demanding than God, and that I would be very happy to be able to change one person, and another, and still another—even if it were just one. And the next morning at breakfast I went over to the table of my colleagues and asked them: "I don't know my way around here. What do you think?" And they said: "If you weren't from the West you would deserve a decoration!"

Do you consciously write in a political vein?

Yes, of course. I am not an animal, I am a conscious person. I have a particularly high level of consciousness, I studied sociology. But let's forget about that for the moment. I write because I am excited from the top of my head to the tips of my toes, about topics such as injustice and whether injustice can be prevented, whether people are slackers, whether people have civil courage, and whether they are "follow-travelers" or whether they are motivated by solidarity. These are the important issues and I am willing to die for them; hence I can write about them. This sort of thing cannot be done by design. A programmed poem is no poem at all. I am against programs. I believe that a poet must pour his heart and his soul into his poems. And I, from the top of my head to the tips of my toes, as someone who once was persecuted, am a person who is afraid of the injustices that are being carried out and being tolerated by others.

This is evident from all my poems, from "Wen es trifft" ["To Whom It May Concern"], the last poem I wrote in Penobscot Bay in Maine in 1953 prior to my return to Germany, and which is a challenge to practice continence from injustice, to "Abel steh auf" ["Abel Arise"], so that everything may begin differently among us; this worry that injustice is tolerated runs like a red thread throughout my work. It is not my only topic, but it can be found time and again in my work, including my prose writings, and later on the topic of belonging, for example in "Lange wurdest du um die türelosen Mauern der Stadt gejagt" ["For a long time you were hunted round the doorless walls of the city"]:

> Lange wurdest du die türelosen
> Mauern der Stadt gejagt.
>
> Du fliehst und streust
> die verwirrten Namen der Dinge
> hinter dich.
>
> Vertrauen, dieses schwerste
> ABC
>
> Ich mache ein kleines Zeichen
> in die Luft,
> unsichtbar,
> wo die neue Stadt beginnt,
> Jerusalem,
> die goldene,
> aus Nichts.

> For a long time you were hunted round
> the doorless walls of the city.
>
> You flee and scatter
> the jumbled names of things

behind you.

Trust, that hardest
ABC.

I make a little sign
into the air,
invisible,
where the new city starts,
Jerusalem,
the golden,
out of nothing.

I would like to make a textual commentary here: naturally I wanted
to write *torelos* ("gateless"), but I had to write *türelos* ("doorless"),
because of the high vowel sound which lifts one's voice. The voice
thus rises when the author wants it to rise, at the word *türelos*. Then
it occurred to me that there are doors in most city gates. The battle is
that of Hector who, because he is running so quickly, cannot get into
the gates, and thus the city is doorless for him.

When I read this poem I thought of Kafka. Was I right?

No, assuredly not. It has nothing whatsoever to do with Kafka. This
is the situation: Hector, who is being chased around the city, is
denied the opportunity of going home. This makes him an exile,
who is driven farther and farther around his homeland to which he
may not return. The land and the city are equated, in the metaphor,
the city and its gates, like a country with its borders. And now we
actually have a country with a wall and with gates, the GDR. Back
then there was no "country with walls," but for me Germany was
walled shut. The turning point of the entire poem is "Trust, that
hardest ABC." In the beginning it is stated that the one who is
fleeing even loses his gift of language. He scatters the letters behind
himself and his language becomes confused. Everything has after all
been identified differently, renamed, or falsely designated. The
essential point is "Trust, that hardest ABC." In the last lines, in this
reference to Jerusalem, the heavenly Jerusalem, are included—as
far as I know—the mosaics of churches such as Santa Prudenziana in
Rome or Santa Prassede, where the Holy City is depicted with these
great walls and with golden clouds. I had not seen these mosaics for
twenty years when I wrote this poem in the winter of 1960–61; I had
left Rome in 1939. You can see that a tremendous amount of time

had passed. But these early Christian mosaics had impassioned me, as has this Holy City, this Holy Jerusalem, which is a heavenly Jerusalem, which has nothing to do with the Jerusalem in Israel or any other earthly city—it is the Promised City. Ernst Bloch would call it utopia, this city which has been promised, the ultimate home of which one cannot be deprived. And that is why I call it "the golden (city) out of nothing." If we talk about gold here, it is the golden color light, of the sun, the last glimpse of the sun, the color of desperation that has been overturned, euphoria in extremis.[1]

I would like to say the following concerning "Schneide das Augenlid ab" ["Cut your eyelid off"]:

Schneide das Augenlid ab:	Cut your eyelid off:
fürchte dich.	be afraid.
Nähe dein Augenlid an:	Sew your eyelid shut:
träume.	dream.

I do not remember when or why I wrote it. I recall that I thought it would turn out to be longer, but it was suddenly completed. When I had written these four lines, nothing could be added, for what could possibly be added to them? If I were to interpret this poem I would say that, because people often blink when they are afraid, I am telling them they should not blink and squeeze their eyes shut, but they should look attentively. To put it metaphorically: they should cut off their eyelids to be able to perceive reality. If they perceive they must be afraid; reality is frightening. Man should not squeeze his eyes shut and look away or close his eyes; on the contrary, he should perceive.

On the other hand, I demand that he also must close his eyes and dream. I mean that he must dream of how mankind should be, both as individuals and in relation to others. And then these two conditions must constantly be compared to one another. Man must do both of them simultaneously.

The poem that was orginally published under the title "Post-ulat" could also bear the title "Challenge":

[1]For a detailed interpretation of this poem, see Hilde Domin, *Doppelinterpretationen*, 3rd ed. (Frankfurt a.M.: Athenäum, 1967), pp. 190–97.

Ich will einen Streifen Papier
so groß wie ich
ein Meter sechzig
darauf ein Gedicht
das schreit
sowie einer vorübergeht
schreit in schwarzen Buchstaben
das etwas Unmögliches verlangt
Zivilcourage zum Beispiel
diesen Mut den kein Tier hat
Mit-Schmerz zum Beispiel
Solidarität statt Herde
Fremd-Worte
heimisch zu machen im Tun

Mensch
Tier das Zivilcourage hat
Mensch
Tier das den Mit-Schmerz kennt
Mensch Fremdwort-Tier Wort-Tier
Tier
das Gedichte schreibt
Gedicht
das Unmögliches verlangt
von jedem der vorbeigeht
dringend
unabweisbar
als rufe es
"Trink Coca-Cola"

I want a strip of paper
as tall as myself
five foot three
on it a poem
that shouts
as one passes by
shouts in black letters
demanding something impossible
civil courage for example
the bravery that no animal has
co-suffering for example
solidarity instead of herd
abstract words
to be made concrete by doing

Man
animal that has civil courage

```
man
animal that knows co-suffering
man abstract word-animal word-animal
animal
that writes poems
poem
demanding the impossible
of everyone who passes by
urgently
irrefutably
as if it were calling out
"Drink Coca-Cola"
```

It is one of the cycle "Drei Arten Gedichte aufzuschreiben" ["Three ways of recording poems"]. This is a poem directed against slackers and was written for a literary forum that Horst Bingel put on in Frankfurt a couple of years ago. Poems were displayed there in the form of posters. One naturally selected posters which would mean *nothing* to the ordinary passerby.

I imagined a poem on a long strip of paper. As some doors open when one steps on an electric cell (as in an airport) or as some art objects are in darkness or bathed in light when one enters a room (as in the Museum of Modern Art in New York), this poem would beckon to the passerby, cry out to him, demanding that he does not remain deaf. In addition it was supposed to demand something impossible—civil courage. And when I assert that civil courage is impossible I am counting on contradiction by those who hear this statement. If I say that civil courage is impossible, he will respond: How come? Civil courage is possible. That is why I call it impossible, because it is so very difficult, though possible (despite the thought of some that it is utterly impossible). And then I continue: "the bravery that no animal has"—and in so doing I define man as an animal with civil courage. To be sure, an animal has the courage needed for survival, to defend itself and its young, but it does not have the ethical daring required for civil courage. Co-suffering, I say "co-suffering" instead of "pity", because pity implies looking down upon someone. *Co-suffering* is a word which you will find in no dictionary, a word which has not been coined previously. It is a term of brotherliness and of identification with one's fellow-man. It puts you on the same level with the person for whom you feel co-suffering.

Akin to the English term empathy?

No, empathy would be less specific. In any case, the word does not exist in German. It is a new word which I have coined. One can only coin words in one's own language. You know, if I were an American wanting to write in German any German schoolboy could speak up and say: This word does not exist, you must delete it.

The poet has the right . . .

No, he does not just have the right, he *can* do it. He has the duty to do it, if he can do it. That is a fabulous gift. He can only do this in his own language. Solidarity instead of herd instinct! Herd equals fellow-traveling, running after a bellwether. I am dead set against clichés and people in the Federal Republic who think daily in clichés really exasperate me. The nonconformer is innovative, but those who run after him are conformers of nonconformity. This is a new type of conformity. The one who repeats an experiment is not an inventor. And he who runs behind a bellwether, whether reactionary or rebellious, is nothing but a member of a herd. One can, of course, agree and go along *from case to case*, but being a member of a herd is something quite different. I say that what is lacking is solidarity instead of the herd instinct. *Loyalty to one's fellow-man, civil courage* and *solidarity*, I maintain, are foreign words; they must be translated into German in the form of action, "by doing". And then I turn it around again and say: "Man/animal that has civil courage"—earlier I had said that this is impossible. Here the problem of defining mankind is raised. Man has been defined as an animal that buries its dead, but this may not be valid much longer. In America they are dumped into the ocean, that is, their ashes are dumped, with funeral music as is seemly. Thus I define man as an animal that has civil courage, is capable of co-suffering, uses words, uses foreign words, and is an animal that writes poetry. That is what man is, as long as he is no robot. And I define the poem as "demanding the impossible," which means the ultimate, something which is startling at the moment, but nevertheless possible. That is what it demands "of everyone who passes by." And I say this as though it were as commonplace as Coca-Cola.

Hans Peter Keller
Born 1915 in Rossellerheide

A native of the Rhineland, Hans Peter Keller lives today in Büttgen, a few miles from his birthplace. He studied philosophy at the universities of Louvain and Cologne. During World War II he was twice seriously wounded, and discharged for disability in 1942. Since then he has been an editor in Switzerland, and he is now a teacher of literature at the Technical College for Booksellers in Düsseldorf.

Hans Peter Keller has been publishing poetry since 1938. His publications also include aphorisms, essays, literary criticism, and anthologies.

He was interviewed in his home on April 7, 1975, and the entire interview was taped. At his request a transcript of the tape, together with an English translation, was sent to him for corrections. This resulted in a number of minor changes in the German text, and these are reflected in what follows.

There is much wisdom in your aphorisms, and they are relatively easy to understand. But in your poems, which consist neither of verses nor of sentences, which do not contain allegories in the usual sense, you make it *much harder for your readers to understand you, even though they instinctively sense them to be poetically beautiful. Why is that?*

To the first point of your question: You say that my aphorisms contain wisdom and are easily understandable. I believe that this is a misunderstanding. These aphorisms—fragments, parceled goods and brittle as they are—do not pretend to convey wisdom. They are word games, thought games designed to challenge the reader to find himself, through the use of language and with the aid of language. The process of being on the move is important to me. That the reader comes to terms with himself is more important to me than a tangible result. A result is always problematical. What is valid today is no longer true tomorrow. But what happens during the reader's exchange of ideas with me, is what I consider significant. I believe an element of the humane comes into play, which is more cogent, which is a level more profound perhaps than the politically ideological and socially critical reflections which are so much in vogue today. I consider the interplay between reader and poet which I am trying to achieve to be of basic significance.

And now to the comprehensibility of my aphorisms. Yes and no. Yes, insofar as many of them, at the first level of understanding, pretend to be witticisms, flashes of insight, jokes delivered with a twinkle in the eye, yes, even puns. But if one thinks a little bit, one penetrates to a second level of understanding, which means that one discovers their latent coherence. I would like to put it this way: These little language and thought games conform to the romantic maxim: "My fragments are designed *to stimulate* thinking." In other words, they are not a *summa existenciae*, a precipitate of experiences; it is not their purpose to communicate experiences but to create experiences. When the reader fills the spaces in these fragments with his own experiences, with substance from his own memories, his fears, sorrows, hopes, dreams, etc.—only in the communication with such a reader is the text completed. As Novalis put it: "The reader is the expanded author."

About my poetic production you said that my poems are composed neither of verses nor of sentences. I do not know how you interpret the term *verse*. If you use it in the classical sense, your assumption is correct. My poems are word groups which on the face of them correspond to a series of sublime personal experiences (I hope you will excuse this somewhat bombastic sounding phrase). I do not know precisely how great the value of these word groups might be for a potential reader. I believe, however, that if one reads these word groups exactly according to their line arrangement, their meaning becomes evident from the image of the text and from their acoustic effect. As you have noticed, allegory in the usual sense is not intended. The same goes for metaphors in their traditional sense. I attempt to induce the reader to achieve understanding, especially understanding of himself, by means of a ventilation [*Durchzug*] of language. In other words, we are not dealing here with ready made, conveniently packaged, transparent goods, but with roughly textured surfaces which remain in place—little stones on which to stub one's toe! Or, if you please, pedagogical literature.

You do have a didactic purpose in mind: to create experiences. Does this creation of experiences by means of your poems also attempt to judge or improve our contemporary society?

Now we have arrived at the crucial question which is asked of almost every author today. When I publish something I naturally first of all want to speak to the individual. Basic work. It is didactic because I want to entice the individual to reflect, by means of my text, about what exists and what could exist. Thus, first of all, analysis of the self and perhaps change of the individual; wherever possible—*pro domo*—reevaluation of all values (big words! You know their source!). And from the individual then germination, radiation onto the neighbor, transfer to society as a whole. But let us stress that this is an internal process, please! No advertisement billboard, no editorial columns, just the appeal to the individual, this most private form of communication. If I multiply this reader, and my texts because of the size of the editions do have the chance to act as multipliers, then my texts can, from time to time, influence matters, conditions and, above all, attitudes over a prolonged period of time. Ad hoc, and in this period of time, as is demanded so often today by slogans such as "relevance in the sphere of society"—I want nothing to do with that! The engagement of an author is less a matter of content than of attitude, at least as I personally sense it. An attitude, in turn, can possibly produce novel contents. Here too the result is, at least initially, unimportant to me; I consider the means of achieving the result important.

So you proceed from the assumption that individuals must change before

society as a whole can change. How do you respond to the following
statement by Reinmar Lenz?

> It is particularly disturbing that the future as a topos seems to have
> been leased by the authors of the German Democratic Republic, while
> the lyric poets of the West evidently do not recognize hope as a
> principle and, at best, contribute dire predictions and prophecies of
> doom when they ought to be discussing that which should happen
> tomorrow.

As I see it, Reinmar Lenz has here panned the scenery quite
carelessly and with too small a lens opening. In the light of day one
cannot seriously fall prey to the notion that the writers of the Ger-·
man Democratic Republic have taken a lease on the future as a
topos. It is a matter of integrity whether I offer chic utopian recipes.
Chimeras are pots that are boiling over; they spoil one's taste for the
realities that are possible. It would be far more upright to begin with
a thorough diagnosis. Western literature, where it is progressive,
has been doing this for quite a number of years. It would be asking
too much to demand that the diagnostician also prescribe the
therapy. History proves that therapeutic cures are not devised in a
jiffy, if we look at the matter objectively. I concede that utopian
measures may legitimize themselves as being productive if they
remain within the realm of the possible. Is this a clever *contradictio in*
adjecto, where nonsense rhymes with consent? What is happening in
the German Democratic Republic at this time is a mysterious
utopianism. A carefully planned sound world is supposed to be
infused onto our pluralistic chaos. Anyone who moves through this
world with open eyes must perceive that we are a long ways removed from a sound world. There is, for example, the problem of
the ecology. It is a question of importance to all of us, to each
personally. It intrudes upon us far more radically than all political
ideologies, no matter what their color may be. The consciousness of
reality—I do not want to judge across the board, this would be a
cliché and thus cheap and unjust—this consciousness of reality of
many authors of the GDR, is programmed from above. It can hardly
enlighten our present condition by means of a credible principle of
hope. It would be far more honest, as I have implied, to divide the
problem areas among the subject matters and the people involved
before one tries to construct. Once again: basic work. One must
begin at the bottom, not in lofty heights with resounding slogans

and catchwords which are enunciated in the morning and which outdistance one already that evening. It is better to go one little step at a time. It is better to take two steps forward and then one backward rather than three steps forward and then trip. Scepticism promotes progress, as the old platitude puts it. Western literature is characterized by greater elasticity, i.e., liberality, since experimentation takes place without restrictions in order to get to the bottom of the questions and the doubtful concepts. A trace of this tendency can probably also be found in my work.

Critics have occasionally accused you of being a cynic. How can you refute this on the basis of what you have written?

I suppose that those critics have not thought my texts through thoroughly enough, have not projected their thoughts sufficiently. I can demonstrate this by means of a brief example. An aphorism from the collection *Panoptikum aus dem Augenwinkel* [*A Sidelong Glance at the Wax Museum*].

> legt ihm keine Sträuße aufs Grab er litt so
> unter Heuschnupfen

> place no bouquets on his grave he suffered so
> from hay fever

When you first read or hear this text it certainly seems macabre, rotten or nasty, as do many others which I have written. I believe, however, that if one thinks for a while the conclusion is inescapable that it is not based on cynicism at all but on a quite different attitude. Here is at least the challenge to adopt an attitude which, to be sure, is not in vogue today: piety, humanism. Big words, but please, "place no bouquets on his grave he suffered so/from hay fever," says nothing more than that one should in commemorating the deceased respect his peculiarities, particularities, his ticks, his neuroses and allergies, in short: his entire personality. At least this is the quite nonpastoral intent of this two-liner. And that is supposed to be cynical? I admit that my texts are often ironic and sarcastic. I consider these to be necessary virtues in this day and age, more necessary than ever to promote a sober perspective.

The poem "Kurzgeschichte aus der Geschichte" ["Short Story from History"] might serve as another example:

der Name tut nichts zur Sache: einer dieser
Altgedienten
schal das Augenlicht
Tränensäcke
hatte eines schönen Tages folgende Idee

schade daß ich nie Zeit hatte
sagte er sich
Zeit zu testen
wie lange der noch die Luft spürt
der da baumelt
wann genau ist er hinüber
und wie denn

schade keine Ahnung wie das
wirklich ist: mit dem
Moment
—müßte doch
auszumachen sein
sagte er sich
und

schade
der seltsame Held
hat uns sein Resultat
nicht hinterlassen

his name doesn't matter: one of these
old soldiers
his eyesight faded
bags under his eyes
had one fine day the following idea

too bad that I never had time
said he to himself
never had time to test
how long someone still feels the air
when he dangles
when exactly he crosses to the other side
and just how

too bad no idea how this
really is: that
moment
—ought
to be explored
said he to himself
and

too bad
that odd hero
did not leave us
his conclusions

This text surely appears to be quite macabre, cynical. Free of emotion, which, in this case, would be quite superfluous by the way it zeroes in on an event from my past experience. An upright, honorable man [*Biedermann*][1], one of the many "honorable men" (firebugs) of the past, was unmasked after years of enjoying the respect of his neighbors. He had belonged to an execution squad in Warsaw and he hanged or otherwise did away with vast numbers of men and women. He succeeded in hanging himself in his cell prior to the announcement of his verdict. I insist that these lines do not represent any form of cynicism; a human-inhumane fact is depicted here which could not have been dealt with by the use of polished phrases. A cold laconism has to be employed to ensure that these lines convey their sense. Only in this way can they stimulate contemplation on the part of the readers. Yes, and self-contemplation, for this "odd hero" undoubtedly serves a model function: the name does not matter, "one of these/old soldiers." How many "old soldiers" are there still among us who, hiding under the mask of an honorable man, collect their pensions even though they are retired firebugs!

An inhumane set of facts should also be sought behind the poem "Stacheldraht" ("Barbed Wire")!

doch	nevertheless
wie gezwinkert ja wie	as though twinkling indeed
mit Zinken	with tines
antik	following ancient custom
um die Kuhweide	around the pasture
gut	well
doch	nevertheless
ich seh schlecht ich	I see poorly I
hör schlecht	hear poorly
schreit's	it calls out
gräßliches	ghastly
Zeug	stuff

[1]The German term *Biedermann* immediately recalls the title of a play by Max Frisch *Biedermann und die Brandstifter* (Biedermann and the Firebugs).

doch	nevertheless
red doch	say it clearly
deutliches	in plain
Deutsch	German
das röchelt ja	I hear a death rattle

Barbed wire is one of the symbols of our age, and I must hasten to add, especially of an epoch which we Germans—no, not *we* Germans but the Nazi Germans—initiated. The words *barbed wire* remind one of Auschwitz, of the infernal concentration camps where millions perished. In my text the words *barbed wire* are first used benignly as an optical phenomenon in a bucolic atmosphere, around a pasture. So far, so good. That simply means that cattle are constrained here not to break out. But then comes the change of mood, the change of voice: barbed wire—in our times this picture no longer implies what it did idyllically in the days of old, but it has acquired a monstrous actuality—people are constrained like cattle. Now I can no longer hear the harmonious sound of alpine cowbells, I no longer see the beautiful cow eyes (in the Homeric sense of that term), but I hear the terrifying cries of tortured human beings, "ghastly stuff." I am compelled to translate this stuff into comprehensible language. And I discover that it is "plain German": "I hear a death rattle."

I said that barbed wire is a symbol of our times. It is—and this beyond the German sphere of culture, please put "sphere of culture" between quotation marks—an even more intensive symbol than the napalm bomb, than all the biological or chemical death weapons. It is the symbol of the period per se.

Your concern with contemporary problems, which seems central to your work, is especially evident in your poem "Zeitzünder" ("Time Fuse"):

es tickt es tickt

ich lese in der Zeitung
im kommenden Jahr
falls nicht etwas dazwischenkommt
werden einige weitere
Millionen Zeitgenossen voll Lebenshunger
umkommen
mit dem Hunger

es tickt und es tickt und es

gibt Gäste zur Nacht lese ich
da zeigen die Lüster mal wieder was
Glanz ist
falls
nicht etwas dazwischenkommt
linde Berauschung kommt aus den Vasen
Bedienung kommt in
Schuhen aus Luft
schalldicht Wände bekommt
das Bewußtsein

und tickt doch wie das tickt

und falls nicht
etwas dazwischenkommt morgen kommt
die Zeitung mit einer
Schlagzeile mehr

erschlagend zeitgenössisch zeitgenüßlich
der Tick

noch ein Prost Herr Minister
ehe endlich der Rausch kommt ehe
Ihr Trick
in Kraft tritt
auch Sie pardon gehn vor die Hunde

immer tickt es immer flinker

jetzt
kommen meine Augen
auf dies Bild in der Zeitung
Haut und Knochen
keine Metapher

es tickt tickt tickt das hält
nichts auf gar nichts falls nicht
etwas
dazwischenkommt

ticktock ticktock

I read in the paper
that next year
unless something interferes
some additional
millions of contemporaries hungry for life
will perish
of hunger

ticktock and ticktock and

there are guests for the evening I read
the chandeliers will once again show what
luster is
unless
something interferes
soothing intoxication emanates from the vases
servants enter on
featherlight shoes
soundproof walls surround
the consciousness

ticktock and how that ticks

and unless something
interferes tomorrow will appear
the newspaper with
one more headline

devastating contemporary hedonistic
the tick

again to your health Mr. Secretary
before ultimate drunkeness before
your trick
becomes effective
you too if you pardon me are going to the dogs

ticktock more and more quickly

now
my eyes notice
this picture in the paper
skin and bones

not a metaphor

it ticks and ticks and ticks nothing
stops it nothing at all unless
something
interferes

This poem was occasioned by an item in the paper, one of those popular statistical analyses. It related to me, after describing the current state of affairs, what was to be expected in the following year, if the world situation did not change. In the same paper I read that a leading politician of the Federal Republic (I can spare us the name; he is very well known, he lives in Bavaria, a combative gentleman) gave a large reception. With a little bit of fantasy I imagined what the reception would be like. This scene serves as an example; it is not limited to this "Free State" [Bavaria], which is so remarkably "conservative." And it ticks on, more and more quickly, skin and bones are not a metaphor—we do not live in a time of resonant metaphors, but in a time of the most blatant realities. And if "something" does not "interfere," and this "something" is most assuredly not just "anything," a total collapse of our society cannot be prevented.

What you have said is irrefutable evidence that you are an engaged poet.

I do not consider this to be a happy choice of phraseology. There are no poets who are *engagiert*. As a contemporary individual I am intimately involved in contemporary events. Daily politics are my business, in the semantically most precise sense of what these words imply, every single day. I cannot do anything other than to "pull my weight." That, however, does not by any means imply that my poetic work has to be solely determined by political realities. It is obvious that my world of literary expression is influenced by my attitude toward the environment. Today I cannot sing a pretty little song like Eichendorff or Mörike did (once again a platitude, I am afraid). I also cannot write poems of the type which Heine wrote, even though he is much closer to us. I could not even articulate as Brecht did, who is still closer to us psychologically. I talk, I must talk about that which burns on *my* lips. But this does not make me an *engaged* writer by any means. My *engagement precedes* everything literary and is *more important* than everything literary (please remember the beginning of our conversation). If this is the way you interpret the term *engagement*, the state of being engaged, involved, then I agree with you.

Do you agree then that literature has both an aesthetic and a moral and social function?

I do not see two functions here but rather a single one. The aesthetic element in the works of an author simultaneously fulfills moral and social purposes. In any case, I would like to have my work accepted in that sense. When I create aesthesis in the Socratic sense this also produces a moral accent which has relevance for the relationship between the I and the Thou. Thou—You must participate in this activity, for otherwise my feat has not succeeded.

Karl Krolow

Born 1915 in Hannover

Karl Krolow studied literature, philosophy, and art history at the universities of Göttingen and Breslau. Since 1942 he has been a freelance writer, first in Göttingen and Hannover, from 1956 on in Darmstadt where he resides in the Rosenhöhe, an artists' colony. He has been a Visiting Professor of Poetry at the universities of Frankfurt and Munich, and he is probably the most widely published lyric poet of the FRG. His earliest poems published during the war, show the influence of Loerke and Lehmann; he then profited greatly from his studies of Garcia Lorca, Éluard, Baudelaire, and Mallarmé. His translations and adaptations of French and Spanish poetry are major achievements. His poems, however, are unmistakably Krolow, characterized by a unique combination of transparency, melancholy, and economy of expression.

In addition to lyric poetry, adaptations and translations of poetry from other languages, he has also published essays, critical comments, prose works, and even written texts to accompany illustrated books.

Karl Krolow was interviewed in his home on March 19, 1975. What follows is a translation from a verbatim transcription of this taped interview.

In 1961 you wrote: "The German political poem is barely productive. The political poem of the western world is the eminently "public" (öffentlich) poem in general. It tells something of the composition of and the relationships and disproportions in human society. Only secondarily does it take sides or mention the word party." Are you still of this opinion?

In principle, yes. We are talking in this quotation about 1961, and I assume that this stems from one of my university lectures in Frankfurt, where I made this statement while serving as a Visiting Professor of Poetry. It deals with the situation prior to the events of the sixties, meaning the international student movement and the other presuppositions for poetry written subsequently. When I said this there was hardly a political poem proffered in our country. One naturally had to refer back to Brecht, and authors like Enzensberger had just become visible. When I spoke of a "public" poem, a term which I would still use today, I in effect referred to a poem that, beyond party perspectives, special interest aspects, preconceived notions and publicity seeking, deals with social conditions and deficiencies, and which is primarily interested in articulating what pertains to our society. From this broad perspective did I view then and do I still view the political, the engaged, poem, *not* the poem that advocates party interests.

Can and should the poet, by means of the engaged poem, attempt to cause his readers to change their points of view?

He should try, to be sure. Among other things a poem is an experiment, nothing more, nothing less. I would not want to go so far as to believe that poems can change the world; naturally they cannot do this. Who indeed can change the world? Some people perhaps, but not people from this corner. But we can arouse interest, and that is very important. Alert people have achieved quite a bit in this world. Perhaps I should add: the sensitive people, but they are the alert ones. I presuppose here a very specific type of reader. But that is precisely what he is: sensitive, attentive, one who projects further that which he has read, including the political or engaged poem. By means of his power of comprehension he absorbs these poems; he then uses his sensitive attitude of readiness to achieve results. How these results manifest themselves becomes evident later. I think that poems can, at the very least, exert an indirect effect like the one I have just described—not a spontaneous effect, a violent effect, a shocking effect; the few examples of this are exceptions. We are talking about the poem of average potential and average capability which, with its average penetrating power—and its thus implied limitations—can be found in a volume of poetry and is then absorbed by a reader of average sensitivity and willingness. This reader "uses" it accordingly, and thus an influence within limitations by the poem is possible, but one should not expect too much of a poem. Today I am no longer entirely of the opinion which I held some years ago that the poem is a structure designed to preserve or create beauty, which is, more or less, a lovely illusion for the eyes and ears, but which is reserved and preoccupied with itself. It does transmit something; it is prepared to give someone a chance. There is a certain power, a momentum. That is my current opinion.

Well—if the poet is aware of this potential of the poem, would it be fair to say that he does not have just an aesthetic responsibility but also a social responsibility?

Yes, one might say that this is necessary. Even if an author does not always want to or can face up to this. To express it somewhat nonchalantly: because of the fact that I write poems something necessarily happens with certain people in certain regions. But this necessity is not of such a magnitude that I sense it as even halfway sensational. At the best it is a very discreet sensation. These are all discreet occurrences directed at individuals. Surely there has been mass effectiveness of poetry. Yevtuchenko was able to achieve this. Here a few were also capable of this during the Nazi period. I do not want to compare the two, although I am doing it. But I am not speaking about this kind of an effect. I am not talking about immediate results. The ballast inherent in this [phenomenon], the atmospheric jamming in which this results, both of these bother me. I still react sufficiently aesthetically to say that this is dangerous, that this is a terrain upon which one should move only with greatest reservations, when one speaks about the effects which may be produced by poems upon people who are receptive.

A famous statement of yours from 1970 states that the politicizing of literature, which can be discerned at the present time, is a misfortune for both forms of social discussion, for politics as well as for literature.

Yes, and I was naturally referring to a certain type of engaged poem.

106

Once again distinctions have to be made. I thought of the so-called *Agitprop* lyrics, which were shrill indeed, foolish, short-circuited so to speak, produced—and, by the way, very quickly excessively produced—by certain people who had excessively high opinions of their significance. It appears somewhat zealous to experience suddenly a change of voice and then to believe that this sort of production would lend masculinity to the effort. The whole business seems pubescent, I would say. However, the heroic phase of the student movement which occurred at this time is understandable to a degree. Something was happening in the streets, and the poem could not change its character as quickly as events do. It is certain that the street happenings were outdistancing the poem. And the shrillness was in essence only the futile attempt of a few people to catch up. Well, subsequent developments show that things have calmed down, that the voices have become scattered. While the *Agitprop* poets have not removed themselves from the scene they have returned to the background from which they came, namely, the background of their insignificance or limited significance. I then thought that this had nothing at all to do with the effectiveness of nonpolitical poems and poems that are less piercingly formulated. I expressed this opinion, which remains the same today, although I have learned since that through these shrill voices something permanent has been infused into the poem, something which had not existed previously, though it was transported, changed, accepted, caught, worn out in the mean time by others who assimilated it, who used it.

I am thinking of something which I myself have tried to accomplish in my activities as a writer throughout the decades. As a matter of fact, I did write a "Korean Elegy" during the Korean War. As a matter of fact, I did write some poems when Hungary was occupied by Soviet troops that had been invited by Hungarian communists. I did take positions, and you can read up on them. But I believe that I can say even today that at the same time I tried to write something that transcended the existing situation clearly. I wanted to depict a general human emergency. I wanted to broach the subjects of excessive power, of terror, of fright—but released, moved by that which had happened, which neither I nor others could prevent: poems of frustration, of forced concession, but not poems that had as their basis the illusion that they would exert an influence in these instances. They were spoken from far away and from a quiet atmosphere, while there things were happening, blood was being shed and those events occurred which I tried to fix in a literary setting. I said earlier that poems cannot keep up with the facts, with the realities of the street and of the wars which march through regions and spread terror. The tempo of a poem is much too slow for this. To be sure the sensibility of an individual can react quickly enough, but such events can only be approved of, registered in fear or rejected after the fact. This is how it was almost twenty-five years ago in the case of Korea and about twenty years ago with the Hungarian episode. They were, you might say, "apropos poems." These horrors, as everyone knows, can happen time and again as long as political and human conditions, politics and their variants do not change. But I have never had the illusion of immediate effectiveness. Some have this illusion, they have seen the loneliness of the individual in a machine called war, called terror, called streetfighting, called fear. The terror which I have described, how it approaches through the suburbs, is carried into the cities, this nightmarish situation on the eve of a war, on the eve of acts of terror which can no longer be prevented, these appear a worthwhile literary topic, unfortunately without an end.

And thus if what you or any real poet writes as the result of an inner necessity does exert a positive influence on the individual, on the lonely reader—for one does usually read poems in a quiet hour—if it contributes to increased awareness of these problems, then this is a positive though not directly intended by-product of the poem, is it not?

Yes. I cannot tell how one of my poems is accepted, I cannot force this, and it is to a degree of secondary importance to me—though I do not mean to imply that it is a matter of indifference to me. I consider it possible that it may reach a single individual; I also consider it possible that it might be a group. In any case a single poem always has only a limited possibility of getting through. It does not spread like a prairie fire. But, as I said, that is not even intended. I count on the intensity of acceptance by the individual, by several individuals, by a group, if you will, but certainly not on an incalculably vast number of people, who do exist at mass meetings and who must necessarily exist time and again in a mass society, when they are drummed together for whatever reason, to demonstrate for or against something. But my poems cannot accede to such a lust for demonstrating; because of their vocabulary, because they are not coarse enough and simple enough and understandable enough and quick enough to get through to the heads of a vast number of people who are yelling in confusion or being silent in confusion, which is almost the same.

I do not expect to reach a large audience. I am not depressed by this, but I am cautious. I am an economical person. It is a part of my economy that I know from the outset that a poem—I have said it several times—has definite limits, very delicate limits, that it cannot transcend certain limits, but that it is capable of achieving something of permanence, perhaps for an entire lifetime or for a major segment of a lifetime, something of lasting value.

Would you please illustrate your concept of the purpose of the poem and the poet by means of some examples?

I will first try it with a poem, a little poem entitled "Die Macht" ["Power"]:

Vorübergehend
eine deutsche Redensart
wie aus der Pistole geschossen—
die Macht.

Anfangs klopft sie
mit dem Knöchel
an die Haustür.
Geduld gehört dazu.

Das ändert sich.
Man steigert die Geräusche.
Die Grabinschriften lauten
immer vorsichtiger.

Temporarily
a German figure of speech
as though shot from a pistol—
power.

At first it knocks
with its knuckle
on the house door.
Patience is necessary.

But this changes.
The clamor increases.
Tomb inscriptions sound
ever more timid.

I would like to call this an elliptical poem, a poem which owes its very existence to economy, a poem which begins with something very incidental, a German expression. We say that someone reacts as though he had been "shot from a pistol," that quickly. This is a quite military figure of speech, is it not? And that which I say at the beginning of the poem is initially only a figure of speech, a German figure of speech "as though shot out of a pistol"—that is how quick, how sudden, overnight, irresistible, is a power takeover and the effect of power, which, having been introduced in the first four lines as appearing suddenly, as though it were appearing on a TV screen, really has not acted all that precipitously, because it had been on the way for some time. Initially it knocked, as it were, "with its knuckle on the door." It came unobtrusively, going from house to house, went to the door, wanted to create the impression that it was not "power" but someone from the neighborhood. This deception requires patience, I believe. I could also have said "planning." I suppose that whatever is inconspicuous needs to be carefully planned, with impatience acting as a counter force. But here a careful and purposeful attempt is underway. From the background, from inconspicuousness, from an everyday setting, thus practically from nowhere this phenomenon appears which after these preparations will suddenly seize power, no longer knocking but with an uproar, a raised decibel level, with violent change, with what is called a "takeover," with the usurpation of power overnight. It does not have to be a certain system. It is a universally applicable phenomenon among men: whoever has power has the right—"as though shot from a pistol"—this right—"might." A clamor is raised, power is exercised; disregard for others is demonstrated; they can be exterminated, if they disagree with the power being exercised, if they resist, if they want to be individualists, want to be human—the inhumanity of power. At first, the inhumane acts quietly: upon the takeover (*Machtübernahme* was the term used here in 1933) individuals are being stalked; the end result is expressed in two lines here, very economically but clearly: the shadows of the dead, and graves with carefully phrased inscriptions. Power is so strong that it transcends the death of the individual who had been seized, terrorized, or dispatched by it. One could say that this force is passed on from one power play to another.

The poem which I just discussed was elliptical, economically structured. In any case, it was an inconspicuous poem which came from somewhere and ended somewhere, namely, in death.

Similarly inconspicuous, emanating from the countryside, but also transcending the countryside, a German countryside, but perhaps resembling a landscape outside of Germany, is the next poem "Angesichts einer Landschaft" ["Upon Contemplation of a Landscape"], a poem about a countryside and yet more than that:

Diese Landschaft wie ein
nationales Lied.

Ihr vielzugrüner Bart
im Wind.
Er ist zu alt
für die Vögel, die sich
in ihm paaren.

Dazu ein Himmel
mit leisen Sohlen,
Gedichthimmel,
großer Augenaufschlag.

Der grüne Anstrich überall.
Er färbt die Finger
und die falschen Töne.

Die national Luft
steigt in die Luft.

This landscape like
a national anthem.

Its all too green beard
in the wind.
It is too old
for the birds which
mate in it.

Add to it a sky
on quiet soles,
a poetic sky,
a wide raising of the eyes.

The green tinge everywhere.
It colors the fingers
and the wrong notes.

The national air
rises into the air.

Yes, this is a central European landscape. I do not just want to say German, but I thought of a German wooded countryside, fairy-tale landscape, landscape of the Grimm Brothers, Löns landscape; it is a landscape which is, on the one hand, sinister, and on the other, fatal, but, in any case, political. Very green—there are quite a few forests in this country. I am thinking of a countryside that is too penetrating, too green. Too green and too old. This landscape is encumbered by its age, encumbered by stories and by what happens in the woods. It is too old for the continuation of life, a shell of a landscape, thus dangerous, contrasted with a "sky on quiet soles" which wants to take possession of this landscape for the duration of one poem, such as this poem, a sky with widely opened eyes, glancing ironically upon this landscape, the landscape with a "national anthem." (It need not be a national anthem—there are many nationalistic songs.) This sky drags the countryside over the coals, though this might be too strong an expression. It tries to achieve an understanding, ironically, approaches it, then withdraws again from this "green tinge," from the penetrating green that dominates everywhere, from the encirclement by the landscape which has become dangerously green because of its age and its history. It is so green that its coloring runs, and despite its age it remains penetrating and persistent; despite the burdens of its history and the fairy-tales with which it is associated, this uneasy mood which rises into the air high above the woods. "The national air/rises into the air"—this tinge colors "the fingers/and the wrong notes." Something does not tally here, has never tallied, when one approached this landscape in a certain way, when one praised it to the sky, when it was placed above everything else and made the subject of a national anthem, when one wanted to immortalize the beauties of a moment in the countryside by making it the subject of a philosophy of life, of a weltanschauung, of all that which may set people against one another under certain circumstances. We have experienced this dangerous Gothic element, this central European penchant for trying to reach the sky with political opinions and churches, and both

112

are potentially explosive. All of these ideas are concealed in this poem about a landscape. They are exposed for a moment, during the ironic, wideopen glance cast by the poem which then closes its eyes once again to look away, to focus upon something else, without forgetting that there were times during which the national air rose very violently, not only here, but occasionally also elsewhere.

"Gar nicht lustig" ["Not a Bit Amusing"] is a poem about a Sunday, which does not necessarily convey a Sunday mood, but which rather describes a desolate place and a treadmill atmosphere, the repetition of this mechanical existence, it is *not a bit* amusing, as the title states:

> Der gar nicht lustige
> Sonntag besinnt sich
> der ins einzelne gehenden
> Sachen: zu viel Zeit
> war für beendete Dinge,
> Anliegen der Kunst
> oder für das Verzeichnis
> zurückzulassender Personen.
> Unaufhörlich sich bewegende
> Bilder standen nun still
> wie Kleinigkeiten, die
> nicht der Rede wert sind,
> vergessene Standuhren und
> versteinerte Passanten—
> Museumsbilder, unbeachtet
> vom Wochenbeginn im Gemüt
> mit seinen ersten
> Straßenunfällen, Tarifverbesserung
> und überhaupt angemessenem
> Sozialfortschritt.

> This Sunday, not a bit amusing,
> recollects facts
> in much detail:
> there was too much
> time for concluded matters,
> artistic concerns
> or for the register of people
> to be left behind.
> Incessantly moving images
> now stood still
> like trifling details

113

not worthy of mention,
forgotten grandfather clocks and
fossilized passers-by—
museum pictures, unheeded
by the start of the week
solely concerned with its first
traffic accidents, tax reforms
and in general appropriate
social progress.

It is as though the world were to stand still for the employee. I am talking about people who are everywhere, and whose Sunday, as everywhere in the world, regardless of religion, even among freethinkers and atheists, could be like everywhere else, namely, bleak. Something to which one is accustomed does not happen on Sunday, the assembly line, and with this weekday assembly line all this good progress stops. It is "not a bit amusing," it is very taxing. There is too much time to look into the wrong direction, there is too much time in the five day or four day week. This is surely true. And on top of all this there is the Sunday. One is prepared for the beautiful, if beauty could be recognized, if these "artistic concerns" could be recognized and those other finished matters, these objects which are extant once and for all, which approach one, which lie about or stand about very orderly like a "register of people to be left behind," like people we thought we had left behind us, whom we considered finished as though they had simply died. But on Sunday they are laid out, as it were, in the death register of a desolate place, in this spreading boredom, this Sunday boredom, in which images otherwise in constant motion simply stand still, where nothing that had kept us breathless during the week wants to move: tax relief, accidents—it looks like we got away this time. We can still read about it. And all of those general images of progress which had kept us all in motion. All that is gone now, and what remains are the props that are not worth mentioning, trifles. Good! We suddenly notice that we have grandfather clocks, which actually indicate the time, which could pleasantly sound like metronomes if we were to use them; perhaps they even still run. But basically we are in a fossilized Sunday world. Everything is stopped, nothing moves. We walk around in a museum, our apartment, our life, our city, our Sunday-city, in the Sunday-apartment—with Sunday-music, Sunday-dinner, or—what is that? And there surely is some evidence of geniality [*Gemüt*] but of a sort which at the beginning of the

114

week will appear differently, when life becomes unpleasant [*un-gemütlich*], but at the same time could easily be more humane, less of a museum, less fossilization, less looking at completed things, fewer "concerns about art," but, as I indicated, connected with some risks. Here there are no risks; Sundays are free of risks. A desolate place is described. A kind of desert. Nietzsche once said that the desert is growing. That is the way it is. I want to say no more. We are in the middle of a desert called Sunday.

Photograph by Hans Georg Schwark

Hans Bender
Born 1919 in Mühlhausen

Hans Bender's studies of literature and art history at the universities of Erlangen and Heidelberg were interrupted by the war. He served in the German Army from 1940–45 and was a prisoner of war in the USSR until 1949. Since 1952 he has worked as a writer, editor, and lecturer (including assignments in Turkey and the USSR as well as a year as Visiting Professor of Poetry at the University of Texas). He now lives in Cologne and edits one of the most influential German literary journals, Akzente.

He has published poetry (the first volume appeared in 1951), short stories, novels, essays, and anthologies.

Hans Bender was interviewed on April 3, 1975, in his apartment in Cologne. The entire interview was taped and, at his request, a transcription of the tape was forwarded to him for corrections. This resulted in minor changes in the text.

I have been familiar with your work for years and have always considered

you a lyric poet, but I noticed that you have published primarily prose in
recent years. Why is that?

It is true, early in my career I was always called a lyric poet, but not
much later a short story writer. I wrote poems as a student, as a
young man, during the war, and while a prisoner of war. Since my
return in 1949 I have been writing primarily short stories. And then,
I believe, came a clearly definable moment where my poetry stopped altogether. This has to do with my work as an editor. I published
an anthology with the title (a title originating with Wolfgang
Weyrauch) *Mein Gedicht ist mein Messer* [*My poem is my knife*]. I
invited poets to think about the art of writing, especially the art of
writing poetry. Why did I do that? Probably subconsciously because
I was dissatisfied with the poetry which was then being written.
And I was beginning to have second thoughts about the poetry
which I had written up to that time. I became critical, skeptical,
perhaps too skeptical. I still remember when I received Günter
Eich's refusal. He wrote in his letter that he did not want to make a
statement regarding the craft of writing poetry; he said that he was
like a centipede who could no longer move if he ever were to think
about his method of locomotion. You might say that I stopped
writing poetry because of a critical attitude toward my own poems
and also toward lyric poetry of the fifties in general.

The various phases of life also enter into this. Some people
say scornfully that writing poetry is a pubescent experience, that the
young write poetry. In his famous speech "Probleme der Lyrik"
["Problems of Lyric Poetry"] Benn cited that derisive remark by
Ernst Robert Curtius who said: "Oh, these young poets are like
birds; they sing during May and in June they stop again." But I do
not want to distance myself entirely from this early epoch when I
was writing poetry. In the intervening years I have occasionally
written poems. Last year, for example, I wrote new poems. And it is
probably true that one can find a lyric attitude in my two novels and
in my short stories. Some critics have commented on this. What is a
lyric attitude [*lyrische Grundhaltung*]? One must proceed from the
perspective of the "I"—from one's personal experiences. I believe
that my poems (which, significantly, I have called *Lyrische Biographie*) are probably much closer to prose, to realistic prose than the
poetry of Gottfried Benn or of Oskar Loerke. And if later on I time
and again expressed my sympathy for Brecht's poetry and for

Brecht's theoretical writings, then this merely manifests the same bias, that poetry, like short stories, like novels, like prose, should have a certain intrinsic value.

Which reminds me of a well-known statement you made in 1971, where you expressed your agreement with Brecht's demand that literature has to produce something, in contrast to Benn who maintained that poetry is directed at a muse, even though this muse does not exist. The term intrinsic value *logically leads to my central theme, engagement. Does the poem (and thus also the poet), aside from an aesthetic purpose, also have to fulfill a social or sociological purpose? If so, why?*

There is a certain history and a certain development in the answers which one could give to this question, answers which all too simplified have been described by the word *engagement* in the twenty-five years during which I have been active literarily. Brecht's engagement implied solidarity with the working class. He wanted to appeal to the workers and write for them, in the hope that what he wrote could be used in their class struggle, etc. About half of this engagement of Brecht has been taken over; the other half went by the board because the situation of the working class has changed in the meantime. The term *engagement* came from Sartre's book *What is Literature?*, where a strict distinction is made between *poésie pure* and *poésie engagée*. *Poésie pure* is totally scorned, above all because it was supposed to have contributed to the events that happened during the time of fascism. Certainly, and surely all too exclusively, only *littérature engagée* was accepted as valid. But I ask myself—and I asked myself the same thing back then—whether one can really impose engagement upon a poem, a short story, or a novel so unequivocally and with such assurance. This would mean imitation of Brecht and Sartre who, after all, had quite different experiences and lived in a somewhat different age.

There was a time when during each poetry reading and each discussion the engagement question was raised. Especially young people asked time and again: "Are you engaged?" I have never sidestepped this question, but neither have I ever answered it as unequivocally as the most ardent questioners had hoped. I have tried to develop a statement regarding my engagement with respect to the subject matter in which I happened to be most involved at the time and on the basis of my experiences in life. In the concluding remarks at the end of my first Reklam-Edition I gave a very concise answer, stating approximately the following: I write realistic stories which communicate certain experiences so that young people today, the younger generation, may read them and may consider them a deterrent. My stories are supposed to serve as a warning, just as one says: "If you touch a hot stove, you will burn your hand." This comparison may perhaps be too picturesque. But one can understand clearly how it is intended and how it can be applied.

But then there came a time when I myself began to doubt this engagement, because it is evident that experiences cannot really be communicated to someone else; that, if older people, fathers and grandfathers, relate their bad experiences to the youngsters in their families, they cannot be certain at all that their warnings have any effect at all, that they would modify the behavior of the young people in any way. Young people have to gain their own experiences. On the other hand, I have always gladly told young people that I, in my youth, was led to both the good and the bad by literature. When I read a war novel during the Third Reich I believed that war is heroic, manly, brave—something which I must experience. And a little bit later I ran across antiwar literature. It too did influence me. It opened my eyes. Thus literature does have a certain effect, and I still believe in this effect today.

When you talk about the effect of antiwar literature between World War I and World War II, I think of Erich Maria Remarque whom we all read, who had a very large reading public, perhaps even today. But how does lyric poetry as a genre fit into this picture, since it is read by a smaller, perhaps even an exclusive reading public?

It is difficult to describe the effect of poetry. Someone once told me that, a couple of days before Rosa Luxemberg was murdered, there had been a poem demanding her murder in a Berlin newspaper. If it could be substantiated that the murderer had read this poem and then acted accordingly it would be striking evidence of the horrible effect which poetry could exert. I believe that all poems, the poems of Schiller and Goethe and Mörike and Stefan George and Rilke, exerted influences, and that the sensitivity, the spiritual attitude of mankind would be entirely different if these poems had not existed. It is naturally very difficult to prove this. I even believe that poems influence people who never read poetry. They are reached somehow, perhaps when on a beautiful fall day someone reads a poem of Rilke or George to them. Then they see and sense how the poets must have felt.

Our entire relationships with respect to love, language, and to our feelings would be different, if poems had not suggested them—at least in part. It is perhaps similar to our experience with paintings: if an Italian landscape has been painted and we visit this area we experience it differently from an area which had never before been shown to us by an artist. These images of fall or of a landscape have been replaced by different images in our century. Now there are poems that give evidence regarding our times, that talk about oppression, about freedom, about certain political stances which one should adopt, about the suffering of mankind in concentration camps and in war. These are less beautiful poems, one might critically comment. But these poems too demonstrate something, pass information on, and in this way they make themselves felt.

Should the poet who can write about such topics on the basis of his experiences write such poems as the result of an irresistible inner urge, or should he sit down deliberately for the purpose of communicating these experiences and of transmitting his weltanschauung, which he naturally considers to be sound, to others?

It seems obvious that this wish ought to be the result of an inner compulsion and that it should stem from his experiences. As far as I am concerned these are self-evident prerequisites. But somewhere he will get to the point where he has to decide how to go about it. Our poets after the war opted for an academic language, a language of the cultured. They took over certain forms. To oversimplify it, they wanted to make their poems as artistically beautiful as possible and fill them with their knowledge and their cultivation.

I would consider it appropriate that the poet ask himself how he could best communicate his personal experience, his subjective engagement. The poet's language has to be stimulated by this subjective engagement. You are familiar with the controversy regarding the "Todesfuge" ["Fugue of Death," by Paul Celan] which was attacked by the dramatist Hochhuth, and, correctly so, from his perspective. He considered this ballad too beautiful to show what really happened in the concentration camps. Celan, of course, had a totally different opinion. Following the principles of Surrealism he wanted to blend beauty and cruelty. I doubt that the Surrealists achieved their goals by this highly cerebrated literary attitude—no, they surely did not succeed in this! This can be demonstrated by their effect: theirs has remained a literature for literature's sake until today. And this is also true of Celan's poem—it is literature for literature's sake. Anyone who reads a factual account about the concentration camps, or who knows Peter Weiss's drama *Die Vermittlung* [The negotiation], has a far more lasting impression than the reader of the "Fugue of Death."

In other words, it is important that the problem be described poetically but nonetheless relatively bluntly. A poem may not be obscure—it should be relatively easy to understand.

You say "obscure"—that just about describes what I am talking about. It also should not be academic, "cultured" [*gebildet*], nor should it be "hermetic"—to which I would like to add that now it also should no longer be harmonious. It might be clearer if I were to say that there should be no poem without a "gesture" [*Gestus*]—no poem without a message, no poem that fails to touch others.

One of the most beautiful gestures is in a very old poem by Matthias Claudius that closes with the words " . . . and our sick neighbor, too." A highly cultured, beautiful, hammered out, stylized poem, which does not mention the sick neighbor or a similar pronouncement, is, to oversimplify it a bit, a useless poem as far as I am concerned. Useless, because it has no effect or does not want to create an effect.

How should a poet ideally use language?

If I were to talk about a simple and uncomplicated language, it would sound very much like conventional, everyday language. There does have to be a differentiation between the language of poetry and everyday language. Poetic language must be more concentrated, more accurate, it must hit the mark—this is difficult to describe. It is difficult to describe, for example, how a simple line in a poem differs from a simple line in a conversation. Some of the younger poets, like Günter Herburger, Nicolas Born, Hugo Dittberner and Jürgen Theobaldy, are struggling with the problem of infusing everyday words, as they like to call them, "normal" words, simple sentences, into poetry. Sometimes they succeed in doing this, and sometimes they fail. Perhaps the word *natural* would not be appropriate here; it implies the contrary and thus a distance from that which I called "academic language" in poetry. Herburger and Brinkmann and others time and again speak of their great yearning for the English language. They say that it is too bad that the

German language is so encumbered with all that has happened; it is too bad that German is not as uncomplicated as English which can assimilate so much more readily and which has a much simpler vocabulary than German. Well, it happens to be the language of Kant and Schopenhauer and Nietzsche and George and others. On the other hand, Goethe managed to write a simple and beautiful German, and Stifter and Fontane and others used it so well. But somehow Herburger, Brinkmann, and others who agree with them, associate German with ponderousness, heaviness, "cultivation" [Bildung].

I consider your poem "Der junge Soldat" ("The Young Soldier") to be an excellent example of the use of natural language in poetry. Despite this relatively simple German, this unpretentious vocabulary, rhythm seems to play a major part in this poem. Am I right?

Yes. What I said earlier about poetry and about the use of natural language is a realization which developed and became strengthened in me over the years. Back then, when I wrote this poem, I do not believe that I could have made these theoretical remarks, nor would I have wanted to do so. I wrote my poems without following a conscious program. I have to accept "The Young Soldier" as I wrote it then and as it is in print. To be sure, it does contain certain embellishments. Somehow it does intend to be an attractive poem. And it surely cannot free itself entirely from the precedents which existed back then in 1949 and 1950. Among these elements is rhythm which was then less under attack than it is now. But it is not an artificial rhythm as in an alcaic-sapphic strophe, or like that of the poets who consciously emulate Greek form, as did our classical and pseudoclassical poets up to and including Weinheber and others. I believe it is a plus of this poem that, when one looks back upon it from today's perspective, it manifests something of these melancholy, gentle epochs. But the words, taken singly and apart—this one can say as an excuse—were not taken from literature, were not taken from other poems.

I know how dependent the young lyric poets, who began when I did, were on Rilke and Loerke and Gottfried Benn and others. But these images of poppies, the forest-path, the cottages, the pleated curtains, the berry clusters, the gladiola stalks, etc., actually happened to me in Russia; I noted some of them in my diary, and I did not at the time intend to use them in a particularly beautiful poem.

Der junge Soldat

In die Blumen ihrer Haare
rieselte die listige Erde.
Auf die Särge ihrer Brust
klopften unsre stummen Würfe.
Sieben gelbe, warme Gräber
trocknen in der Julisonne.

Wiesenweg durch heißen Mohn.
Wälderweg durch kalte Tannen.
Weg, der blind im Sumpf ertrinkt.
Ungewisser Minenweg—
Dann vorbei an hellen Hütten.
Vorhangfalten, Fensterglas.

Beerentrauben in den Gärten.
Rosen, Gladiolengarbe.
Brunnen, dran der Eimer schwappt.
Vor den Zäunen steife Mädchen.
In die Löcher der Pupillen
Haß, vom Schreck hineingebohrt.

Trauer durch den Sommer tragen,
Schultergurt und rauhes Tuch.
Handgranate, Spaten, Helm,
das Gewehr und die Geschosse.
Messer, eingekerbt die Rille
für das Blut der stumpfen Rücken.

Sieben fette Krähen wehen
aus den Ästen roter Föhren.
Sieben schwarze Federn fallen
in die Raupenspur des Tanks.

(Als er vom Begräbnis
seiner sieben Kameraden
zur Front zurückging.)

The Young Soldier

Into the flowers of their hair
drifted the cunning earth.
On the caskets of their breasts
resounded our mute clumps of sod.

Seven yellow, warm graves
drying in the July sun.

Meadow-path through sunbathed poppies.
Forest-path through cool firs.
Path of no return, drowning in a swamp.
An uncertain, mined path—
Then past bright cottages.
Pleated curtains, window panes.

Berry clusters in the gardens.
Roses, gladiola stalks.
A well, on which a pail clatters.
Before the fences girls stand stiffly.
Hatred, drilled by terror
into the recess of their pupils.

Sorrow carried through the summer,
shoulder harness and coarse cloth.
Hand-grenade and spade and helmet,
and a rifle and munition.
A bayonet, grooved to shed
the blood of blunted backs.

Seven sated crows are drifting
from the branches of red pines.
Seven dull black feathers fall
Into the caterpillar tracks of tanks.

(When he returned to the front
from the burial of
seven comrades in arms.)

The strophe that begins with the words:

Sorrow carried through the summer,
shoulder harness and coarse cloth.
Hand-grenade and spade and helmet . . .

remains my favorite, because it succeeds in describing the skeptical attitude that then prevailed. As you know one later spoke of the "clearing of the thicket" [*Kahlschlag*], a term which Wolfgang Weyrauch first used. It was difficult to find examples for this. Günter Eich's poem "Die Inventur" ["The Inventory"] was cited time and again, but the question was generally asked: Where are examples of this much touted *Kahlschlag*? We know today that the term was subsequently used incorrectly and interpreted incorrectly, but I believe that these three lines (and here I am using those terms again) which represent quite the opposite of academic and cultivated poetic language do contain an element of *Kahlschlag*. In contrast, the last lines which begin with "Seven sated crows are drifting" are reminiscent of a legend, of a fairy-tale—I believe that I wrote them like this because that is the way I experienced them. As a writer of poems, as a writer of anything, one is chock-full of what one has experienced, what one has read, what is cherished, of religion, and, in this case, also of fairy-tales in which the number seven has special significance, usually as an unlucky number. These things are within a person, and if he writes they come to the fore.

What about other poems from this period, when you were most active lyrically?

I think they are easy to explain. I wrote down what I had experienced. This event, where I had taken part in the funeral of seven soldiers, has a parallel in the funeral of a prisoner—the worst experiences of my life occurred whenever one of our prisoners died. During the first winter perhaps six or seven prisoners died every day in our camp. The procedure was totally shameful, how mechanically these bodies were loaded onto a sled and pushed outside of the camp and then secretly buried on a hill without a marker. The Russians had prohibited the registration of these deceased. There is not a list in existence to this day. This boiled down to a totally anonymous death of hundreds of thousands of prisoners of war. But in a poem this cannot be represented in the terms which I have just used, but must be concentrated, and I tried to do this in "Der tote Gefangene" ["The Dead Prisoner"], which is even more unadorned than the poem about the burial of the soldiers where what happened is simply recounted.

Geschoren,	Shorn bald,
entkleidet,	naked,
auf den Schlitten,	onto the sled,
tief im Schnee,	deep in snow,
nackt gebunden	tied on naked
mit zwei Schnüren.	with two cords.
Ein Hungernder zieht,	The one who pulls is hungry,
ein Spitzel schiebt,	an informer pushes,
ein Priester	a priest

ohne Kreuz,	without a cross,
im Spurgeleis der Schienen.	in the rut of the runners.
Der Himmel	The sky
hinter Krähen.	behind crows.
Die Erde	The earth
Eis.	ice.
Zwischen Faust und Schrunde	Between fist and crevice
der Spaten bricht.	the spade breaks.
Leichnam	A corpse
fern von allem,	far away,
ewig—	eternally—
auf den Nägeln	on the nails
fremden Schnees.	of foreign snow.

Let us look at the second strophe as an example:

The one who pulls is hungry,
an informer pushes,
a priest
without a cross,
in the rut of the runners.

This is nothing but an enumeration of facts. The hungry one pulls the corpse out of the camp because he will afterwards get a supplementary ration; an informer, one of the prisoners who snitches to the guards, has the same motivation; the priest without a cross symbolizes the clergymen who, in this situation, often displayed a totally unworthy conduct. They were just as hungry, just as miserable, just as pitiable as the rest of us . . . that was intended to be expressed by these lines.

Another very intense experience—I told you my poetry was published in a volume entitled *Lyrische Biographie*—was the return home, this return which in the literature following World War I had always been described as something marvelous, something heroic, which was, however, a very divided experience. On the one hand, the prisoners were looking forward to getting home. They had imagined to return to familiar surroundings, but time had marched on. New things had taken place. And they suddenly realized that this return was not concentrated in one day, but that they were marked men for four or five or more years because they were not present during all the events that had happened in the intervening years. And I tried to capture this predicament in the final lines of my poem "Heimkehr" ["The Return Home"]. Because I was born in a village and spent my childhood there, returning home was always associated with rustic images:

Im Rock des Feindes,	In an enemy tunic,
in zu großen Schuhen,	in shoes too large,
im Herbst,	in the fall,
auf blattgefleckten Wegen	on leaf speckled roads
gehst du heim.	you come home.
Die Hähne krähen	The cocks crow
deine Freude in den Wind,	your joy into the wind,
und zögernd hält	and your knuckle stops
der Knöchel	hesitatingly
vor der stummen,	before a silent
neuen Tür.	new door.

What I said earlier in ten or fifteen prose sentences is concentrated in the last six lines, and corresponds approximately to my concept of an ideal poem. Not all poems are so clearly manifestations of a certain point in my life, but I must note nevertheless (as should the critics) that they have been reprinted time and again. From this one could deduce that they strike a responsive chord because others, who had similar experiences in their lives, recognize something of themselves in these poems and thus feel attracted to them.

Nevertheless, it must be pointed out that neither these poems nor other poems of that era can truly convey what really happened. On the other hand, we also know that figures, cumulative cruelties, statistics, and didactic treatises also have little, if any, effect. We take notice of them, while the individual example, which the poem tries to capture, perhaps makes a greater impression. One single individual, like, for example, Anne Frank in Amsterdam, creates a deeper impression than a book dealing with the horrible collective fate of the inmates of an entire concentration camp. And I believe that a poem can produce something akin to this Anne Frank effect. This really suffices.

Your last remarks would serve splendidly as the finale of this interview. But I am tempted to ask you one additional question because you, as the editor of Akzente, *have a particularly good overview over the poetic scene in the Federal Republic today. How could you summarize it for the American reading public?*

We like to use the term *pluralistic*. This means that different tendencies, methodologies, and types of poems are evident simultaneously. Active poets fall into many age groups. There are some in their seventies, fifties, thirties, or even younger than twenty, and this does make a difference. The German poem—and I know that I am using a cliché here—constantly questions its identity. The development is away from that which I have called the academic and cultivatedly hermetic poem. It has become simpler and more natural. It has become a poem which makes a gesture, carries a message [*Gedicht mit Gestus*]—and when I say this it may be because I am influenced by what I said earlier in this interview. I particularly like the poems of the younger writers, whose first poetry volumes are being published and who are sending poems to me, because they are continuing ot beginning to implement the ideas which I have just expressed, though perhaps with some modifications.

Wolfdietrich Schnurre

Born 1920 in Frankfurt am Main

Wolfdietrich Schnurre grew up in Berlin where he still lives today for about half of each year, spending the balance of the year in Porto Valtravaglia in the Northern Italian lake district. During his military service (1939–45) he was incarcerated several times because of his "defeatism." After he failed in an attempt to desert in 1945 he was assigned to a "punishment company" (Strafkompanie). *He began his literary activities in Berlin in 1945 by writing book, theater and movie reviews for a number of journals and newspapers. He was a cofounder of the "Gruppe 47." He has been working as a freelance writer since 1950. In 1961 he resigned from the P.E.N. center of the FRG because he considered it to be too tolerant of the GDR.*

Immediately after the war he began to write short stories. He has published prolifically in many genres, including children's books, radio and television plays, essays, and poems.

Wolfdietrich Schnurre was interviewed in his apartment in Berlin on April 21, 1975, and the entire conversation was taped. Except for

129

elimination of a few redundancies the translation follows the German original verbatim.

In 1961 you wrote: "In Poland, in Hungary, in France, in Italy, in almost every country in Europe the writers are the conscience of their nation. In Germany it is desired that they be silent." This raises two questions: 1) Is it the responsibility of writers, including lyric poets, to serve as the consciences of the nation? and 2) Who in Germany demands that the poets be silent?

Permit me to say the following. It is *not* the task of an author to be the conscience of his nation, and there really is not anyone, as far as I know today, who wants writers to keep silent.

What I said in 1961 was written in a period of a definite political repression. I said it enthusiastically, perhaps somewhat too hastily, because of the wall the German Democratic Republic had built in Berlin. I would want to explain this statement today, but I could hardly excuse it any longer. When I think back now I reconstruct the situation like this: I was indignant regarding the entire circumstances, but seen from the perspective of realpolitik the erection of the wall was understandable, though by no means acceptable. If one were to deduce now that an author had to feel absolutely obligated to raise his voice in protest, then I would raise the additional demand that it would not prejudice his cause one bit if he first of all swallowed his indignation and considered the prehistory of this wall. While it did not have its origin with Adam and Eve, its genesis certainly dates back to Hitler. Besides, the Americans contributed to it just as much as did Ulbricht and the West German government. This is how the understanding of the wall should be revised. At the moment it was considered in bad taste if one said anything at all, and especially if one accused the West German government of bearing a share of the guilt for the wall. This, though somewhat exaggerated, is how the situation as it existed back then ought to be understood.

You wrote that the responsibilities of the writer, of the poet, include "a number of uniquely important functions and ethical obligations." Have these obligations changed in any way, have they increased or diminished in the last fifteen years?

The function of the poet has not changed. I only believe that I grossly overestimated it back then. Basically it is the function of the writer—I cannot define it, I am trying to paraphrase it by means of a temporary description—to be an eyewitness and an earwitness of that which occurs around him. Perhaps he can be a seismograph, perhaps he can point toward what is likely to happen tomorrow—this might be true ideally, but it does not have to be. In any case, he perceives what is happening today, perhaps even a tiny bit earlier than his reader. He should not be expected to recognize more than that, since more than that is not his task. Without violating aesthetic and other laws he should attempt to include in his poem, in an almost imperceptible fashion, ethical or humane or humanistic elements—these are big words, and this is a big job. But I would like to minimize my position, taken fifteen years ago, considerably. The experience gained since then has taught me that such extensive demands are too ambitious. Too much is asked of the reader or consumer of a poem if I slug him with tremendous formulations and try to realize these formulations by attempting to write a poem that would do justice to all of these demands. The result would no longer be a poem. It would be an endless, perhaps rhythmically segmented, thought-sausage [*Gedankenwurst*]. But I do not believe that the result could be a poem.

So you do confirm then (and I am once again quoting you) that "recent anger is not a valid stimulus for writing." You once said—and you must forgive me for confronting you continuously with your own words—that you write "l'art pour l'homme" and not "l'art pour l'art." These are big words that constitute a deliberate distancing from the tradition of a Stefan George, for example.

This does indeed constitute a disassociation from Stefan George and some other gentlemen, though I consider many of Stefan George's poems very beautiful. But I do not consider these to be big words. It may surprise you, but *"l'art pour l'homme"* ought to be the most obvious motivation for an author who hopes to be understood reasonably well, though he may not always be aware of this when he is writing, when he is chewing on his pen or on his typewriter. Naturally I initially write any poem first of all for myself, not immediately in its final form. I have associations which my reader cannot always understand. But then I rework these associations, boil them down on my little genius-cooker [*Geniekocher*], to ensure that the potential consumer, the potential reader, can get aboard my train of thought. I even provide him with crutches, if the poem, its rhythm, its construction, permits this, and I hope that these crutches are artistically concealed—I write for him, *"pour l'homme."* In no case do I write *pour l'art*. That I try to master *l'art* reasonably well, try to use it as a tool (or degrade it to that purpose, as the *l'art pour l'art* artist might judge me), is obvious. For me, art is a means to an end, and that end is my desire to be understood—perhaps not by everybody. Writing a poem and being understood are two different things. But I surely would like to try to be understood by those who know how to read a poem at all. Thus my modest formulation: *"l'art pour l'homme"* and not the immodest *"l'art pour l'art."*

"L'art pour l'homme" means to me that a poet's responsibility is more social and ethical than aesthetic in our present day society. Do I understand you correctly in this regard?

I know what you are driving at. But I do not understand why, if I say *"l'art pour l'homme,"* if I think of my fellow man when writing, this should immediately be interpreted in a social sense. I do not think socially at all. When I write I am totally asocial. I want to be understood and write for a potential listener or reader. But I do not give a tinker's damn (*einen feuchten Dreck*, as we say in Berlin) whether my reader lives in a slum or sits on a velvet pillow when he reads my work. It is only important that he understand me.

A second question is the content of my poem. Naturally this content is less directed at the reader on the velvet pillow than at someone who leads a miserable life, and I must hasten to express a limiting factor here: the individual who is deprived has less of a chance of understanding me. Why? Because he, as a result of the way he lives, has less of an opportunity to read poems. It is a fact that literature is written for a limited reading public, and that even fewer of them read poetry. The concept "social"—if I take it seriously and look at it from a literary perspective—has in my opinion nothing at all to do with poetry.

You have raised an issue which is particularly interesting for the literary scholar, that poetry is read by a relatively small public. As far as the general reading public is concerned, poetry seems to be an elitist genre.

This may sound as though I am contradicting myself. I do not believe that it is elitist, and I am of the opinion that the writer, the poet, the lyric poet, should do everything in his power to undermine this appearance of elitism. Getting back to something I said earlier, he cannot reasonably expect that he will be understood by the masses. He must presuppose a certain basic understanding of poetry on the part of his readers. For someone who has rarely read poems it is not all that simple to discern a lyric style. There is no need to cite Celan right off the bat. Let us take another example. I would like to mention Ingeborg Bachmann. As far as I am concerned, Ingeborg Bachmann by no means wrote in an elitist manner. As an example, her poetry volume *Anrufung des großen Bären* [*Appeal to Ursus Major*] is made of the literary stuff that permits it to be understood by a large number of readers. I believe that a writer, a manufacturer of poems, a producer of poems, should strive for enlarging this group. It will not get really big because a poem contains thought structures which not everyone can follow. But I can help my readers without violating the laws of poetry—that is a requisite. This is why I believe that, although elitism seems to be the rule, the author of poems should feel the obligation of violating this rule as often as possible for the benefit of that larger number who will then understand his poetry.

In the poem "Strophe" you use a falcon as the central figure. This falcon reminds me of the Lay of the Nibelungs *and of "der von Kürenberg." Were you thinking back this far when you wrote the poem?*

Als der Falke	When the falcon
der Taube	thrust its claws
die Fänge ins Fleisch schlug,	into the flesh of the dove,
sank eine Feder	a feather drifted
der Welt auf den Mund.	onto the mouth of the world.
Reglos hing sie	Motionless it clung
an den dörrenden Lippen	to those parched lips
und harrte des Atems.	awaiting a breath.
Er kam nicht; es	It did not come; it
war der Abendwind,	was the evening breeze,
der sie fortnahm.	that carried it away.

It could be that I subconsciously remembered this. I believe, however, that I wrote this type of poem deliberately, though I must concede that the subconscious, the less than fully conscious, may have played a trick on me. A poet really should not be unequivocally interpretable. What you are suggesting is entirely possible. But I do believe that, if you take the poem at its face value, it clearly indicates that this falcon, which is thrusting its claws into the dove, represents a warlike being. It is not just a hunting falcon which, when its hood is removed, attacks the heron or the dove. This dove is akin to the dove of peace, and the falcon almost seems to personify war. When I think of the "parched lips" upon which the feather from the dove falls, then this, I believe, refers to a human being, perhaps humanity per se. The poem ends quite pessimistically: an evening breeze comes. No breath comes forth any longer. The human aspect addressed here almost seems to have died. As a result the falcon image, as optimistically as it often has been depicted, appears to have been reversed and it should be interpreted here as a harbinger of death rather than something identifiable with a hunt or similar activities.

In your volume entitled Kassiber *(Thieves' Latin)—and you have written a number of poems bearing the same title as this book from the year 1956—a poem begins with the words "A cloud of dust approached . . ." ("Eine Staubwolke kam . . ."). When I read this poem I think of the atomic bomb. I have a problem with the third line from the end, "Women experienced convulsions of passion" ("Frauen fielen in Krämpfe der Wollust").*

The atomic bomb interpretation is not wrong, but, when I think back to the time this poem was conceived, it was not in my mind.

Kassiber

Eine Staubwolke kam,
eine rote;
lastend,
ein Dunstleib,
sank sie herab.
Die U-Bahn blieb stecken,
der Bus drückte die Wand ein,
es war Mittag, und war
eine rötliche Nacht.
Und roch nach Leder,
nach Steppe und Tierschweiß.
Frauen fielen in Krämpfe der Wollust;
Kinder erstarrten im Spiel;
und es regnete Sand.

Thieves' Latin

A cloud of dust approached,
a red one;

crushing,
embodied haze,
it settled down.
The subway came to a standstill,
the bus flattened the wall,
it was noon, and it was
a reddish night.
And it smelled like leather,
like steppe and the sweat of animals.
Women experienced convulsions of passion;
children grew still at play;
and it rained sand.

This is a poem of personal experience, if I may call it that. It refers directly to the condition in which I found Berlin, the city in which I had grown up. I came back to Berlin. I had experienced in other cities the entry of the Russians, which is not intended as a value judgment here. Neither is it in this poem. But the basic impression created by the steppe, this basic impression, has nothing to do with the Russian soldier. It has to do with those other bombs (not yet the atom bomb, although the first one had fallen by then in Hiroshima) which had fallen here and had devastated the city. Where there had been the State Chancery there was not only a pile of rubble, but in this debris hedge-mustard and moss were growing. They were messengers of the steppe—moss, reindeer, whatever associations you might choose. And, in addition to that, soldiers came. To be sure, they had been enticed here by us, for we had been the original aggressors, and they were now following us back—but they are here totally detached. You mention having had a problem with that one line. This is a cold-blooded reflection, that there were any number of people of the female sex—to formulate it coyly—who for a potato, something which I know to be a fact and can fully understand, gave themselves to those people who were marching in, who were prepared to spend some time with them, to state it delicately, and to be recompensed for this. That was the basic impression gained by anyone returning: the steppe, a new garrison which was suddenly here; and people who were willing to do anything to still their hunger. It smelled like the steppe, it smelled like the sweat of animals—there were horses in a city that used to be populated by cars. That was the first impression of Berlin in 1946, to reduce it to one denominator.

Only eleven years passed between Kassiber *(1956) and* Abendländer
(Occidental Countries). *But when I compare the poems contained in these
two volumes the difference among them is greater than one might expect
chronologically. Why is that?*

I will take the risk of putting you out by remarking that the author of
Kassiber may well have sat down one day after completion of this
volume to start writing the poems contained in *Abendländer*. It is thus
not the span of time that accounts for the differences, but rather the
style, how these poems were patterned. I make a very strict distinction, I might almost call it obdurate, between purely literary poems,
like the two examples we have just discussed, and utilitarian poetry
[*Gebrauchslyrik*]. This is not a denigrating concept. But utilitarian
poetry, as it is contained in *Abendländer*, and I will soon think of a
couple of good examples, is designed for a similar purpose as the
other poems, only more so: to reach a large audience, to reach
individuals who could not be reached as easily when I employed
satire (which requires a certain degree of being privy to the author's
train of thought). Two poems come to mind, "Wohnzimmer"
["Living Room"] and "Geschäftsmann" ["Business Man"].

Let us discuss the latter first:

Wieder ein Hochhaus
fertiggestellt der
Altersversicherung Regine.

Ach, wie verläßlich
schützt diese Gralsburg
doch nun unser Leben!

Stünd nur nicht so tot
und grundhäßlich
die Synagogenruine
daneben.

Once again a skyscraper
of the life insurance company Regine
has been completed.

Oh, how reliably
this castle of the grail
protects our lives!

If only the ruins of the synagogue
were not so dead
and so hideous
beside it.

Things were really happening fast during the reconstruction period
after the war in Germany. What was built first? Not apartment
houses. Skyscrapers! And I noticed especially new insurance company office buildings. When this trend began I do not remember
exactly, but it was relatively early. But I do know that at the same
time—not only back then, but also today, and this is 1975 after
all—the ruins of synagogues in Germany were and are not being
reconstructed because the Jewish congregations no longer exist,
because Jewish citizens are not interested in coming back here, even
if they survived, and that number is frighteningly small. I can think
of many cities where this is true. Berlin is an exception; here the
synagogue has been rebuilt. It too had been burned out, like all of
them in Germany—they are closed now and just stand there, while
the insurance company buildings of which I am speaking in this
poem are sprouting up like castles. This is a fact which anyone can
verify. I do not have to presuppose much. If I bring these two ideas
together in a short poem, and what is more, employ a certain kind of
irony, then I can expect that far more people will understand me and
grasp what I am driving at than if I wrote a political editorial.
Certainly the businessman, of whom I am thinking, who looks and
regrets most unfortunately—and isn't it disgraceful!!—that the ruin
of the synagogue is still standing. In certain cases I will even get
through to him and he will honor me with a shabby smile, but he will
somehow have grasped what I am after. This, then, is the reason for
one of these two poems.

The second poem "Living Room" is similarly constructed and
written out of a similar motivation:

Nun steht das Foto des Vaters
(SS-Offizier, gefallen bei Woronesch)
prall in der Sonne: Sohn Herberts
Koppelschloß gegenüber glüht auf.
Urgroßvaters Kegelpreisbecher
reflektiert das Geflimmer
und wirft es zurück.
Opas Mensursäbel pariert;

langsam sickert das Rot
die Klinge hinab und versprüht
im Nacken des Enkels; der spielt
auf dem Teppich Soldat.

Now the foto of the father
(SS-Officer, killed near Voronezh)
is in the full glare of the sun. Son Herbert's
buckle across from it flares up.
Great grandfather's bowling trophy
reflects the glittering
and throws it back.
Grandpa's duelling saber parries;
slowly the red oozes
down the blade and splatters
the neck of the grandchild; he is playing
soldier on the rug.

If I look at this poem correctly it seems to be dealing with three generations of Germans. A child plays soldier on a rug; the picture of the father, who fell in battle near Voronezh, is mentioned. Obviously he was in the SS—this too is mentioned. And grandpa's duelling saber parries, which is expressed through the reflection of light on neck of the boy who plays on the rug. This expresses, and I believe that it does so in a concise form, that the military tradition continues through three generations down to the child, who was then small, and is now, in 1975, presumably fifteen or sixteen years old, and who will probably follow in the same footsteps. I believe that this expresses the theme more effectively in only twelve lines, coupled with the irony of the poem and with the poetic distance that is maintained, than could be done by other means. Here too I hoped to reach some of those poeple so that they, in contrast to the author, might not experience this fear some day, a fear that this may be inherited from generation to generation.

Perhaps your best known poem is "Wahrheit" ("Truth"):

Ich war vierzehn, da sah ich,
im Holunder aß eine Amsel
von den Beeren der Dolde.

Gesättigt flog sie zur Mauer
und strich sich an dem Gestein
einen Samen vom Schnabel.

Ich war vierzig, da sah ich,
auf der geborstenen Betonschicht
wuchs ein Holunder. Die Wurzeln

hatten die Mauer gesprengt:
ein Riß klaffte in ihr,
bequem zu durchschreiten.

Mit splitterndem Mörtel
schrieb ich daneben: "Die Tat
einer Amsel." Man lachte.

I was fourteen when I saw
a blackbird in an elder
eating berries from the umbel.

Sated it flew to the wall
and scraped on the stones
a seed from its bill.

I was forty when I saw
an elder growing on the burst
concrete. The roots

had ruptured the wall;
a hole gaped in it,
large enough to walk through.

With shattered plaster
I wrote nearby: "The work
of a blackbird." They laughed.

It seems obvious that you are thinking of the famous Berlin Wall, but the poem does seem to imply far more than that.

If I wanted to be nasty, and I am nasty, I would say: you guessed correctly! I must disappoint you. Even though your assumption is reasonable, I absolutely did not think of the Berlin Wall when I wrote this poem. It is nothing but a description of a phenomenon: a blackbird is scraping its bill. (Actually it does this quite rarely, and then usually against wood—I had some ornithological training from my father.) I was reluctant to say that it shit on the wall, which is probably what it would have done. I am not being ironical—I say this entirely factually. The actual phenomenon is that when a bird

(What is the proper term here? I think that *Losung* only applies to large game) craps on a wall, it will deposit seeds. Birds do digest large numbers of seeds, and you can observe time and again how much potential strength there is in an elder seed, when it falls into a crack in the earth or into a little bit of sand that has accumulated between stones. The seed begins to sprout roots and one day there is a little plant. I have observed this hundreds of times on rubble or on normal walls, that a tiny plant or a tree (usually they were birchseeds that had been left by birch siskirts, or had been spat out or crapped, as I said) managed to survive and to develop further. After two or three years, if one remembered the place, one could see how cracks ran through the wall, cracks caused not by the weather but by the development from the little seeds transported there by birds, which had begun to cause the walls to burst. While I have never seen this, it seems obvious that it should be possible for this little bush or little tree to grow so much that it totally shatters the wall. Whether this is the Berlin Wall!! It could just as well have been part of the wall of the Warsaw Ghetto. There are many walls in this world that do not have the right to exist. There are other walls, walls formed by debris, which are the result of bombardments—but that is not what I am talking about. My topic is the phenomenon that something lacking in strength, something weak, can achieve a strong result. A blackbird is a very weak bird—it can accomplish virtually nothing. But the author writes with chalk next to the crack in the wall: ''The work of a blackbird.'' A blackbird can accomplish more, not by singing but any answering the call of nature, than any politician can, than is within the power of who knows what on this earth. And suddenly the wall is destroyed if one is patient. Patience is absolutely necessary. That is what this poem is all about. It also contains some evidence regarding the passing of years: at first I am fourteen, and then I am forty, as I recall. And in between a considerable amount of time passes. If people can muster this courage, and live with the victor or the tyrant, attempt to survive him, they may experience the joy of victory without using a big bomb. If you put your money on the powerless and the nonviolent you can accomplish something great. And that is what my poem tries to express.

Photograph by Renate v. Mangoldt

Walter Höllerer

Born 1922 in Sulzbach-Rosenberg

Walter Höllerer was drafted in 1941 and served in the Mediterranean. He was a prisoner of war, and after his release studied theology, philosophy, literature, and history at the universities of Erlangen, Göttingen, and Heidelberg, culminating in a Ph.D. in German literature. He traveled and lectured extensively in Western Europe and the United States (he currently holds an appointment at the University of Illinois, to which he returns from time to time to conduct seminars in German literature). He has taught at several German universities, including Frankfurt, where he wrote his inaugural dissertation (Habilitationsschrift, a post-Ph.D. major research project), and at the Technical University of Berlin, where he serves as Professor of German and Chairman of the Department of Literature.

He has published poetry, short stories, essays, and a novel, and has edited literary journals. His first poetry volume, published in 1952, contained poems written since 1942, including a number that depicted his wartime experiences.

Walter Höllerer was interviewed on April 23, 1975, in his office at the Technical University of Berlin, and edited the transcription of the tape.

Under the title "Progress" in Hans Bender's anthology Mein Gedicht ist mein Messer *(My poem is my knife) you write: "A poem could effect change, even if it were read only by a few; then it would be a necessity. It changes the perspective of the individual. It attempts to influence the attitudinal scene of an era and the actions which are possible within or are prevented by this attitudinal scene . . . ." From this I assume that you are of the opinion that the poem as a genre can be an effective instrument for the accomplishment of social and political changes.*

I wrote this statement when I was much younger and less experienced than I am now. I still agree with the basic premise of these sentences, but I know that there are many difficulties connected with any attempt to effect social changes through lyric poetry. I am convinced that I, when I write poetry (and I can only speak for myself), can only create a good poem when I myself am touched by the topic. And the feeling of being touched [*Betroffenheit*] is the difference. It sets me in motion, not only superficially by inducing me to engage in speculations, but it sets my rhythm in motion, my *creative thought* and my *imagination regarding future possibilities*. The feeling of being touched is the Alpha and Omega, which is why I believe that a poem which was written out of this feeling has the possibility of also touching others. They sense from the rhythm of the poem, from its liveliness, from the fact that it has escaped superficialities, that it is of concern to both me and them, that it stirs up both of us. Through such a feeling I reach many contemporaries who are sensitive and not already beyond any involvement, who do not simply consume or are being consumed. That is the decisive point, the possibility of transmitting something to others which, in turn, leads to certain cognitive processes, to certain processes of change.

Does the lyric poet who is touched in this way have a duty to use his creative talent to serve as a signpost to a better future? Or may he still today produce art pure in a society that seems to be at the brink of collapse?

Whenever one regiments a writer, whether he writes poems or novels or plays—whenever one tells him he *may* do this and he *may not* do that—in every such case this will lead to no results at all. In the event of the existence of such prescriptions—this is permitted, and that is not permitted—he will either conform to these restrictions, in which case he will certainly not produce that of which he is optimally capable, but merely what one can read in the newspapers every day; or he will not conform, and then he will soon be in a situation where he won't say anything anymore because one has forbidden him to say what he *wants* to say. In other words, such rigidity is no way of dealing with literature. An author will say what he has to say. Perhaps *l'art pure*, out of opposition of consumerism. But this is not for me! But one cannot set up any generally valid schemes. People's gifts vary greatly.

I look at contemporary literature as a large complex ensemble with many possibilities. And as such literature has every opportunity of accomplishing a lot. One should not expect that each author excels in everything, that he, for example, simultaneously is highly innovative and widely understandable. Good for him, if he can do both!

Within literature as a whole, within this vast ensemble, there is a place for authors who are so innovative that they are not widely accepted and who initially appear to be purely esoteric. And it may well develop that such authors were on the right track but ahead of their times, that they furnished the impetus for reflections which, to be sure, are not popular as yet, which have not been widely accepted, but which subsequently make possible the consideration and formulation of ideas and facts, which had not been considered previously and could not be formulated earlier. True in the case of Kafka, for example. And in the nineteenth century in the case of Georg Büchner. What they wrote was initially understood and valued by virtually no one, but later they became the most significant and important authors of their centuries, but were not recognized as such until later.

And others immediately have the possibility not only to supply innovation, which subsequently wins wide acceptance for initially just a few, but they have an immediate opportunity to appeal to a wide audience and to convince many. One should not tag them as writers of trivia: there are other possible explanations. Here literature simply follows a different course. There are writers like Heinrich Böll. He writes bestsellers and fulfills a valid function in contemporary society although he is perhaps not very innovative at all. He says much that needs to be said in a generally understandable style, within established tradition. Thus, he is neither a better nor a worse author than someone who elects a different course. They all are a part of literature, and literature can use these many possibilities to achieve its purposes. If literature is so polynominal, it also has the opportunity to exert its influence in the direction of innovation as well as in the direction of broad acceptance, of communication.

If you ask me about myself on the basis of what we have just discussed I will put it this way: *I try to be understandable*. I do not have a natural proclivity for esoterica. But I would like to say what I want to say—and I do not want to be mistaken for or confused with many of the "old truths," which I am not trying to convey. I therefore try to use *that* language which excludes confusion as much as possible. This is occasionally quite difficult for some people. They talk to me and ask: Did you mean it *this* way or *that* way? It seems to me that a process that leads to questions is not all that bad. One should not strive to record prepackaged answers on a piece of paper, in the form of a poem, to offer them to the readership in this form as a consumer good. A lyrical text that provokes questions has the possibility of leading the reader away from the superficial consumer life of our times.

You have talked about "understandable" style. It has probably always been one of the problems of lyric poetry that it appeals to a relatively exclusive public. You have also said that one should not categorize, that unlimited creative possibilities must exist within literature to ensure that a broad spectrum of poetic thought will be offered. How do you feel today about your essay regarding the "longer" and the "shorter" poem, which created quite a stir when it appeared?

I wrote this essay to ward off a narrower and narrower development of poetry. There was a lyric code language, ever more in evidence, which communicated by means of a metaphoric shorthand. These metaphoric grammalogues, I believe, were no longer the results of spontaneous impulses, of the feeling of being touched, but they were a part of an available, prefabricated repertoire of images. There was a mechanized assembly line, a sort of lyrical freewheeling. I mean that the post-Surrealistic metaphoric poems contained genitive metaphors such as "mustard of mourning" [*Senf der Trauer*] and similar devices, that in a stereotyped manner connected an abstraction with a concretion, which was supposed to exemplify the difficulties of reality. It was a process of writing in riddles. I was referring to these poems which moved in such a rarified atmosphere when I referred to poems that are "too short." In other words, I said that poets should consider the world in which we live instead of continuing by rote in a lyrical modernistic convention, producing these somewhat hermetic and rarified secretive poems. I advocated that poets should return to the spoken language, that they should part ways with pretentious artificiality. And I thought that one way to get away from the language of such post-Surrealism would be to realize that there are indeed poems which have something to say to the person the poet is facing, to his neighbor. I also thought of an American tradition, ranging from Walt Whitman to Beat Generation poets like Allen Ginsberg, where poems were designed to express a direct appeal to an individual or to many people, using the spoken language and avoiding subtle stipulations. Naturally the "long poem," the syntactical poem contains stylizations, rhythm, and imagery, but the poet does not isolate himself in a sphere of lyrical secret messages and farfetched metaphors—as I found from personal experience. Naturally anything theoretical which I wrote had something to do with my own development. I always said to myself: write a long poem which is more communicative and which does not introduce baffling word games—which is what I described in my essay. But I have also stated that a long poem should not be measured with a ruler. A "long poem" merely describes a *type* of poem; it is a poem that employs syntax and breathing intervals rather than closed metaphors.

My theory of the long poem was an attempt to get away from the tradition of symbolism and to approach a spoken poem, one that verbalizes oral German instead of the written language filled with involutions and sublimations. I am reminded also of the poems of the American William Carlos Williams which make eminent sense to me. Such somewhat longer spoken poems are not necessarily in the German tradition. There was a start in that direction in the *Phantasus* of Arno Holz, but the best examples come from America, the poems of Walt Whitman and his followers, and from Russia, the poetry of Majakowski, for example. Such poetry appeared to provide a salvation from the bungled situation created by an ever shrinking and less communicative type of poetry. My ideas created some turmoil and some misunderstandings among poets and critics, as though I had wanted to impose regimentation. There were arguments pro and con, but I stick by these theses, as long as they are not interpreted dogmatically—they were not intended to be dogmatic—and they were not formulated dogmatically. And at the end I stated that the long poem would then be the first step toward short poems, after the instruments had been retuned by employing different writing devices. I believe that there has in the meantime been a good beginning: We prepared a special issue of *Akzente* (2, 1965) where we demonstrated that the "long poem" does indeed have a place and a chance in modern poetry.

I do not want to deny that my theory also gave me an opportunity to make the transition from poetry to prose. I next published a novel, *Die Elephantenuhr* [The elephant clock]. I tried, by using a very specific prose which is rhythmically arranged and at the same time includes conversational elements, to "touch" a greater number of readers, but without compromising what I wanted to say. One critic, and I believe that he is correct, has tagged this novel as a five hundred page "long poem." Basically it is characterized by the same phenomenon that permeates my poetry from 1952 to the present day. They were poems of inconvenience, i.e., poems which were inspired by my being touched by inconveniences; thus the novel is a long "poem of inconvenience."

My theory of the long poem was not just a theory for its own sake, but it stemmed from my praxis, my observations, and my own writing experiences. Lyric poetry constantly takes bearings on attitudes, grasps situations anew, faces up to present conditions, and changes its vocabulary and instrumentation.

Poetry that imitates, that only confirms what already exists, runs the danger, in my opinion, of existing only for its own sake, of mumbling to itself. It loses spontaneity. It loses its lively coloration, its dynamism, the very ground under its feet—which is why I think that the discussion about the long poem was salutary at this point in history.

The changes in your point of view are easy to recognize. When I compare your poetry volumes Der andere Gast [*The other guest*] *and* Systeme [*Systems*] *the degree of change is astounding. In* Der andere Gast *you wrote in the tradition of the first half of our century, using rhyme and occasionally difficult symbols, while* Systeme *seems to approach concrete poetry but without obscurity. I would appreciate it if you would comment on the stylistic changes in the work of Walter Höllerer and illustrate this by use of a few examples.*

I never considered form as a separate matter, separate from the situations that aroused in me the feeling of being touched. For those moments which touched me, or, to restate it somewhat differently, for those inconveniences which touched me, I had to find the right language for poetic expression. I do not even consider whether I use a more traditional language or more modern modes of expression. There is always a right language for a given situation, and it will vary depending upon different situations. I sensed the situation after 1945 as quite different from that of today, of 1975. Naturally I too have changed, the information available to me has changed. The worst thing which one could do would be to *lie*, simply to deny the existence of this or of that and not to include it into the lyrical process. One must give what one has in himself. Certainly not less. It would be to give *less* if one were to cling to a stage of development and were to operate within it at any cost, just to be consistent would lead to self-imitation. But above all one should not try to give more than one has. One should not talk about things which one has not experienced and does not understand, just to create the appearance of being modern and as interesting as possible. Honesty is a matter of self-discipline. Failure to be honest results in self-doubt. I have tried to remain honest, which explains why the poems written in 1952 look different from the ones written in 1965 or 1972; conditions changed, and poems are stations along the way of the poet. I cannot imagine a poet who passes through various stages and yet retains the same tone. He does not stand still and therefore the key in which he writes must also change. If there is such a thing as a relationship between the intonation of one's verses and the poet's feeling of being touched, a change in key must be possible. Such changes should not be held against a poet; but, on the contrary, the reader should be skeptical if a poet keeps on writing in the same manner, monotonously giving expression to the same ideas. Such a poet is either moving in circles or has become stuck somewhere, which would make me very suspicious.

In my case I do not find it astounding at all that the poems have changed. You said that it appeared as though my poetry of 1952 was traditional and now, in the volume *Systeme*—how did you put it?—almost concrete. Naturally everyone has his predecessors. No one begins as a *tabula rasa*, but rather with what one knows. My first poetry volume [*Der andere Gast*, 1952] noticeably reflects what I had learned; influences can be identified. My free rhythms, for example, were inspired by classical odes. But I do not believe that these poems are so very traditional. They are formulated quite simply. My *penchant for directness* was as evident then as it is now. It is a function of my background, my birth, my environment. It was not as difficult then as it is now to formulate ideas simply, for we are now surrounded by both specialization and uniformity. We are in a very complicated manner ambivalently conscious of this sort of civilization. To express the current situation simply is surely more difficult than it was back then, when one breathed a sigh of relief to get out of prison at the end of the war, to have been released from a dictatorship and a bureaucracy. The reaction: Good, let's get started toward a new understanding! This created the possibilities for *Der andere Gast*.

In the second poetry volume, *Gedichte Wie entsteht ein Gedicht* [Poems how does one create a poem, 1964], the "longer poem" is first perceptible. Not just single moments are fixed, as they had been in *Der andere Gast*, but moments are depicted in their relationship to one another and in what might be called fluctuation within a poem. It is more difficult to identify parameters, there is more movement. The next stage was *Der weiße Hopfengarten* [The white hops garden], one long poem in three parts, published in 1967 by Wagenbach in one volume.

Regarding *Systeme* (1969) I should like to comment that at first glance these poems may look like concrete poetry. However, I never did subscribe to concrete poetry because I am of the opinion that language has greater possibilities than limiting itself to its own structure. Language is a means of communication and exists within a social framework; it also has a tradition. Therefore, it seems to me that I here do a number of things other than merely recording concrete lyric constellations on paper. What, perhaps in contrast to concrete poetry, fascinates me especially is that one can signal a lot to one's readers by introducing the right breathing intervals visually into a poem, which explains that unusual arrangement of the lines. It is supposed to enable the reader to read a poem in the manner in which I imagine that I would read it. As with Charles Olson's poetry, breathing intervals are indicated by the printed arrangement of the poem. The rhythm hesitates where the lines are broken off, so that the reader may sense the rhythm in which these poems were written. Such a writing system is merely an aid which is supposed to signal that this is how the rhythm of my life progresses—do try to follow me! It is not just important that you understand the grammar and the sense, but you should also understand the rhythm.

As early as in my first poetry volume, rhythm was very important to me, a means of communication. From the point of view of line analysis [*Semiologie*] it could be stated as follows: Rhythm makes language basically understandable as a series of signals. Even before I use a certain term, the rhythm I am using can communicate what I am trying to express to the subconscious or the preconscious of someone else. I thus consider it to be of ever greater importance that poems must be printed in a way which unmistakably signals their rhythm. I believe that this idea corresponds to the views of the American poet Charles Olson who expressed a similar theory. He said that the syllable is of utmost importance. What is intended to be expressed must be conspicuously recognizable from the constellation of the syllables on the paper. Then the reader cannot read it incorrectly but is guided to a correct rendering. How the poem is printed is not as much of an aesthetic problem or a problem of taste as it is part and parcel of the attempt to achieve accurate communication and thus understanding of the poem.

By contrast, concrete poetry is more interested in the exterior perception and tries to signal certain abstract language structures. I am interested in the sum total of what I want to *say*, not only in what language implies abstractly.

From my first volume, *Der andere Gast*, the poem "Der lag besonders mühelos am Rand" ["He lay especially effortlessly on the edge"]. It is not an accident that this poem has been cited and discussed time and again. Here occurred what I mentioned in the beginning: the writer's strong feeling of being touched can be sensed by his readers. For this to happen, it was necessary that the feeling of being touched be expressed without much ornamentation. I therefore believe that this is not a traditional poem. One cannot categorically differentiate between "traditional" and "avant garde" poems. There are poems which signal a timely feeling of being touched—then they *hit the mark*. There are others which miss to some degree; there the reader feels that something is lacking. The same key does not fit every occasion. Within a certain framework, I have found the right key for me, resulting in a continuum which is evidenced by a connection between the poems from *Systeme* and those from *Der andere Gast*: they are frugal in the use of ornamental expressions. They try to be concise, to understate rather than exaggerate, to stick to the point in such a way that the message becomes obvious, in order that they may become examples for events that touch many people. And such is true in this early poem.

Der lag besonders mühelos am Rand

Der lag besonders mühelos am Rand
Des Weges. Seine Wimpern hingen
Schwer und zufrieden in die Augenschatten.
Man hätte meinen können, daß er schliefe.

Aber sein Rücken war (wir trugen ihn,
Den Schweren, etwas abseits, denn er störte sehr
Kolonnen, die sich drängten) dieser Rücken
War nur ein roter Lappen, weiter nichts.

Und seine Hand (wir konnten dann den Witz
Nicht oft erzählen, beide haben wir
Ihn schnell vergessen) hatte, wie ein Schwert,
Den hartgefrorenen Pferdemist gefaßt,

Den Apfel, gelb und starr,
Als wär es Erde oder auch ein Arm
Oder ein Kreuz, ein Gott: ich weiß nicht was.
Wir trugen ihn da weg und in den Schnee.

He lay especially effortlessly on the edge

He lay especially effortlessly on the edge
Of the path. His lashes hung
Heavily and contentedly into the shadows of his eyes.
One could have thought he was asleep.

But his back was. (we carried him,
The heavy man, somewhat farther away, for he disturbed
The columns that were hurrying by) this back
Was only a red rag, nothing more.

And his hand (then we couldn't tell the joke
Very often, we both
Quickly forgot it) had, as though it were a sword,
Grasped the solidly frozen horse manure,

The apple, yellow and stiff,
As though it were earth or perhaps an arm
Or a cross, a god: I don't know what.
We carried him away from there and into the snow.

It is a poem about the war, but one which touches us also in the time of peace when one considers how humanity is being hurt and how one reacts to these injuries. The key is self-observation and the recognition that these injuries should lead to a clearer judgment of and attitude toward political processes and social processes. The mere fact that the poem talks about someone who is lying "effortlessly at the edge" signifies that one is concerned about things which are not in focus, about peripheral situations, outsiders and their problems. I believe that this concern can be sensed from my earliest poems on. It is a part of the continuum of my poems, this question about the status of the weak and the oppressed. I cannot identify with those who move along with the mainstream regardless of what happens. Political and social engagement need not be connected with party slogans—it nevertheless retains its political and social aspects.

Thomas Mann once said, and this makes eminent sense to me, that people who want to look at human relations from only one perspective, perhaps purely politically, run the strong risk of violating both humanity and democracy; they have a tendency to submit to a dictatorship. Thus the most idealistic engagement may accomplish quite the reverse of what was intended and support that against which it was originally directed. This observation should always be kept in mind. Engagement must be critically analyzed. I am for the principle of engagement, but I am against an engagement that is understood incorrectly, formulated in a misleading fashion or too limited in its objectives, and which then becomes counterproductive. To avoid this pitfall constant self-analysis is necessary. In my poem the engagement stems from the feeling of being touched by a life that has been disregarded and has ended in death. It is recorded precisely as the writer experienced it. He is touched by the process and he observes the reactions of himself and others. He notices that he himself first tries to ignore it nonchalantly:

And his hand (then we couldn't tell the joke
Very often, we both
Quickly forgot it) had, as though it were a sword,
Grasped the solidly frozen horse manure.

This was a self-defense mechanism among soldiers, not to become emotionally involved in that sort of thing but to try to pass over it lightly. This is a part of the reality which this poem takes up. And when the poem then near the end reads, "As though it were earth or perhaps an arm/Or a cross, a god: I don't know what," this is a hint that big words or big ideologies would have been futile in the situation, that one deliberately pushed them aside in order to see what was going on—to remain honest with oneself. The last sentence, "We carried him away from there and into the snow," first of all reports *the facts*, but secondly also the *feeling of being touched* by the fact that in this snow, which creates the impression of one big completely empty space, a man is lying, a man has been moved aside away from other human beings, as though he were an inanimate object. This scene demonstrates what it is all about, what touched me.

The end of this poem has been attacked. The poet and critic Werner Kraft, to cite an example, wrote to me and accused me of cynicism, of a lack of feeling for writing something like this. I am convinced that he misunderstood the poem. It demonstrates precisely the opposite. Rather than cynicism and lack of feeling it communicates how touched I was by this act of war and by this violation of a human being. The fact that it is expressed in a language which befits the situation demonstrates that the issue is not dodged by humanitarian rhetoric or artificially transplanted symbolism. The fact of having been touched is fixed within the parameters of feeling of this touching moment. It is all the more uncomfortable and all the more difficult to cover up with illusionary hope. Not every poem should show that each cloud has a "silver lining," for this would not only not improve the poem, but it would contribute to untruths and misunderstanding.

Jordan Chimet, a Romanian poet, has published an *Anthology of Innocence*. He defines innocence not as moral immaculacy, but as that which one formulates spontaneously from within, which is not camouflaged by rationalizations or by abstract systems; it is something which is spontaneously correct. There are indeed some poems where one demonstrates one's innate innocence, one's innermost intentions—and I would include my poem among them.

Perhaps that is the reason why so many others felt touched by it. One reason, of course, is that many others could understand the premises, had been in similar situations and still are, because war remains a fact of life. At this very moment, as we are talking together, such situations are happening.

A poem has the opportunity of presenting a situation open-endedly, of being continued anew time and again, where each person with his background and his experiences adds to the poem, creates it anew when he is reading it. Such reading is a part of the poetic process. A poem without a reader would be deaf-mute, would not justify its existence as a poem at all.

The poems from *Der andere Gast* describe *particular moments*. Thus, they are different from those in the second poetry volume, *Gedichte Wie entsteht ein Gedicht*, where many moments are placed in juxtaposition. As a result the later poems are first of all somewhat more difficult. "Wie die hohe Mauer auch heißt" ("Whatever the high wall may be called") may serve as an example:

Unzulänglich
   zwischen leeren und vollen Bogen
      eine Fahrt lang die Worte
   hintragen vor dein Ohr!

Und wenn es nichts weiter war als Hörbarkeit,
Die Minuten vernommen, Secunden
                abgespielt—
Und wenn es nichts sonst wär als Projection,
Als einige Schatten werfen in dein Haus,—ich
Traf dich an den Rändern des Grundstücks an.

Beweglichkeit
   zur Fläche
      vor der wir fliehen,—du
kannst den Zwiespalt fühlen, beim Aufwachen.

Wie die hohe Mauer auch heißt,
Und wie das Schweben über die Mauer hingeht,
Wie die großen Vögel paarweis herabkommen,
Heutzutage, da nicht mehr getötet wird,—

Laß uns die Stadt einhüllen in gelben Sand,
   Da drückt der Wind die Sandspur ans Fenster,
   Da wachst du, fiebrig. —
      Wenn wir vergessen, was uns hält,
      Wenn wir gelben Sand und Wind nicht schmecken,

      Wenn wir Fieberhitze, wenn wir
         gekrümmte Rücken,
Wenn Runzeln wir und spärlich Bedeckungen,
      die grauen Rinder auf dem Sand
      Nicht zählen,

Wars doch Möglichkeit—
    Mehr als Wort gegen Wort,
       Als alltäglich Dürre oder)die Harmonie⟨,
    Dies, zwischen Traum und Aufstehen
Atem ziehen.

Inadequately
  between empty and full sheets
      throughout the trip to carry
    the words into your ear!

And if there were nothing other than audibility,
The perceived minutes, passing
                    seconds—
And if there were nothing but a projection,
But to cast a few shadows into your house,—I
Met you at the property lines.

Mobility
    toward the surface
      from which we flee,—you
  can feel the discord, when awakening.

Whatever the high wall may be called,
And how there is soaring beyond the wall,
How the large birds descend in pairs,
Now, that there is no more killing,—

Let us envelop the city in yellow sand,
    There the wind presses traces of sand against the window,
  There you awaken, burning up.—
      If we forget what keeps us,
    If we don't taste yellow sand and wind,

If we don't notice the heat of the fever, if we
    Don't count bent backs,
Wrinkles and, scarcely protective covers,
    the grey young cattle on the sand
    If we don't count all those,

It was still a possibility—
    More than one word against another,
      Than recurring drought or "harmony,"
    This, the breathing between dream
  And awakening.

Of all of my poems this is one of those I like best. It is an attempt to depict in a monologue the many experiences which one has had, to reconstruct one's inner landscape as it then existed. Because inner landscapes depend upon outer landscapes, they are reversed. All that demanded one's attention in the outer landscapes reappears here, such as a high wall which was encountered in the outer landscape, perhaps in Berlin—but it would not have to be the political Berlin Wall, it could just as well have been one of the firewalls that characterize this city. One cannot help but notice how many divisions are created here by means of walls. Or the configuration of the surface upon which one is moving about: there is no straight road—one is forced to look in many directions to avoid losing one's way. And the earth is but a little star in the midst of many possible directions of vision and motion. Our perspective of the world is no longer that from a country road or from a mail coach. We no longer see in straight lines, neither with our outer eye nor with our inner eye, when we contemplate the landscape of our knowledge and our dreams. This poem has to do with these experiences. It is a love poem, addressed to someone who sits or lies nearby. This someone is addressed with the familiar pronoun *du* ["thou" translated here as "you" because of the awkwardness of "thou"]: " . . .—you/can feel the discord, when awakening." It is an attempt early in the morning when one is still half asleep to tell the other person everything that one has experienced, which is why the images are presented in a dreamlike outline. They flow into one another. The rhythm too is that of a dream:

> Inadequately
>> between empty and full sheets
>>> throughout the trip to carry
>>> the words into your ear!

The "into your ear" is meant quite literally: the communicating of what has happened, into the ear of one who is so close by early in the morning. This communication occurs again at the end where the poem reads:

> It was still a possibility—
>> More than one word against another,
>>> Than recurring drought or "harmony,"
>> This, the breathing between dream
> And awakening.

155

Thus, the "situation" of the poem is between dreaming and arising—a morning monologue for the loved one nearby.

Everything of special concern is mentioned. No one moment has been singled out from the many moments; this is a ballet of moments, motion toward the plane from which we escape because it is endangered, the plane of life which is awaiting us that day: you can feel the conflict when you awaken! All this is said in the morning, now, at the moment when I am not yet once again blanketed and surrounded by newspapers, television, radio. In this moment I can still sense the conflict, until telephone calls and mail and all else that is awaiting me takes over once again. Once this has happened I can no longer sense the dichotomy—I am back in the treadmill of life. The high wall, whatever its name, whether it be a political wall (an ideological wall) or a wall of misunderstanding between individuals, perhaps the wall between me and the person nearby at this very moment—this wall can be surmounted in this moment:

> . . . how there is soaring beyond the wall,
> How the large birds descend in pairs,
> Now, that there is no more killing. . . .

All these are appeals to try to establish a connection across the wall, across the borders, across the wall between two individuals, across the border between two ideologies, two nations, between the two halves of one city. This attempt at communication is on this morning by means of this monologue carried to the ear, into the ear of someone who is listening. The monologue thus becomes an attempt at communication even though it remains a monologue. It represents the difficulty of achieving understanding, but also the hope that this may succeed. I could well imagine that this is a poem which not only demonstrates my feeling of being touched but which also can be interpreted as a manifestation of social engagement. In other words, if we can no longer communicate there will once again be catastrophes everywhere, both in private life and in politics. The poem tries to promote the right way of reaching an understanding, not in a superficial channelized manner. The latter has always led to misunderstandings. To me the purpose of such poems is to promote understanding, even though they may not initially be easily understandable.

A few comments regarding *Systeme*. The short poems from *Systeme* undoubtedly puzzle the critics, since I, who first published theories regarding the long poem, am here writing short poems. The reason is that I consider these poems in their context to be a logical extension of what I had said in my essay. They are speckles [*fleckenartige Gedichte*] which, when taken together, form a larger poem. And these speckles, at least in the first cycle which bears the title "Flecken," result when extended on various planes in all directions in a larger entity. They are all interrelated and depict our present life: whether it is the poem that discusses the "rectangles" [*Geviert*] to which one is "admitted," where everything is cemented over, where there is one parking lot and one drill field next to another, one airport next to another, everything "secured with wire fences," and where—lo and behold!—one discovers a green speckle which, upon closer examination, also turns out to be square—as well as the sewage collecting area! This is a poem which observes and reports the state which we have created for ourselves by the quadrangulation of the landscape, the use of a geometric form that runs counter to our brain structure, in which our brains must atrophy; and our structure keeps chafing because of an architecture, because of city planning, because—if one transfers the concept—of a rectangularly ordered ideology which does not correspond to our needs. These are critical poems, such as the one with the "bang" [*Knall*]:

> da ein Knall
>   und dort einer
>   was aus der Leitung platzt
>   unter Gebimmel
> traurige Krähen . . . .

> here a bang
>   and there another
>   what erupts from the transmission line
>   accompanied by ringing
> sorrowful crows . . . .

The bang signals the overworked system, in need of renovation, of which we are a part, where everyone is supposed to respond to a bang and a clang and a telephonic message and a computer printout: "humming machines/on the plains" [*surrende Maschinen/auf den Ebenen*] or "many pipes/windpipes and veins" [*viele Röhren/ Luftröhren und Venen*]—systems which are basically out of harmony with our psyche, but to which we are exposed from morning to evening, whether it be the system at a university, a thinking pattern, or the manner in which we ourselves set up our days by means of slips of paper and appointment calendars. It seems to me that this over organization does not permit us to achieve the kind of life for which we could optimally hope. These *Flecken* also contain other poems such as "Landschaft mit Satellit" ["Landscape with a Satellite"]—a juxtaposition of what happens here and what happens in space.

I would like to mention another "poem of innocence" which is contained in *Systeme*. I wrote it on the spur of the moment and then did not have to make changes at all: "Kinderlied für Florian gegen Wut zu singen" ["Nursery Rhyme for Florian an Antidote for Rage"]. I consider it to be a political poem even though it is identified as a nursery rhyme:

auf der Bank	on a bench
sitzt ein Pfau	sits a peacock
kommt die Frau	comes a woman
malt ihn blau	paints him blue
sagt der Pfau	says the peacock
liebe Frau	dear woman
ich bin lieber	I'd rather be
rot als blau	red than blue
kommt ein Kammer-	comes a royal
jäger her	hunter
gibt dem Pfau	gives the peacock
ein Gewehr	a gun
wird der Pfau	peacock turns
puterrot	turkey-red
schießt den Kammer-	shoots the court
jäger tot	hunter dead
fährt der Pfau	sails the peacock
in einem Boot	in a boat
wird der Wannsee	turns the Wannsee[1]
purpurrot	crimson-red
kriegt der Pfau	gets the peacock
einen Schreck	quite a scare
springt von Deck	jumps from the deck
und ist weg	is gone fore'er

[1]lake in Berlin

158

The poem conveys the insight that one can easily steer a course which leads one to the antipodes of one's original goal. On the first level, it is a nursery rhyme which I wrote for my son Florian because of the way he used to rage from time to time. But, on the other hand, it is also written from the experiences gained with students. Subconsciously also on my mind as I was writing this, was the student movement, where one could see that much that had been motivated by good intentions was done thoughtlessly and led students, because of their rage, in an ominous direction, so that these youngsters approached the brink of disaster—just like this peacock in the poem who, at the end, jumps out of the boat and disappears, disappears completely, because he cannot control the situation, because he sees nothing but red, because in this condition of mindless agitation he becomes totally confused and thus totally neurotic. This poem tries to convince people whom I like—and I do not like only my own child but also others who have spontaneity—tries to plead with them rhythmically, that they should ponder their situation and what the results of their actions might be. Such a nursery rhyme is more likely to get through to them than pedantry would because it is loosely structured and humorous. It strikes the right note for them. I think that it is an important part of the engagement of a poet, who does have a reading public and is able to address it, to tell people whom he likes where he believes them to be on the wrong track. It is a poem of innocence because it is not obscured by any secondary reflections, but it devolved out of its own rhythm and the poet could say: yes, that is it, I will leave it just the way it is. This happens from time to time when one writes poetry.

Finally, I want to discuss one of my favorite poems, "der hat die Koffer getragen" ["he carried the suitcase"]:

> der hat die Koffer getragen
> der hat Schuhe poliert
> der hat mit Händen geredet
> der ist auf Strecken geritten
> der hat vor sich hingesungen
> der hat im   Gefängnis   gesessen
> die hat Liedzeilen zitiert   für einen Pfennig
> der ist dem Festzug vorangeritten   in Unterhosen
> der hat Bonzen beschimpft
> der hat   in einer   Stadt
> laut protestiert   als man ihn abholte:
> "wer wird euere dreckigen Straßen kehren?"

diese Versammlung auf einem Fleck
dieser Fleck läßt mich nicht
einstimmen in Definitionen—
die blutigen Narren
hinter Tisch-
platten die
ihre Definitionen ausgeben

he carried the suitcase
he polished shoes
he talked with his hands
he rode for stretches
he sang to himself
he has   been   in prison
she quotes lines from songs   for a penny
he rode at the head of the ceremonial train   in underpants
he castigated big-wigs
he   in a   city
protested loudly   when they hauled him off:
"who's going to sweep your dirty streets?"
this gathering on a spot
this spot does not allow me
to agree with definitions—
the bloody fools
behind table-
tops who
hand out their definitions

(Translation by A. Leslie Willson)

This poem belongs to the species "engaged poetry." It points out what I am for and what I am against. Of all the poems this is the only one that is printed in a visually symbolic form. When you first glance at it you see an urn. All the people who are mentioned here, the one who talked with his hands, the one who rode for stretches, and so forth, they all are people who were arrested in my hometown during the Third Reich and who were subsequently exterminated because they were "living beings unworthy of life" [*lebensunwertes Leben*]. I am talking about the insane bureaucracy which annihilated people outside of the mainstream. I am talking about outsiders, people at the edges of society—streetcleaners, porters who were allegedly feebleminded. But who was to know? Who could tell who was insane? Who was not insane? These outsiders were declared superfluous, not worthy of living by the norms then

160

in use, a narrow-minded absolutist system that simply stated: This is valuable, and that is not worthy of living. They were then annihilated because one "knew exactly" what was worthy of life and what was not according to the classification system which had been so neatly developed. These outsiders are the figures which are conjured up in this poem. It speaks up *for them* and *against* those who want to systematize and define. It seems to me that ideologies and systems which are so sure of themselves that they know precisely what is *good* and what is *bad*, what is *wrong* and what is *right*, lead to horrifying results, that people can be killed because one knows exactly that these are the people who should be killed. I think the poem makes clear my resistance against "the bloody fools/behind table-/tops who/hand out their definitions."

This resistance to rigid categorization is the crux of my engagement at all times. In the university too, for here similar things happen, and in politics. I keep repeating my objection when they come to me, totally convinced of some rigid system. They may be well motivated and may believe that they can improve the world. It appears to me that all hope of improvement is lost whenever this arrogance of absolute knowledge rears its head, these classifications that cannot be doubted. Then conditions only get worse. These are the thoughts behind this poem, because it is a poem of experience and, at the same time, expresses very clearly what its implications are for the future. Thus it not only refers to the Third Reich, but it also cautions against any repetition of similar conditions. I believe that it is especially important to say such things in Germany, because the Germans are enormously thorough, enormously fond of orderliness, to the point where they become fanatical, and it is in such a society where inflexible systems produce their worst results, since nothing is tempered by slovenliness as in Austria, by corruption as in Italy, or by a heterogeneous society as in the United States where dissent is a way of life. Here there is no leavening; here such inhumane principles can produce far-reaching results. That is why the poet, the writer, anyone who is reasonably thoughtful must say time and again that he opposes such rigid doctrines. Even if the poem is nothing more than the creator of a certain degree of turbulence, a disquieting factor, even if it merely destroys harmony in a world which is either too uniform or in the danger of becoming too uniform, it has achieved a social function, it has accomplished something. No matter from which direction it does this—it is effective.

161

Photograph by Maria Rama

Günter Grass

Born 1927 in Danzig

Günter Grass was drafted into military service at age sixteen and ended the war as a prisoner of war. He worked briefly as a laborer, as an apprentice stonemason, and as a sculptor. From 1949–53 he studied sculpture at the Academy of Fine Arts in Düsseldorf, and in 1953 he entered the Academy of Fine Arts in Berlin, where he worked in metal sculpture and independently pursued writing and painting. His first novel, The Tin Drum, *published in 1959, established him as a twentieth century Rabelais. He has traveled widely in Europe, the Middle East and America (perhaps the most recent of his many honors is an honorary Ph.D. awarded by Harvard University in 1976). Before he became disenchanted, he campaigned vigorously for the election of former Chancellor Willy Brandt. He lives in Berlin.*

He published his first poems in 1956 (in a volume illustrated by himself), and has since published in many genres: essays, plays, novels, poetry, political and cultural commentaries.

Günter Grass was interviewed on April 17, 1975 in his studio-office in his home. What follows is a verbatim translation of the taped interview.

For centuries it has been traditionally expected that the German poem should provide its reader with edification, comfort, and helpful guidelines. Why and in what way has this changed in our time?

I do not believe that the poem at all times has had exclusively this function of giving comfort. There have been poets from the very beginning—let's say since Walther von der Vogelweide—who wanted to sound an alarm, who raised political protest. Of course there are periods, especially in the baroque poem, where the giving of solace runs parallel to the exposure of the terrible conditions prevalent during the Thirty Years' War. But it is evident that lyric poetry became more and more political with the formation of a German state, even earlier, when belatedly the effects of English and French enlightenment made themselves felt in Germany. Interestingly enough, the earliest advocates of enlightenment juxtaposed in their poetry the concept of patriotism to the fragmentation of Germany into minor states; even before it came to political unification in Germany they, as authors, attempted a unification of the language, and in this endeavour they often employed lyric poetry, as Schubart did, for example, but also Klopstock and Lessing.

In Protokoll zur Person [Personal protocol] you say that of all literary genres lyric poetry, with which you began, is closest to you, that it remains a more precise tool to take measure of oneself and to come to grips with detailed problems. Do you still feel that way today and, if so, may we soon expect the publication of another volume of poetry from you?

This is even more true than before because of the variety of my activities; aside from writing and drawing I have also been active politically in recent years. This makes for a great danger of fragmentation of one's efforts, of frittering away of one's abilities. In such situations the poem is most helpful. It forces the writer to concentrate, it forces one to take measure of one's own position. One must examine anew the language which loses its cutting edge particularly when it is employed in the realm of politics. In my case there is an additional facet—there always has been: drawing and the writing of poetry usually occur parallel to one another. I often cannot remember whether I first recorded a metaphoric image graphically or in writing. And then it often happens that metaphoric language when examined by graphic means cannot stand up to such an exacting attempt of graphic recreation. Thus, drawing acts as a proofstone for me, especially when it comes to lyric work.

You have just mentioned political activity. You have said that artistic work is a special kind of egotism. On the other hand, since 1961 you have devoted uncounted hours for political purposes, hours which could have been employed in artistic endeavours. It thus seems that despite the somewhat-pardon the expression-"cynical" remark which I just quoted, you are basically an idealist, does it not?

This is not an all encompassing egotism. Once one has discovered that artistic work—not just writing—requires this special egotism, this concentration upon oneself, upon one's own nervous system, one must then maintain or create political conditions which permit and safeguard this luxury (which is no luxury from my perspective, but may be a luxury in the eyes of the powers that be). What I have tried to accomplish politically—and often with some success or at least with more visible success than literature per se can achieve—I have also undertaken as a citizen who, after all, lives in his time, something which one senses especially acutely in Germany. But I would not entertain the idea of promoting with poems a political party, which I would like to assist, such as the Social Democrats here in Germany, or a specific program, such as the reform of our hospitals. A poem cannot achieve this. If it tries, it becomes the handmaiden of political propaganda, well intentioned as it may be, and simultaneously an unsuitable tool. A political speech demands knowledge of political facts, a certain amount of political passion, and likewise an appropriate use of language. It demands that the speaker, its author, understands, comprehends, and effectively deals with the needs that are brought to his attention in their social context. But none of this is a prerequisite for the writing of lyric poetry. Viewed from the outside the writing of lyric poetry can be a totally asocial process, a process which refers only to one's own particular situation which, however, once the result has been obtained (and even though this may not have been the intention of the author), becomes accessible to a larger circle of people, is transferable, and thus does produce a social effect. But the initial impetus is not social in nature.

Thus when, as you have said, your poems are occasional poems, the primary stimulus was a lyrical inspiration which, because you are a member of society, ultimately led to a treatment of a timely topic. But you did not sit down consciously and write a poem to cope with a specific situation or to change a specific situation.

That is correct. And there are naturally stimuli from without that cause a poem to be written. But this does not always have to be the proximate cause. Only when a situation which exists outside of the poet as a person aggravates a potential conflict already existing within the writer can this type of creative process occur.

You have represented the point of view that the writer (and thus, I assume, also the lyric poet) should not presume to act as the "conscience of the nation," but that he instead, as a "citizen with special abilities," should participate in the political process. You have further said that the professional designation "engaged writer" reminds you of such tags as "pastry-cook to the royal court" or "Catholic cyclist." Could you formulate the thought behind these two terms of yours into a concept that represents your current thinking?

As a writer, or rather as an artist—because this does not only concern literature—I am not valueless or above values, that which outsiders like to call a "creative person," but I am, however, a product of my time, steeped in traditions and historical developments, not only in political, but also in literary and artistic developments. I am a *part* of a literature and naturally know that I have learned by experience, that I am dependent, that the concept of the "independent" artist, of the "independent" writer is only wishful thinking and perhaps not even a particularly desirable concept at that. I am dependent upon language. And language is constantly being transformed by me and my colleagues—especially the German language, everyday German is subject to a continuous process of change. Politics are but one factor of this process. Thus politics, social conduct, socially responsible conduct, also influence the language of *that* writer who consciously turns away from these processes, who tries to live in isolation. Even the determined nonengagement of a writer is, though with an inverted prefix, a sort of engagement. I thus have derided the professional designation of "engaged writer"—it seems redundant to me.

An artist is, whether he wants to be or not, interwoven in his time, obligated to his time. And even if he is ahead of *his time*, which often is the case, he is—after all—ahead of his time, which too is a measure that relates him to his time.

I am in principle opposed to the idea that writers and other artists should be treated as priests, as though they were characters with the mission of blessing and speaking and seeing from a lofty perch. They are perhaps more sensible fools than the normal fools who live all around us. They are more nervous instruments, resonate more sensitively, and are more extensively dependent upon artistic means in order to exist, to be able to prove themselves. But they are simultaneously, and often in a very cumbersome manner, citizens of their contemporary society. Especially those who use language as their artistic tool are exposed to many temptations, above all the temptation of power. There have always been political forces—and these exist today more than ever—who want to exploit literature. This is especially evident in the Iron Curtain nations, in all nations that are under a communist regime in which Trotsky's warning that literature should not be used as the handmaiden of the revolution has been disregarded flagrantly. There the attempt is made—and this with partial success and by the use of appropriate pressure—to create an apologetic and affirmative literature. Socialist realism does not question in principle; literature however, by its very nature must question. This goes for other art forms too. These phenomena are sometimes obvious, sometimes disguised. But the same dangers naturally exist with respect to various churches and other power structures which are organized similarly to the central committee of the Communist Party; i.e., hierarchically. Certain hairsplitting consensuses have developed to which many authors have yielded, even important ones.

In "Irgendetwas machen" ("Do Anything") you seem to be telling the poets of protest that they must do more than just impotently object verbally, that they should become active.

Irgendetwas machen

Da können wir doch nicht zusehen.
Wenn wir auch nichts verhindern,
wir müssen uns deutlich machen.
(Mach doch was. Mach doch was.
Irgendwas. Mach doch was.)
Zorn, Ärger und Wut suchten sich ihre Adjektive.

Der Zorn nannte sich gerecht.
Bald sprach man vom alltäglichen Ärger.
Die Wut fiel in Ohnmacht: ohnmächtige Wut.
Ich spreche vom Protestgedicht
und gegen das Protestgedicht.
(Einmal sah ich Rekruten beim Eid
mit Kreuzfingern hinterrücks abschwören.)
Ohnmächtig protestiere ich gegen ohnmächtige Proteste.
Es handelt sich um Oster-, Schweige- und Friedensmärsche.
Es handelt sich um die hundert guten Namen
unter sieben richtigen Sätzen.
Es handelt sich um Guitarren und ähnliche
die Schallplatte fördernde Protestinstrumente.
Ich rede vom hölzernen Schwert und vom fehlenden Zahn,
vom Protestgedicht.

Wie Stahl seine Konjunktur hat, hat Lyrik ihre Konjunktur.
Aufrüstung öffnet Märkte für Antikriegsgedichte.
Die Herstellungskosten sind gering.
Man nehme: ein Achtel gerechten Zorn,
zwei Achtel alltäglichen Ärger
und fünf Achtel, damit sie vorschmeckt, ohnmächtige Wut.
Denn mittelgroße Gefühle gegen den Krieg
sind billig zu haben
und seit Troja schon Ladenhüter.
(Mach doch was. Mach doch was.
Irgendwas. Mach doch was.)
Man macht sich Luft: schon verraucht der gerechte Zorn.
Der kleine alltägliche Ärger läßt die Ventile zischen.
Ohnmächtige Wut entlädt sich, füllt einen Luftballon,
der steigt und steigt, wird kleiner und kleiner, ist weg.
Sind Gedichte Atemübungen?
Wenn sie diesen Zweck erfüllen,—und ich frage,
prosaisch wie mein Großvater, nach dem Zweck,—
dann is Lyrik Therapie.
Ist das Gedicht eine Waffe?
Manche, überarmiert können kaum laufen.
Sie müssen das Unbehagen an Zuständen
als Vehikel benutzen:
sie kommen ans Ziel, sie kommen ans Ziel:
zuerst ins Feuilleton und dann in die Anthologie:
Die Napalm-Metapher und ihre Abwandlungen
im Protestgedicht der sechziger Jahre.
Es handelt sich um Traktatgedichte.
Gerechter Zorn zählt Elend und Terror auf.
Alltäglicher Ärger findet den Reim auf fehlendes Brot.
Ohnmächtige Wut macht atemlos von sich reden.
(Mach doch was. Mach doch was . . .)

Dabei gibt es Hebelgesetze.
Sie aber kreiden ihm an, dem Stein,
er wolle sich nicht bewegen.
Tags drauf ködert der hilflose Stil berechtigter Proteste
den treffsicheren Stil glatter Dementis.
Weil sie in der Sache zwar jeweils recht haben,
sich im Detail aber allzu leicht irren,
distanzieren sich die Unterzeichner
halblaut von den Verfassern und ihren Protesten.
(Nicht nur Diebe kaufen sich Handschuhe.)
Was übrig bleibt: zählebige Mißverständnisse
zitieren einander. Fehlerhafte Berichtigungen
lernen vom Meerschweinchen
und vermehren sich unübersichtlich.

Da erbarmt sich der Stein und tut so,
als habe man ihn verrückt:
während Zorn, Ärger und Wut einander ins Wort fallen,
treten die Spezialisten der Macht
lächelnd vor Publikum auf. Sie halten fundierte Vorträge
über den Preis, den die Freiheit fordert;
über Napalm und seine abschreckende Wirkung;
über berechtigte Proteste und die erklärliche Wut.
Das alles ist erlaubt.
Da die Macht nur die Macht achtet,
darf solange ohnmächtig protestiert werden,
bis nicht mehr, weil der Lärm stört,
protestiert werden darf.—
Wir aber verachten die Macht.
Wir sind nicht mächtig, beteuern wir uns.
Ohne Macht gefallen wir uns in Ohnmacht.
Wir wollen die Macht nicht; sie aber hat uns.—
Nun fühlt sich der gerechte Zorn mißverstanden.
Der alltägliche Ärger mündet in Schweigemärsche,
die zuvor angemeldet und genehmigt wurden.
Im Kreis läuft die ohnmächtige Wut.
Das fördert den gleichfalls gerechten Zorn
verärgerter Polizisten:
ohnmächtige Wut wird handgreiflich.
Die Faust wächst sich zum Kopf aus
und denkt in Tiefschlägen Leberhaken knöchelhart.
(Mach doch was. Mach doch was . . .)
Das alles macht Schule und wird von der Macht
gestreichelt geschlagen subventioniert.
Schon setzt der Stein, der bewegt werden wollte,
unbewegt Moos an.
Geht das so weiter?—Im Kreis schon.
Was sollen wir machen?—Nicht irgendwas.

Wohin mit der Wut?—Ich weiß ein Rezept:

Schlagt in die Schallmauer Nägel.
Köpft Pusteblumen und Kerzen.
Setzt auf dem Sofa euch durch.
   Wir haben immer noch Wut.
   Schon sind wir überall heiser.
   Wir sind gegen alles umsonst.
   Was sollen wir jetzt noch machen?
   Wo sollen wir hin mit der Wut?
Mach doch was. Mach doch was.
Wir müssen irgendwas,
mach doch was, machen.
   Los, protestieren wir schnell.
   Der will nicht mitprotestieren.
   Los, unterschreib schon und schnell.
   Du warst doch immer dagegen.
   Wer nicht unterschreibt, ist dafür.
Schön ist die Wut im Gehege,
bevor sie gefüttert wird.

Lang lief die Ohnmacht im Regen,
die Strümpfe trocknet sie jetzt.
Wut und Ventile, darüber Gesang;
Ohnmacht, dein Nadelöhr ist der Gesang:
   Weil ich nichts machen kann,
   weil ich nichts machen kann,
   hab ich die Wut, hab ich die Wut.
   Mach doch was. Mach doch was.
   Irgendwas. Mach doch was.
   Wir müssen irgendwas,
   hilft doch nix, hilft doch nix,
   wir müssen irgendwas,
   mach doch was, machen.
Lauf schweigend Protest.
Lief ich schon. Lief ich schon.
Schreib ein Gedicht.
Hab ich schon. Hab ich schon.
Koch eine Sülze. Schweinekopfsülze:
die Ohnmacht geliere, die Wut zittre nach.
Ich weiß ein Rezept; wer kocht es mir nach?

Do Something

We can't just look on.
Even if we can't stop anything
we must say what we think.

(Do something. Do something.
Anything. Do something, then.)
Indignation, annoyance, rage looked for their adjectives.
Indignation called itself righteous.
Soon people spoke of everyday annoyance.
Rage fell into impotence: impotent rage.
I speak of the protest poem
and against the protest poem.
(Once I saw recruits taking the oath
unswear it behind their backs with crossed fingers.)
Impotently I protest against impotent protests.
What I mean is Easter, silence and peace marches.
What I mean is the hundred good names
underneath seven true sentences.
What I mean is guitars and similar
protest instruments conducive to records.
I speak of the wooden sword and the missing tooth,
of the protest poem.
Just as steel has its booms, so poetry has its booms.
Rearmament opens markets for anti-war poems.
The cost of production is low.
Take an eighth of righteous indignation,
two eighths of everyday annoyance
and five eighths—to heighten that flavour—of impotent rage.
For medium-sized feelings against the war
are cheaply obtained
and have been shopsoiled ever since Troy.
(Do something. Do something.
Anything. Do something, then.)

One lets off steam: already righteous indignation goes up in smoke.
The small everyday annoyance makes the safety valves hiss.
Impotent rage discharges itself, fills a balloon with gas,
this rises, rises, grows smaller and smaller, is gone.
Are poems breathing exercises?
If that is their function,—and prosaic
as my grandfather, I ask what their function is—
then poetry is therapy.
Is a poem a weapon?
Some, too heavily armed, can hardly walk.
They have to use their dissatisfaction with circumstances
as a vehicle:
they reach their destination, they can hit the mark:
first the weekly paper, then the anthology:
The napalm metaphor and its permutations
in the protest poem of the 'sixties.
I mean poems that are tracts.
Righteous indignation enumerates terrors and miseries.

Everyday annoyance discovers the rhyme for no bread.
Impotent rage sets people talking breathlessly about itself.
(Do something. Do something . . .)
There are laws of leverage.
But they hold it against the stone
that it will not budge.
Next day the helpless style of well-founded protest
acts as a bait for the well-aimed style of smooth refutation.
Since in the cause they are always right
but all too easily slip up over details
the signatories tacitly half-dissociate themselves
from the authors and from their protests.
(Not only burglars buy gloves.)
What remains is: resilient misunderstandings
quote one another. Erroneous corrections
learn from guinea pigs
how to breed so that no one keeps track.

The stone takes pity and acts
as though it had been moved:
while indignation, annoyance and rage interrupt one another,
the specialists in power
appear smiling in front of the public. They make well-informed
    speeches
about the price demanded for freedom:
about napalm and its deterrent effects;
about well-founded protests and understandable rage.
All this is permitted.
Since power respects only power
impotent protest is allowed to carry on
until, because the noise is disturbing,
protest is no longer allowed.—
But we despise power.
We are not powerful, we keep assuring each other.
Without power we enjoy our impotence.
We do not want power; but power has us.—
Now righteous indignation feels misunderstood.
Our everyday annoyance ends in silence marches
that have first been announced and permitted.
Our impotent rage runs around in circles.
This provokes the equally righteous indignation
of angered policemen:
impotent rage becomes aggressive.
The fist grows into a head
and thinks in terms of low blows hooks to the liver knuckle-hard.
(Do something. Do something . . .)
All this becomes institutionalized, and by power
is caressed beaten subsidized.

Already the stone that was to be moved
gathers moss, unmoved.
Can we go on like that?—Yes, in a circle.
What shall we do?—Not anything.
How express our rage?—I know a recipe:

Strike nails into the sound barrier.
Behead dandelions and candles.
Assert yourselves on the couch.
   We still feel rage.
   Already we're hoarse all over.
   We're against everything, vainly.
   What else can we do now?
   How shall we express our rage?
Do something. Do something.
We must do something or other,
do something, do it.
   Come on, then, quickly protest.
   That fellow won't join our protest.
   Come on, then, quickly sign.
   You've always been against it.
   Those who don't sign are for it.
Lovely is rage in the paddock,
before it is fed.
For a long time impotence ran around in the rain,
but now it is drying its socks.
Rage and safety valves, about them a song;
Impotence, your needle's eye is a song.
   Because I can't do anything,
   because I can't do anything
   I'm full of rage, I'm full of rage.
   Do something, then. Do something.
   Anything. Do something, then.
   We must do something or other,
   does no good, does no good,
   we must do something or other,
   do something, do it.
Silently march in protest.
Have done it once, have done it.
Write a poem, then.
Have written it, have done it.
Cook some brawn. Pig's head brawn:
let impotence jell, rage quiver in sympathy.
I know a recipe; who'll follow it cooking?

Translated by Michael Hamburger.

This is less intended as a challenge to the poets of protest to do this
or not do that in their role as poets or verbalizers of dissent than as an

attempt to point out that a poem emanates from uncertainties. Once I have thought a political matter through to my complete satisfaction, once the process of cogitation and examination has been concluded, it would not occur to me to transform these conclusively formulated ideas into a poem. On the contrary, I would become active politically with this insight, away from my desk. There are other forms of discussion more suitable than the poem for political discussion. Among these are the speech, the essay, the editorial. When such conclusively formulated and correct political insights are expressed poetically, then these poems often become like treatises. On the one hand, they place exorbitant demands upon lyric poetry, and, on the other hand, they underestimate that which makes lyric poetry more sensitive, more delicate, more ambiguous than the editorial or the political speech, to cite a couple of examples, both of which are necessary and far more effective in a political sense.

Furthermore, this kind of poetry, by its very nature, deals critically with a trend. This poetry of protest is a challenge to the mediocre to versify diligently, since it always uses a political certainty as its point of departure, and the very important prerequisite of lyric poetry, self-doubt, indecision, the desire to depict something vague precisely, has been set aside.

This poem says nothing against the attempt to express by poetic means political conflicts, social conflicts, sociological conflicts, which is possible and is also a part of what I try to do. But the insight that the war in Vietnam, beginning with the first European and then the American participation, has been a crime with all the consequences implied. This insight, if I wanted to employ it politically, would not induce me to write a poem about such a topic, but rather to attempt, within the limits of my possibilities, to strengthen those political forces which share my opinion more or less. And there a difficult political fight begins, full of contradictions, replete with compromises and with setbacks. It is a battle which can only be won if one does not rely solely upon protest as one's weapon. Protest is quickly down at the heels. Protest quickly disintegrates. What usually remains is resignation and disenchantment. But the political work of some American journalists, the stick-to-it-iveness of some journalists, for example during the Watergate affair—that was no spontaneous process, but one which had to be pursued tenaciously, which demanded political detail-work and, as I just said, stick-to-it-iveness. I do not believe that an outraged protesting poem, or even a plethora of poems, would have succeeded, in the face of the lies of President Nixon, in lifting this man from his saddle.

Naturally because of the experiences which we have gathered, a poem could reveal to what degree we all—and this is where poets have often lent the impetus—are prepared to manipulate power, to manipulate language, for the purpose of exposing deception. But here we have come full circle to the sensible questioning of our own premises without which a poem cannot exist.

"Irgendetwas machen" is thus a timeless poem although it was motivated obviously—at least in part—by conditions of our times. In this poem you are dealing with a macrocosm. When I read the poem "Pünktlich" ("Punctually") I have the feeling that you are describing the microcosm of the people living in one and the same house as a symbol for society as a whole.

Eine Etage tiefer
schlägt eine junge Frau
jede halbe Stunde
ihr Kind.
Deshalb
habe ich meine Uhr verkauft
und verlasse mich ganz
auf die strenge Hand
unter mir,
die gezählten Zigaretten
neben mir;
meine Zeit ist geregelt.

One floor beneath
every half hour
a young woman
beats her child.
Therefore
I have sold my watch
and rely entirely
upon the stern hand
under me,
the counted cigarettes
next to me;
my time is regulated.

Yes this is quite often the case with me: a minute occurrence, which inspires a poem takes on a different dimension in that poem. I really can say no more than that about this topic.

174

Your poem "Neue Mystik" ("The New Mysticism") is probably somewhat more difficult for the reader, especially the American reader, than are the two poems which we have thus far discussed. Would you please comment on it?

Neue Mystik
oder: Ein kleiner Ausblick auf die utopischen Verhältnisse
nach der vorläufig allerletzten Kulturrevolution.

Als unsere Fragebögen lückenhaft blieben
und die formierten Mächte sich ratlos näher kamen,
begann die Verschmelzung aller Systeme mit der Telepathie.

Während noch Skeptiker abseits standen,
wurden schon volkseigne Tische gerückt,
Geister gerufen, mit Hegel
und anderen Mystikern gefüttert,
bis es klopfte und leserlich Antwort gab.

Auf jener Tagung spiritistischer Leninisten in Lourdes,
deren Arbeitsgruppen das fortschrittliche Tibet
und die Errungenschaften der Therese von Konnersreuth
mit Hilfe der Schrenk-Notzing-Methode behandelten,
wurden die Vertreter aufklärender Dekadenz gemaßregelt:
Fortan fiel Pfingsten auf jeweils den 1. Mai.

Im folgenden Jahr,
während der telepathischen Karwoche,
überführten Zen-Pioniere,
geleitet von den vierdimensionalen Sozial-Jesuiten,
gefolgt von indischen Kühen
und den großen Sensitiven astraler Hindu-Kombinate,
des Stalin wächserne Leiche in Etappen nach Rom.
Als man, nach paladinischer Weisung
(Eusapia Paladino, geb. 1854 in Neapel,
mediale Vorkämpferin der Neuen Mystik)
auf der windigen Insel Gotland
ein gelbhaariges Medium gefunden hatte,
wurde es zur Heldin des sozialistischen Mystizismus erklärt
und kurz nach jenem tragischen Autounfall,—
versprengte Sozialdemokraten
und marxistische Revisionisten
gestanden später den Anschlag, —
heiliggesprochen.

Die in Texas und in der Äußeren Mongolei
zwecks Umschulung an Schutzlagertischen

konzentrierten Konterrevolutionäre
nehmen fortan
von Sitzung zu Sitzung ab.

Ständig tagt unser Vollzirkel dialektischer Psychokinese.
Denn immer noch gibt die Heilige Antwort.
Um einen Tisch sitzt die Welt und holt Rat bei ihr.
Sie, die irrationale, rüstet uns ab,
sie, die telekinetische, hilft uns, das Soll zu erfüllen,
sie, die okkulte, ernährt und verwaltet uns,
nur sie, die parteiliche und unfehlbare,
sie, die gebenedeite und schmerzensreiche,
sie, die liebliche Sensitive,
füllt unsere Fragebögen,
benennt unsere Straßen,
säubert uns gründlich,
erlöst uns vom Zweifel,
nimmt uns das Kopfweh.

Fortan müssen wir nicht mehr denken,
nur noch gehorchen
und ihre Klopfzeichen auswerten.

New Mysticism
or: A little survey of the utopian conditions
after the temporarily ultimate cultural revolution

When our questionnaires tended to show gaps
and the established powers, puzzled, sensed a rapprochement,
all the systems began to be merged with telepathy.

While sceptics still stood aloof,
nationalized tables were turned,
spirits invoked, then fed
on Hegel and other mystics,
until there were knocks and legible answers.

At that assembly of spiritualist Leninists at Lourdes
whose working parties dealt with progressive Tibet
and the achievements of Teresa of Konnersreuth
with the aid of the Schrenck-Notzing method,
the spokesmen for enlightened decadence were called to order:
Henceforth Whitsun always fell on the first of May.

In the following year,
during the telepathic Passion Week,

176

Zen pioneers,
guided by the four-dimensional Socialist Jesuits
and followed by Indian cows
as well as the great sensitives of astral Hindu Corporations
transported Stalin's wax corpse by stages to Rome.
When in accordance with paladinian instructions
(Eusapia Paladino, born 1854 in Naples,
medium and forerunner of the New Mysticism)
on the windy Isle of Jutland
a yellow-haired medium had been found,
she was proclaimed heroine of socialist mysticism
and shortly after that tragic motor accident,—
scattered Social Democrats
and Marxist revisionists
later confessed to the coup,—
she was canonized.

The counter-revolutionaries
concentrated in Texas and Outer Mongolia
for the purpose of re-education at the desks of protective camps
now diminish
from meeting to meeting.

Our plenary circle of dialectical psychokinesis is in permanent session.
For still the saint answers questions.
Around one table the world sits and asks for advice.
She, the irrational, disarms us,
she, the telekinetic, helps us to fulfil the norm,
she, the occult, feeds and administers us,
only she, the partisan and infallible,
she, the blessed and sorrowful,
she, the charmingly sensitive,
fills in our questionnaires,
gives names to our streets,
cleanses us thoroughly,
delivers us from doubts,
takes away our headache.

From now on we need no longer think,
only obey
and decode her knocking signals.

Translated by Michael Hamburger

Yes, and this is probably because, at the time when I wrote this
poem, the self-assurance of the Americans was still very much intact
in a negative sense. Purged perhaps by the experiences of the last

decade, the Vietnam War, by defeats and by doubts of the "American way of life," of the great puritanical ideology, which has led to so many defeats outside of the United States proper, more sensitivity and understanding for this poem may have developed. Here too, in Western Europe, when I first recited it, it was barely understood or, at best, understood very one-sidedly. And then, in the middle of the sixties, when I made a trip to Prague and Budapest, and each time recited this poem before an audience of writers and students, it had a shocking effect upon the party bosses, while others found it liberating because it expressed a presentiment. It was my purpose in this poem to point out how great is the inherent danger when all absolute ideologies collaborate with one another. The Alliance of the Intolerant! They may contradict one another in details—whether they are capitalists or communists—but they agree on one thing: intolerance toward reformers. And later, after I had written this poem, there were gruesome examples of this, whether it was in Czechoslovakia—the occupation of '68—or in Chile, where a democratically elected government was destroyed because of the objections of the intolerant, also because the United States supported a putsch. All this is evidence of how intolerance, no matter what its ideological base, achieves similar effects in its exercise of power and terror.

Five lines in this poem are especially perplexing for the American reader. You say:

> The counter-revolutionaries
> concentrated in Texas and Outer Mongolia
> for the purpose of re-education at the desks of protective camps
> now diminish
> from meeting to meeting.

Why Texas?

As I said before, the claim to power, the belief in the one unshakable truth, which one represents, whether this is the communist ideology or the perception of sturdy Americans that their "way of life" is the only one to bring happiness to mankind, these function similarly in their methods and in the use of terror.

You simply used Texas symbolically, not with reference to a specific occurrence?
I could well imagine that Texas is especially well suited as the site for

"protective camps." Perhaps Americans can think of other and even better suited locations. But that was not what I was driving at. I merely wanted to point out that this claim to ideological omniscience, no matter what its source, leads to acts of inhumanity.

What is the future of lyric poetry as a genre in this sober consumer-society in which we live today?

Poetry is independent of this. It may well be that the novel, a relatively new aesthetic form, will wither away, because there are other means of entertainment, both in a positive and in a negative sense. But lyrics, the poem, this is an existential form of expression which is subconsciously practiced by many, even if this does not result in a text, i.e., in a recorded text. There is the desperate stammering of a lonely person, whether it be a child or an old man, or even the individual who talks to himself while walking down the street—they all operate within the framework of this form of parting with their innermost thoughts.

Lyric poetry is as elementary and as existential as excrement, as a bowel movement. It naturally—to continue this comparison— manifests itself in different colorations, composition, can appear healthy and give testimony of a good digestion, as the pleasing excrement of children, but can also be permeated by traces of blood, be bubbly, show evidence of illness and pestilence, and be black and watery. And since you ask about the future of lyric poetry I might conclude with the following remark: as long as human beings shit they will stammer poems and sometimes commit them to writing.

Photograph by Mechthild Gräfin von Courten

Walter Helmut Fritz
Born 1929 in Karlsruhe

Walter Helmut Fritz studied literature, philosophy, and modern languages in Heidelberg and became a high school teacher. Since this did not give him sufficient time for writing, he is now working as a freelance writer, critic, and college lecturer in his native Karlsruhe.

His first poetry volume appeared in 1956 and has been followed by short stories, sketches, novels, translations and adaptations from French. His poetry volumes are characterized by a remarkable economy of language, achieving maximum effectiveness with minimum expenditure of words.

This interview took place on March 7, 1975, in his apartment, and on March 8 during an excursion to Sesenheim, where we visited a number of sites familiar to any reader of Goethe. Walter Helmut Fritz did not want to be taped and felt that the taking of extensive notes would detract from our conversations. He consequently suggested that he would write up the substance of our discussions and mail a draft to me for my comments and corrections—exactly the opposite of the procedure followed in the other

180

interviews. His memory is remarkable: what follows contains all of the substance of our conversations, though—characteristically for Fritz—they are stripped to the bone. Needless to say, I changed nothing, but merely translated his draft into English.

Do you consider literature to be an end in itself?

No. It makes little sense to consider it in isolation.

I would appreciate your comments regarding my topic, literary engagement.

All literature is engaged, even the most serene poem, because literature, by the fact that it is—among other things—devoid of practical utility and therefore opposes functionalism, schematization, rigidness, utilitarianism; because it creates freedom, permits involuntariness, eliminates tutelage, provides breathing room, and promotes doubts and the patience to be skeptical; it strives for solidarity and attempts to lessen indifference; it renders feasible a language which does not merely want to be informative.

Can literature change reality?

No, but—as a prerequisite—the concept of reality.

Have you always had the fundamental expectations, impulses, motivations, and goals which you are now describing?

They naturally became tangible over a period of time, a number of years, during my work. First of all, because you can gain an overview of your work only after you are in the midst of it, perhaps even after the fact, and, secondly, because I had to confront with ever greater frequency the question of what I was trying to accomplish by my writing.

How many imponderables remain?

Many. Even though a number of answers become clearer as time goes by one must never forget how many new uncertainties crop up; how many surprises—fortunately—do occur; how gingerly one progresses and experiments at the beginning, and how long it takes before the road just a few paces ahead seems clearer; how great a difference remains between what one believes to see ahead when implementing new plans, and what ultimately results. It makes no sense to try to bridge the gap by any sort of reassurances, to try to force together that which is diverging, to try to create an illusion of harmony where there is none. These various difficulties mount with each attempt. But, at the same time, there is always the renewed impetus to accomplish something, to progress a bit farther.

Please comment on the development of your poetic work.

The preface of my first poetry volume *Achtsam sein* [*Be on Your Guard*] which appeared in 1956 was written by Karl Krolow. Other poems are in collections entitled *Bild und Zeichen* [*Pictures and Signs*], *Veränderte Jahre* [*Changed Years*], *Die Zuverlässigkeit der Unruhe* [*The Certainty of Anxiety*], and *Aus der Nähe* [*Seen from Nearby*]. I believe that my poems have become more laconic over the years.

In addition you have written sketches which occasionally approach lyric poetry.

There I tried to understand imaginary exercises as manifestations of logic, as an internal imaginative process. They were first collected under the title *Zwischenbemerkungen* [*Incidental Remarks*].

I think this also applies to Bemerkungen zu einer Gegend (Comments Concerning a Region). *Would it be fair to say that these two volumes attempt to effect a synthesis of two genres, the short essay and the poem?*

Yes.

You wrote that paintings, watercolors, and sketches of Paul Klee inspired the Comments Concerning a Region.

Correct, but these are neither descriptions nor interpretations of pictures; they are thoughts, questions and answers concerning Klee's titles. In the volume *Changed Years*, by the way, is a cycle of poems entitled "Von Bildern Lyonel Feiningers" [While contemplating paintings by Lyonel Feininger] which was also conceived as a commentary, as poetic equivalencies, as a mimetic form in its own right.

Aside from poems and poetic prose—if I could thus tag the contents of the two books we just discussed—you have also written a number of stories and novels, Umwege (Detours), Abweichung (Variation), Die Verwechslung (The Mix-Up), Die Beschaffenheit solcher Tage (The Nature of These Days) *and* Bevor uns Hören und Sehen vergeht (Before it Takes our Breath Away). *While prose is not central to this discussion I would like to ask one question that does also have bearing on your poetry: Do you see a great difference between poetry and narrative prose?*

No. I could write certain pages of this narrative prose only after I had had some experience with poetry.

In your narrative prose you also work very economically, not wasting many words. But let us get back to your poetry. I would like to discuss a few of your poems with you, such as "Das Wort Friede" ("That Word Peace"):

Zäune laufen	Fences crisscross
über die Erde.	the earth.
Was begonnen hat	That which has begun
das Unglück	unhappiness
dauert fort.	continues.
Und doch will	And yet
das Wort Friede	that word peace wants
überall erscheinen.	to appear everywhere.

To what kinds of fences are you referring?

To those that limit the philosophy of life, to ideological fences, cordons, obstacles, all of which make the contact among human beings and mutual understanding more difficult.

Because there are such fences "unhappiness" continues. But the poem does not end in resignation: You say that the word peace *at least wants to "appear," that it is waiting in the wings for its opportunity to come forward as soon as the "fences" disappear. This reminds me of another one of your poems, "Vorwände" ("Pretexts"):*

Zwischen uns und den Frieden
haben wir Vorwände geschoben.
Sonst würden wir ihn entdecken,
mitten auf der Ebene,
über der unaufhörlich Schnee fällt,
verlassen und bereit, sich zu nähern.

Between us and peace
we have pushed pretexts.
Otherwise we would discover it,
in the midst of the plain,

on which snow falls ceaselessly,
abandoned and ready to draw near.

The word Vorwand, *which is translatable into the English term* pretext, *contains in German also the implication of a wall in front of something and seems to have a dual meaning here.*

Yes. For one thing it is used in the usual sense which implies an apparent reason, but, above all, also in the sense of a real wall which has been pushed between mankind and peace. If it were not for this wall, which corresponds to the "fences" in the first poem we discussed, one would soon seen peace approaching across the vast, snow covered plain.

You use snow frequently in your poems.

As something which implies isolation, alienation, distance, and similar concepts.

Let us turn to your poem "Bald ohne Namen"("Soon Without Name"), strophes in which you talk about the borderland between East and West Germany:

Grenzland, nicht erfunden
das altert von Hof bis Travemünde.

Argwohn, unnachgiebig, erstickend,
zwischen Minenfeld, Wachturm und Drahtverhau.

Geleise, im Gestrüpp, das die Schritte hemmt,
endend und rostend.
Leere, der nichts widerspricht.

Den Wald haben sie niedergebrannt,
weil das Schußfeld unübersichtlich war.

Tarnungen, Komplizin Nacht.
Die Häuser wenden sich ab,
wenn man vorbeigeht.

Land der vergessenen Straßen, der Pendler,
Land, bald ohne Namen.

Borderland, not invented,
aging from Hof to Travemünde.

Mistrust, unyielding, stifling,
between minefield, guard-tower and barbed wire.

Rail-track, in the foot-tangling thicket,
ending and rusting.
Uncontradicted void.

They've burned the forest down
to get a clear field of fire.

Camouflage. Night an accomplice.
The houses turn away
as you pass them.

Land of forgotten roads, of secret smugglers,
land, soon without a name.

Translated by Ewald Osers

The borderland appears as something ghostly, sinister, which is simultaneously a harsh reality; it is "not invented," as the poem puts it. This poem, too, is laconic, with its abbreviated sentences characterized by key words. Only two sentences are complete, one of which reads "The houses turn away / as you pass them." You do not say that the houses, which are probably empty and decaying, create a sad, repelling impression, but transport this feeling into the gesture of turning away. I think there is a crucial metaphor near the beginning. Can land "age"?

Here this means stagnation, diminution of the capacity for renewal. The linguistic expression of this stagnation is in the prevalence of participles: stifling, ending, rusting, burned down, forgotten. The aging country between the borders is in danger of losing its "name," its condition or state of being land [*Land-schaft*].

Finally the poem "Dezember 1944," [December 1944] which you published only in 1972:

Ein Tag, durchflogen,
durchworfen von Schnee
—der fiel durch die Augen der Menschen—
verstand kaum noch den andern,
den gerade gewesenen.
Die Leere wuchs, sie wog schwer.
Der letzte Angriff fand
am zweiundzwanzigsten statt.

Überall in den Kellern
sind die Toten beisammen,
schrie eine Frau,
aber sie sehen sich nicht.

One day flown by,
riddled with snow
—which fell through the eyes of the people—
scarcely understood another
the one that had just passed.
The emptiness grew, it weighed heavily.
The last attack took
place on the twenty-second.
Everywhere in the cellars
the dead are together,
cried a woman,
but they don't see each other.

I wrote it late, twenty-five years after the night of the air attack.

Was there a special reason for this?

No.

Did you "invent" the ending of the poem, the last four lines, or are they a quotation?

A quotation. The words of this woman remained verbatim in my memory. I have often thought about the fact that this woman expressed a foregone conclusion, namely, that the dead do not see one another, but that what she had said was nevertheless peculiar, especially because she had previously stated that they were "together" and then connected her two sentences with "but."

In the first part of the poem you say that one day scarcely understood another. The observation that the emptiness, of which you speak, weighed "heavily" might be a bit hard to understand.

This is an attempt to express an idea by means of a paradox.

One last question: Must literature justify itself?

No. Max Frisch once said that literature has lost its chance whenever it tries to justify itself.

Hans-Jürgen Heise
Born 1930 in Bublitz

    After living in Berlin as a youngster, Heise was evacuated to his native Bublitz (in Pomerania, now a part of Poland) to escape the air attacks on Berlin, but he returned to Berlin in 1945 to escape from the advancing Soviet troops. His education was interrupted by the war and the ensuing chaos, and he is thus largely an autodidact. From 1949–50 he worked on the East Berlin journal Sonntag, *then fled to West Berlin, and subsequently moved to Kiel where he now works in the Institute of World Economics of the University of Kiel.*

    His first poetry volume appeared in 1961. He has also published essays, literary criticism, newspaper articles, reviews for the media, and a volume of travel impressions of Spain (in collaboration with his wife, the poetess Annemarie Zornack).

    Hans-Jürgen Heise initially declined to be interviewed, but suggested that written answers to my questions be included in this book. As a result of subsequent correspondence, a visit with him at his home, intended to be purely social, took place. During this visit on May 12, 1975, he changed his mind and consented to a taped interview but requested that he be sent a transcript before preparation of the English version. What follows are the positions he took in writing in January of 1975 and a materially shortened, but in substance accurate, version of the personal interview.

Responses to written questions received under a cover letter, dated January 14, 1975:

What is the task of poetry—criticism of political conditions or development of a utopian design? What should characterize the type and quality of utopian poetry and, if the occasion arises, any utopian poetry which you might produce?

I consider literature, and especially poetry, to have not just a critical function. Poetry is also, is above all, spontaneous expression. It is intuitive exclamation. It is metaphorical protest against conceptually hardened speech, as it is used daily in politics, economics, and business. Utopia, as I perceive it, should also anticipate concrete present-day possibilities. Utopia must infuse into our frustrated lives particles of feeling and experience which are more intense than any other emotional states or imaginary elements. To put it differently, utopia may not be consigned just to the status of an ideological substitute player. It must function as an always available connecting link between the temporary reality of our everyday lives and an imagined better reality.

How do you react to the statement: "Literature . . . intends to act and agitate, but all it really does is react."

A literature which exclusively reacts critically to society is reactive indeed. In order to criticize a critic descends to the niveau of the object of his criticism. And any artist who totally consigns himself to politics will ultimately become a politician—with all the characteristics that make a politician and thus differentiate him and his externalized manner of thinking from the more subjective sensitivity of a potential artist.

"It is particularly disturbing that the future as a topos seems to have been leased by the authors of the GDR, while the lyric poets of the West evidently

do not recognize hope as a principle and, at best, contribute dire predictions and prophecies of doom when they ought to be discussing that which should happen tomorrow." Your response?

I do not believe that the authors of the GDR have a better grasp of the future than do the authors of the Federal Republic. An ideological projection offers no guaranty that the future can in actual practice be managed. The problems of our contemporary western consumer and throwaway society will be the problems of socialist and communist societies of tomorrow and in the future. The principle of hope is a philosophical conglomerate of the Jewish expectation of a Messiah, Hegelianism, and Marxist historical materialism. Since in the meantime the limits of growth have become evident worldwide, the principle of hope can no longer be a blindly acceptable postulate for the eastern nations, including the GDR.

"The poet as a leader tries to approach an ideal step by step and attempts to bring this ideal to reality through his own person. The engaged poet disrupts the concentration upon himself, looks toward his fellow man and investigates the prerequisites and tools for action . . . ." Is this an acceptable statement?

The poet should be less of a leader toward higher ideals than a leader into the almost lost catacombs of the psychic. If poetry can exercise an interhuman function it is its ability of injecting certain remnants of "savage thought" into society at a time when abstract thinking is excessively exerted. "Savage thought"—Levi-Strauss has made this clear—is less a primitive form of thought, less the thinking done by primitive people, than a type of articulation stemming from the bioactive subconscious which has become foreign to us. I believe that a writer becomes most intensively engaged when he converses ever more intensely with himself. If possible a poet should not illustrate political programs or "personify" ideas. He should rather convert the inner psychic into a sociological exterior and, in this manner, confront society with something of which it would not become aware without him: the interior of the social creature called man.

What do you think about the assertion that poets are physicians and what they write is the handwriting on the wall?

I do not believe that writers are the physicians of mankind. I rather believe that, without themselves becoming in the least pathological or pathogenic, they serve as indicators of the symptoms of diseases which afflict mankind collectively and which, under certain circumstances, have been caused by collective mankind. Foucault said something very remarkable when he pointed out that we have only tended since the period of enlightenment to banish insanity from public life, from the streets and from the family environment, and to lock up the insane. Why did this come about? What sort of ideas, what kind of an ideology, causes this demand to make insanity invisible and to hide the insane behind walls? For some of us it has become more than just a presentiment that it might have been rationalism itself which, because of a lack of confidence in its own reasonableness, excommunicated and banished its irrational portrait. In any case, the artist still today has the opportunity of expressing a bit of that counterrationality which, prior to the elimination of the emotionally disturbed, had been a part of a more complex, more honest, and perhaps even healthier social reality.

Can we afford the luxury of creating new beautiful works of literature unless we first call the attention of mankind to the dangers extant in our present-day society?

We do not deprive mankind of anything when we create artistic works of beauty. On the contrary, in a world which is becoming ever more uniform, we thus increase the number of original objects. Even if, after all the upheavals, after all the political and economic power struggles, we were to succeed in creating a socially reasonably fair world (an aim, to which every moral artist subscribes), what would be gained if the price for such material satisfaction were a global cultural wasteland and total didactic equalization? An artist creates values which are not utilitarian—at least not primarily utilitarian, until they get into the hands of the tradesmen. It is true that utilitarian technical objects can be beautiful, can have beautiful form. But this does not mean that conversely the beautiful in art is utilitarian. It is rather a psychic and spiritual necessity. Art, as I understand it, is not a form of social luxury but an emotional necessity for its creator and—I would like to add—also for the one who uses it, who "consumes" it.

Must "tendentious" be synonymous with "inferior"?

No. But the tendentious work of art, the tendentious poem, does contain the inherent danger of lacking in creative originality and imagery. To put it differently, it may be dominated by mere political rhetoric, by pure propaganda, by naked demagogism.

You sent me a collective written answer to nine additional questions which I will let stand on its own merit. (These questions are numbers 4–12 in the Appendix.)

Because there are many poets who consider the writing of poetry nothing but a verbal game, the entire lyric genre has acquired the reputation of being nothing more than the marketplace of elitist conceits. The fact that, because of shyness, some of the most sensitive poets appear to be more and more hermetic, contributes further to the image that any poetry which is not specifically politically engaged is nothing more than a metaphoric costume ball. These misunderstandings and errors can only be eliminated by a very laborious examination of each individual case—perhaps in monographs, as I did in my volume of essays *Das Profil unter der Maske* [*The Profile Under the Mask*]. It is and remains the greatest handicap of the lyric poet that he is read almost exclusively by the so-called "cultivated," and that even they do not usually really understand him—which is why lyric poets are solely interested in the formal and aesthetic aspects. Cult of words and fetishism for language serve as a substitute for lack of excitability, for a defective understanding of the psychological and social prerequisites of art, including lyric poetry. On the other hand, many who have a natural inclination toward poetry are prevented from recognizing in the fluctuation and desolate cyphers of modern imagery the correspondency to their own alienation, because of the nature of the cultural marketplace, partly because of the academic and partly because of the commercialized forms of dissemination.

Interview of May 12, 1975:

When reading your poems I gain the impression that your engagement involves many problems: politics, the environment, the fate of mankind in our somewhat difficult times. I would like to ask you to illustrate this by means of some sample poems, to tell a little about the history of their origin and to explicate them.

Politics, the environment, the fate of mankind. I first would like to say a few words about the environment. Naturally man has always lived in some type of an "environment," although he did not note this fact nearly as consciously nor reflect upon it as intensely as in our scientific, almost excessively scientific, times. On the other hand, our highly trimmed consciousness can now largely experience reality only through the filters of abstraction.

We no longer have a natural, unconstrained relationship with the world. Our attitude toward the environment has become disturbed and dissected, meaning that we no longer consider ourselves to be mere creatures of nature, but rather shapers, *makers*, of history. And in recent times this has led increasingly to a feeling of being injured, of being victimized, because there have been numerous unfortunate events, ecological problems and the like, and because we are now aware that we are approaching the limits of our creativity.

I have used this situation in which we all live and under which we all suffer more or less as the theme of a number of poems, first (and this without striking any responsive chords at all) in certain verses of my first poetry volume *Vorboten einer neuen Steppe* [*Precursors of a New Steppe*], published in 1961. In recent years I have treated the subject of the environment in a number of absurd-parabolic poems, such as "Quer" ("Diagonally"):

Die überfüllten Städte
wandern
in den Geschichtsatlas aus

Wir laufen
quer über die Schallplattenrillen
ans Meer
         Einen zappelnden

Golf an der Leine
vielleicht
holen wir die Fische
zurück

The glutted cities
emigrate
into the historical atlas

We run
diagonally across the record grooves

192

to the ocean
A wriggling

gulf on the line
perhaps
we bring back
the fishes

I will now attempt an interpretation of my text, but do this with much hesitation, with strongly felt inhibitions, because it makes me uncomfortable to comment on my own writings, and because I realize that the transposition of a metaphoric structure to a discussion niveau causes not only changes in language, but also changes in the essence, a certain watering down.

But let us consider the beginning of "Diagonally:" "The glutted cities / emigrate / into the historical atlas," which means that the world today, in the century of overpopulation, is threatened by such a total urbanization and excessive settling that the end of history has become thinkable, certainly the end of our civilization which depends so completely on technology. My poem is a menetekel, a Cassandran prophecy. It anticipates what threatens to happen soon—that the cities will grow rankly, destroy the landscape, and use up the environment and what resources still remain. Even the oceans, which were once the symbols of freedom and limitless expanse, are now threatened by the danger of being fished empty and of becoming sewers. Now the reaction which I describe appears entirely possible: we, together with our thoroughly confused contemporaries, run away from our artificial world (symbolized by a record with its vast number of grooves) toward the ocean, an act of irrational rebellion or fulfillment of a secret longing. And there we try "A wriggling / gulf on the line" to recapture what has been lost, the natural, the living, or—expressed differently—the fishes which have been scared away and decimated.

This is how I would interpret my poem "Diagonally," though I must hasten to add that here, as in all other cases, I was not conscious of the direction my intuitive mental adventure would eventually take as I was writing it down. At the basis of my metaphoric excursions lies a certain unrest, not a premeditated goal. Once a matter has been developed clearly it can only result in an essay, not in a poem. Metaphoric poems can only be interpreted ex post facto—this, at least, is the opinion of the author who, I believe, will not always be able to discover *all* the implicit interpretative possibilities in his work.

This is similar to an abstract painting. You leave it up to the reader to reach conclusions that are meaningful to him, in contrast to a classical ballad whose ultimate thrust is recognizable at once.

In contrast to an abstract painting, a metaphoric poem does not give absolute freedom of interpretation to the reader. While the metaphoric poem is not an empty frame into which the intuition of the viewer can insert any conceivable picture, it can be interpreted far more associatively than easily comprehensible, didactic, or otherwise *intentional* poetry.

I believe that the well known "Dich" ("You") is one of your poems that has often been interpreted incorrectly. It has been asserted that it was inspired by the infamous Berlin Wall, to which it might be applied. But I do not believe that you had the Berlin Wall in mind when you wrote it, did you?

"You" was written in June or July of 1960, approximately one year prior to the erection of the Berlin Wall. This text goes back to personal experiences and to historical events, which had to do with the banishment and killing of relatives, of two innocent civilians. Thus, this poem has nothing to do with the wall even though I myself crossed the border in Berlin as a refugee in 1950, at a time when the wall did not exist as yet. My flight from East Berlin and the emotional trauma connected with it undoubtedly contributed to the imagery contained in this poem, though they did so subconsciously.

I have been queried about this poem time and again. On the Italian radio Professor Marianelli described it as "perhaps the most painful symbol of the partition of Germany." And when the poem was reprinted in the *FAZ* [*Frankfurter Allgemeine Zeitung*] a number of students surmised that it was a plea for the Palestinians. From a certain moment on, it became clear to me that this creation had become divorced from the specific circumstances of my biography, both in the external and emotional sense, and that I, the author, could only make a limited contribution to its interpretation. This is why I now believe that it can be applied to any appropriate situations, no matter where these might occur.

Dich haben sie erschossen	You were shot dead by them
mich vertrieben	I was expelled

194

Und nun verteidigen sie	And now their rifles
mit Gewehren	defend
dein Grab	your grave
gegen meine Blumen	against my flowers

Translated by Ewald Osers

You deal not only with politics, not only with the environment, but also with the general problems of mankind in our times. Unfortunately "Song of Yourself," a poem which I consider particularly interesting, is too long for this volume. But in "Aktennotiz" ("Memorandum for the Files"), a poem which was published just two years ago, you also consider mankind in modern society.

"Memorandum for the Files" is simultaneously a personal and a public poem. It is personal because I have subjectively experienced it, lived through it; public because the conclusions reached apply to many others.

Mit Büroklammern	Faces
zusammengehaltene	held together
Gesichter	with paper clips
Man zieht ein Farbband	One pulls a typewriter ribbon
durch die Lippen	through one's lips
und stellt sich	and draws up
im Löscherschatten auf	in the shadow of the blotter
Abgeheftetes Licht	The detached light
der Neonröhren	of neon tubes
auf der elektrischen	on the electric
Schreibmaschine	typewriter
setzt sich der Traum	the dream continues
als Geschäftsbrief fort	as a business letter
Und um dem Quader	And to remove all emptiness
allen Raum zu nehmen	from the block
akkreditiert sich nebenan	a mortuary is
ein Beerdigungsinstitut	accredited next door

In many ways this text is self-explanatory, at least as I see it. Anyone who goes to an office five times per week, eight hours per day, and then, in an atmosphere of an unreal paper-world, reduced life and limited communication with others, fights an obstinate secret battle against the (time) clock, does not speak metaphorically but entirely realistically when he says:

> Faces
> held together
> with paper clips . . . .

The next stanza:

> One pulls a typewriter ribbon
> through one's lips
> and draws up
> in the shadow of the blotter . . .

illustrates this frustrating condition with additional details. Modern bureaucrats are alienated. They do not have a relaxed relationship with the environment in which they work, where they earn their money. When someone pulls a typewriter ribbon through his lips this demonstrates that he has become a mere accessory of his technical equipment. And since there is no possibility of leaving the treadmill of this thoroughly programmed daily routine, the depersonalized individual has no other choice but to take refuge in the shadow of the blotter. Man has become a utensil among utensils. The pitilessness of the business world is also expressed in the following images:

> The detached light
> of neon tubes
> on the electric
> typewriter
> the dream continues
> as a business letter . . . .

The office worker is the least important, the most easily exchanged part, of the functional objects that surround him. Individual feelings founder in the clatter of electric typewriters. The dream degenerates into the empty opening phrase of the business letter that must be written. Goal directed, rational thinking reaches the culmination of perverseness. Only the last stanza leads from the interior of this office-induced anxiety into the outside world. But here too is no sudden revelation of freedom; on the contrary

> And to remove all emptiness
> from the block
> a mortuary is
> accredited next door . . . .

In place of a transcendental view or—at least—an illusory perspective all there is to see is a mortuary, a funeral parlor, which represents the realm of death just as soullessly and factually as the world of officialdom and business represents the sphere of commercialized life.

What is the future of the poem as a means of communication in our time of mass media?

I am inclined to think that the poem is one of the few art forms that retains a function in the time of the mass media, simply because the poem, as a small linguistic entity, can express emotional states, spontaneous pronouncements. The novel could conceivably be replaced in the future by scientific examinations of group behavior. Besides modern man is not a particularly interesting subject for an epic poet. In a time when everyone does the same and experiences the same, both during his work and his leisure time—perhaps while watching television—there is little original material for novelists, short story writers, and writers of ballads. Behavior has become standardized and interhuman relations boring. The active subject, the protagonist of the old gripping stories has been replaced, as it were, by the anonymous pronoun "one" *(man)*—and what of significance can still be told about this person without characteristics [*Mann ohne Eigenschaften*]?! It is different with our feelings. Within each one of us something special, unique, something which cannot be repeated, occurs. In the psyche each is and remains a more or less scintillating personality. This is where I see the possibility for the lyric poet. This is where I perceive, even in the time of mass media, where works of art can be reproduced technologically, a remaining chance for the poem.

Courtesy Verlag-Eremiten Presse

Christoph Meckel

Born 1935 in Berlin

Christoph Meckel spent his childhood in Berlin, Erfurt, and Freiburg im Breisgau. With a number of interruptions he studied graphics and painting for four semesters at the academies of fine arts in Freiburg and Munich. In between and since then he has traveled extensively in Europe, Africa, Central America, and the United States (including a Visiting Professorship in German Poetry at the University of Texas). He works not only as a freelance writer but also as an artist and has illustrated a number of his own literary works. He divides his time between his native Berlin and a summer residence in France.

His early poetry was influenced by Krolow and Eich: the first volume was published in 1956. Since then he has not only published poems, but also ballads and prose works.

Christoph Meckel was interviewed in his apartment in Berlin on April 9, 1975, and edited the transcript of the tape with the result that what follows is slightly cut in length but remains unchanged in substance.

When reading your poetry I gain the impression that the loneliness of man is your central theme. Why is that?

I do not believe that it is an important motif of just my poetry; it is a central motif of world literature, perhaps since time immemorial. But "loneliness"—that is putting it too simply. The problem is how man asserts himself, how he comes to terms with others, how he survives in a social structure, is unable or unwilling to live in it, in what way he exposes himself, or how he tries to prevent exposing himself. Loneliness is a tremendous driving force. For this reason I do not consider loneliness to be merely a defense mechanism. Every individual can overestimate his loneliness. It is possible that writers have been overestimating their loneliness. I do not consider myself as lonely; on the contrary, I have become increasingly aware of the fact that I am far less lonely than others, less isolated, because I—in contrast to many others—have the opportunity of using this loneliness to write.

Critics have time and again described your literary work, especially that of the first ten years, as pessimistic. Now that I have met you personally I find this even more difficult to accept than before. Are these critics correct—or were they correct?

I know neither what pessimism nor what optimism means. They do not seem to be distinguishable from one another. Besides we could all victimize one another by the use of such terms. But there is a skepticism extant today which is inevitable and necessary if one considers the future. I believe that the formerly occurring individual skepticism has long been replaced by a collective skepticism. We have more of a past behind us than of a future ahead of us; the earth is old and exploitable. I never cease searching for possibilities of how I and others can continue a life worthy of a human being in a future suitable for humanity. What an author writes humiliates slogans (probably also that which I am now saying), invalidates all clichés, and causes vocabulary items like "pessimism" and "optimism" to disappear.

Would you describe these dispensers of clichés as Agitprop *poets?*

I really do not know these people or their work well enough. This may be just the constantly beating drum of those who want to be tendentious. I am convinced that the poem has the chance to synthesize all spheres of human experience, the intellectual, spiritual, biological, etc., in one comprehensive statement. If any one element is lacking in a poem—let us say, for example, timeliness—this is comparable to a human being who is minus a vital organ of his body. Such a poem could not live. *Agitprop* poetry would be poetry which lends itself only to a political interpretation. But as far as I am concerned there can be no poem which is exclusively political in nature, just as there cannot be a poem that concerns itself solely with nature or with love. A living poem has an infinite number of foregrounds and backgrounds. Poems are charged with energy like batteries and these elements of energy can be understood by the perceptive reader even when they do not occur in his vocabulary. When these elements of energy are lacking a poem is nothing but a literary mirage.

Would you extend your assertion that all dimensions are contained in every poem even to Eichendorff's famous "Mondnacht" ("Moonlit Night")?

It can perhaps be determined today that the apparent absence of a plainly political dimension in a poem by Eichendorff or Mörike does constitute a political statement. Among the lyric poets of classicism and romanticism there was a political sensibility, a critical attitude toward their own time in a broader sense which was not expressed directly. Furthermore, Eichendorff wrote some sonnets which clearly manifest his attitude toward the politics of his time. And in the case of Mörike you find not only the profound, celestial musicality of such poems as "An eine Äolsharfe" ["To an Aolian Harp"] and "Erinna an Sappho" ["Erinna to Sappho"], but also the very incisive and clearly critical poem "An Longus" ["To Longus"]. When some poets turn away from their time this too constitutes a political decision.

The concept of the "idyll" was raised time and again in literary discussions in Germany during the fifties and sixties. This term was used with reference to the attitude of those authors who had not confronted contemporary events unequivocally or head-on. There was talk about the "retreat into the idyllic." Perhaps this was necessary after World War II. But this was never a useable concept for me. There are not any idylls left today, and there is not any possibility at all of a retreat. I do not know a single lyric poet of merit to whom this concept could be applied. Even in an apparently peacefully meandering poem by Peter Huchel, in a vocabulary that is virtually completely limited to terms describing nature lyrically, there is a far clearer decision for or against the times than the *litterateur* who reads it too quickly or who operates with blinders may want to believe.

I can follow your idea that omission can also represent a statement. But does not this make it very difficult for the average reader, for the consumer of the product called poetry, who may not discern this? And does not this create the danger that a poet may lose a part of his potential public? In other words, for whom do you write?

It is not a matter of omitting something. On the contrary! The important thing is to omit nothing, nothing at all! I believe that I alluded to that earlier. For me, a contemporary poem is alive when it contains all dimensions which are accessible to experience and insight. I try to make a poem as complex, inclusive, opulent, and extensive as possible. Furthermore, he who writes lyrics cannot calculate the effect of this language. You see, like any other created object a poem depends upon distribution, upon publishers, binderies, reviewers. Every literary text is caught in this multitude of dependencies; it is a product which has to assert itself in an irrational mechanism consisting of advertising, proclamation, and ignorance. A lyric poet can do nothing more and nothing less than to say what he has to say as comprehensively, clearly, and uncompromisingly as possible. There would be absolutely no sense in my roaring more or less loudly into this general cacophony. I represent what I am, and I write what I know. To be sure, I am confident in one respect: that there are readers, and this is no blind confidence, but it is based on experience. I do not know precisely who reads these poems—I do not want to talk about "my reading public"—but I know that poems reach readers, sometimes via incredible detours and after long delays in time. Poems can cope with any kind of dependency upon a cultural or economic structure. As an aside, the scholar who considers himself an authority on poetry and language may well be least capable of comprehending both. The comprehension of lyrical language is very little dependent upon a literary education, upon one's level of education in general. It also has nothing to do with feeling. I cannot distinguish between feeling and intellect, and there can be no differentiation between emotional poetry and anything else. A far greater number of people are capable of comprehending poetry because of their experiences, their involvements, and their sensitivity. People in general are far more gifted than they know and than one leads them to believe.

I take it then that your engagement is not a conscious effort. You do not sit down and say to yourself: I will now write a poem about this grievance or that one? Your engagement is merely a part of that which compels you to write in the first place?

I can answer this question only about myself, and I would like to leave out the word *engagement* because it has been talked to death. The personal involvement and the taking of a position by a lyric poet are prerequisites, are a part of his responsibility, and are dangerous for his life. There is a constant personal risk involved. Undoubtedly there must be a decision against any kind of fascism, against getting into a rut, against haughtiness, lack of understanding, destruction of human possibilities, and against oppression—but in such a self-evident manner that it need not be stated or emphasized time and again.

Your style seems to intertwine the perspicuous and the surreal (and I hasten to add, that this is by no means an original observation on my part).

Look, it is a matter of indifference to me what all I may have intertwined literarily or otherwise. There are others who can carry out literary investigations better and more thoroughly. For me, poetry is the possibility of liberating myself from all limitations. In other words, it is quite the contrary of that which is happening in German literature and probably also in other literatures: all these limitations and taboos, this commitment to a certain type of poem or language (usually provincial and temporary); all these dicta regarding the functions of literature, how a poem should be structured, long or short, transparent or otherwise—all of these demands and assertions directed at authors I consider meaningless. A poem does not always have to do something! A person does not always have to do something from dawn to dusk, does not have to say or consider something all the time. A poem need not always comply with any kind of principles. It is the opportunity of the poem to be totally free from all this. The question whether a poem is conservative, avant-garde, opportune, or tendentious is of secondary importance at best. A poem which sets aside in like manner all slogans, categories, demands, and fashions corresponds to my conception. Furthermore, a poet and a poem which is really a poem accomplish much more than could ever be elicited by any demands.

You have written sonnets, poems that rhyme, completely "modern" poems that defy classification. Are you of the opinion that there is no necessary connection between form and content?

It is naturally useful for a lyric poet if he has mastered the various techniques of his craft, if he can write a sonnet or use the meter of Klopstock. I consider the writing of sonnets today quite possible, not necessary or desirable, but possible—if the right man undertakes this. It depends on how one does this and what energies motivate it. I do not write sonnets at the present time, but it is possible that I may do so again some day because, as I said, I consider this form to be quite useable. I do not agree that a certain form is needed to express a specific thought. One can use existing forms. They are in any case transformed into something new; each poet creates his own language. A poet should have complete freedom in the use of what already exists, just as he would be if he were writing in a language which does not exist as yet.

Since we are talking about content just now: it seems to me that you are very often concerned with the unmasking of counterfeit sentiments. Are counterfeit sentiments one of the chief problems of our time?

The lyric poet by his very nature directs his efforts against all types of stupidity, illusion, and uninspired repetition. There are such problems as the terrifying ideological illusions, the presumptuous and dangerous way in which political opinions are formed, the manner in which government, the press, the literary establishment, and the media take advantage of and dominate the public—wherever one listens and looks there is deception. Against this I pose my share of freedom: to do forthrightly what I consider to be correct. I do not have to make a decision time and again against that which limits the existence of mankind—I have made this decision a long time ago. I am not interested in case by case dealing with an obvious or hidden social, political, or other grievance, but I insist upon personifying this kind of protest for the remainder of my life, irrevocably and thus irrefutably—and I do not intend to do too much talking about this.

In your most recent poetry volume, Wen es angeht (To Whom It May

Concern), *I am especially intrigued by the poem "Was dieses Land betrifft"* *("Concerning this Country"). You just said that you are no pessimist. But* *when I read this poem I do gain the impression of a certain degree of* *pessimism.*

Was dieses Land betrifft: hier ist kein Ort, für die Zeit
die kommt, einen Grundstein zu setzen. Dies ist kein Ort
für mehr als ein Dasein in Kälte, ausgeschieden
einsilbig und überstimmt. Wenn dein Knochen wandert
in dir auf der Suche nach Leben und ausbricht, hungrig
nach Freude und Zukunft, aber zurückkehrt
ruhlos, weltwund, todnah—wo ist der Genosse
ohne Vertrag, der Bruder ohne Berechnung? Wer hat
seinen Traum nicht zertrampelt oder verkauft, seine Sprache
nicht abgestimmt auf jedermanns Vorschrift und Vorteil?
Wer hat seinen Kopf nicht eingezogen, wer schleicht nicht
mit halber Sonne unter dem Hut in sein Loch
wo die Ohnmacht Staub ansetzt und die Liebe,
ein Haustier, sich ausschläft. Wo ist ein Mensch
der Handschellen weder trägt noch anlegt, wo ist
der Ort, für die Zeit die kommt, einen Grundstein zu setzen?

Hier bleibst du stehn und lässt dir nicht sagen: verschwinde.

Concerning this country: here is not the place
to lay a cornerstone for the future. Here is not the place
for more than an existence in the cold, rejected
laconic and overruled. If your bone moves
within you in search of life and breaks out, hungry
for joy and a future, but returns
restless, scathed by the world, close to death—where is the voluntary
companion, the uncalculating brother? Who has not
trampled or sold his dream, failed to tune
his language in conformity and to everyone's advantage?
Who has not pulled in his neck, who does not crawl
into his hole with but half a sun under his hat
where the dust of impotence prevails and love
is sound asleep, like a house pet. Where is someone
who neither wears nor dons handcuffs, where is
the place to lay a cornerstone for the future?

Here you stop and let no one tell you: disappear.

This poem is a challenge, directed by the poet toward himself and toward every other individual personally—thus not toward all collectively, but toward each individual personally—not to accept the fact that this country does not seem to be the location where the cornerstone for the future may be placed. And that is precisely why I can see no pessimism here, because we are talking about someone who is unwilling to accept things as they are; and as long as *one* person is unwilling to submit there can be no talk about pessimism. Your question whether I would like to add something to this poem I must answer negatively. I do not want to limit or spoil my own work by a subsequent interpretation. I would like my poem to be open-ended, not even restricted by my own opinion. I do not believe that this poem is in any way enciphered; it is simple. That which must be said has been said. Each reader can relate it to himself.

It seems obvious that reviewers of Wen es angeht *will want to make a comparison between "Was dieses Land betrifft"("Concerning this Country") and your poem "Hymne." Please comment on the similarities and differences between these two poems.*

It seems to me that you are unduly optimistic regarding the literary practices in Germany. Scarcely a single critic will take the trouble of considering what an author has previously written, of taking notice of changes in his work. One quickly and superficially evaluates whatever is on one's table. So we are out of luck here. But let us talk about the poem "Hymne."

> Ich lebe in einem Land, das seine geschundenen
> und geflickten Garderoben den Spiegeln des Himmels
> vorführt ohne besondere Koketterie,
> in einem Land unter Tränengloriolen,
> dessen ewige Grenzen Klagemauern sind.
>
> Ich lebe in einem Land, das verliebt ist in den Tod,
> seine Erde ist mit zahllosen Särgen möbliert
> und ausgestattet mit Knochen, die abgeklärt
> den Schankwirt des Todes um neue Gefährten bitten,
> dem Himmel des Landes steht die Sonne gut,
> doch seine Sterbefabriken schließen sich nie.
>
> Ich lebe in einem Duft von abgestandenen Seufzern,
> der Gewißheit des Todes, der Ungewißheit des Lebens,
> zwiefach unwillig verbunden und verpflichtet
> durch Angst und unausweichliche Vorsicht,
> die ein Zirkusaffe auf dem Rücken
> eines Elefanten braucht, um nicht zu stürzen.

Ich lebe in einem Land, das verliebt ist in den Tod,
ein Tränenkrug ist sein Wappen und Souvenir,
ein Blutegel sein Maskott, seine Fahnen Vogelscheuchen,
der tausendste Enkel meiner Hoffnung kam um.
Der letzte Schild meiner Zuversicht ist zerborsten.

I live in a country which displays its exploited
and mended wardrobe to the mirrors of heaven
without any special coquetry,
in a land under a halo of tears,
whose eternal borders are wailing walls.

I live in a country in love with death,
its earth is furnished with innumerable caskets
and fitted out with bones which, self-possessed,
ask the innkeeper of death for new companions,
the sun looks good in the sky of this land,
yet its death-factories never close.

I live in an aura of stale sighs,
in the certainty of death, in the uncertainty of life,
twice involuntarily fettered and obligated
by the fear and inescapable caution
which a circus monkey needs
on the back of an elephant in order not to fall.

I live in a country in love with death,
an urn full of tears is its coat of arms and souvenir,
·a leech its mascot, its flags are scarecrows,
the thousandth grandchild of my hope has perished.
The last shield of my faith is split asunder.

I was born in 1935, was five years old when World War II began and ten years old when it ended. Then came the postwar years, the time of my youth and of my first points of reference. I belong to a generation which faced the world, sought it out, and believed itself able to participate in totally new experiences. It was a time of incredible hopes. There also seemed to be once again an inviolate bourgeois concept of art. But it became evident very quickly that the German recovery devoured everything. This reconstruction period after the war made a strong impact upon my youth, especially upon my protest against what was happening. And in this poem "Hymne" you find a young man with an expression of early despair because nothing really moved ahead—everything retrograded into

a stifling, petty bourgeois, quickly degenerating status quo. In the
meantime sixteen or seventeen years have passed. I am older and
have had the chance to broaden my perspectives. Today it would be
unthinkable for me to become the victim of desperation, or, to
express it more accurately, for me to adopt an attitude of resignation. Desperation is another matter, something vital and painful: the
desperate person strikes out with fists. That which led during the
German reconstruction period to resignation in this and a couple of
other poems is unthinkable for me today. I would like to personify
protest, and I have tried to do this all my life and in an obvious
manner. Poetry is protest.

*Your most famous poem "Der Pfau" ("The Peacock") must be mentioned
here because of its affinity with the poems which we have just discussed.*

Ich sah aus Deutschlands Asche keinen Phönix steigen.
Räumend mit dem Fuß in der Asche
stieß ich auf kohlende Flossen, auf Hörner und Häute—
doch ich sah einen Pfau, der Asche wirbelnd
mit einem Flügel aus Holz und einem aus Eisen,
riesig wachsend, die Flocken der Feuerstellen
peitschte und sein Gefieder strählte.

Ich sah aus Deutschlands Asche alte Krähen kriechen
und borstige Nachtigallen mit heiseren Kehlen
und Hähne mit Schwertfischschnäbeln und kahlen Kämmen,
den Ruhm des Vogels zu pfeifen und zu singen.
Ich sah sie in aller Feuer Asche schnobern,
in die der Wind fuhr und kalten Rauch
abtrieb über Breiten, wo wenig nur Gold war, was glänzte.

Ich sah aus Deutschlands Asche keinen Phönix steigen,
doch sah ich einen Pfau in der Leuchtzeit seines Gefieders,
ich sah ihn strahlende Räder schlagen
im Gegenlicht eisgrauer Himmel und Wetterleuchten
und hörte den Jubel der Krähen und Spatzen und sah
*Elsternschwärme in seine Goldfedern stürzen
Läuse finster aus seinem Gefieder wachsen
große Ameisen seine Augen zerfressen*

I saw no phoenix mount from Germany's ashes.
Rummaging in the ash with my foot
I turned up charred fins, horns and sloughs—
yet I saw a peacock, swirling up the ash

with one wing of wood and other other of iron,
growing enormous, and he whipped
at the flakes where the burning had been
and he fanned out his plumage.

I saw old crows creep out of Germany's ashes
and stubbly nightingales with hoarse throats
and cocks with swordfish beaks and bald combs
to whistle and sing the praises of that bird.
I saw them snorting in the ashes of all fires
where the wind was driving, pushing cold smoke
over broad places where little was gold that glittered.

I saw no phoenix mount from Germany's ashes;
yet I saw a peacock in the time when his plumage shone,
I saw him spread a tail in glorious radiances
in the counterlight of icegrey skies and lightnings
and heard the jubilation of crows and sparrows and saw
magpie flocks plunge into his plumage of gold,
lice darkly evolving out of his plumage,
big ants feeding on his eyes.

Translated by Christopher Middleton

Your engagement, as you said earlier, is expressed in the poem which touches upon all problems of mankind. Your concern for the ecology manifests itself very early, much earlier than in the case of most lyric poets, in "Flaschenpost für eine Sintflut" ("Bottle Mail for a Deluge") which today, sixteen years after its first publication, seems most timely and appropriate.

Ihr Überlebenden auf großen Flotten
feudaler Archen über den Wasserschächten
einmal kommender kleiner oder mächtiger Sintflut,
ihr Zuhälter des Todes, Schmeichler Noahs, würdet
unsrer nicht mehr gedenken, die in den Böen,
in Rauch, Schlamm und Gestank, an den wellenvermummten
Orten des Zähneklapperns verblieben, wenn diese Flasche nicht
heute oder morgen an eure ungleich goldneren
Häuser schlüge, wo ihr beim Mahl
der inzwischen wieder geschlachteten Taube
lacht und euch sicher dünkt auf der Empore Welt,
würdet unsrer nicht mehr gedenken, wenn nicht
zahllose solcher Flaschen voll Nachricht für euch noch
im Wasser trieben, von Welle zu Welle getragen,
und nicht die ein oder andre euch eines Tages
plötzlich vor Augen oder Ohren käme, eure

Tagesordnungen häßlich unterbrechend,
worin geschrieben steht, was ihr ohne Schlottern
nicht lesen könnt: "Ihr Überlebenden
auf großen Flotten feudaler Archen
über den Wassern der wieder zerronnenen,
auf uns herabgesunkenen Sintflut, die wir geopfert
an verschollenen Orten des Zähneklapperns . . . "

You survivors on great fleets
of feudal arks above watery abysses
of a small or mighty deluge, which someday will come,
you pimps of death, you wheedlers of Noah, would
not remember us, who remained in the squalls,
in smoke, mud, and stench, at the carefully muffled
sites of chattering teeth, if this bottle did not
today or tomorrow knock on your incomparably
more golden houses where you are laughing
while feasting on the dove, slaughtered in the meantime,
and believe yourselves secure on the gallery of the world,
you would not remember us, were there not innumerable
such bottles full of news for you drifting
on the waters, carried from wave to wave,
and if one or the other of them some day
suddenly did not come within your sight or hearing,
hideously disrupting the orderly course of your days,
conveying a message which you cannot read without
trembling: "You survivors
on great fleets of feudal arks
above the waters of the deluge, which
has subsided again and sunk down on us, who, sacrificed
in lost sites of chattering teeth . . ."

Back then poems of this kind were often described as "seismographic." Today literature no longer has this possibility to such a great extent—science has usurped this function. I personally consider the ecological catastrophes to be far more far-reaching than the well-known ideological controversies. No one can be indifferent to what is happening today and what, as a consequence, will be occurring tomorrow. There are concepts and slogans that suddenly appear when a subject becomes of vital concern. For example, quality of life, sensibility, and solidarity. These three concepts began circulating when all this was brought into focus. The quality of life has been curtailed, and for many people it does not exist as yet or has already been lost. Solidarity is requested more often than it is granted, and sensibility—who know what we will experience in that regard.

But is it not the function of the poet to serve as a prophet? Is not what he writes, as Wolfgang Weyrauch once put it, "the handwriting on the wall?"

I am convinced that writers get wind of a thing, that they, and not only they alone, can pinpoint a problem. They know what it looks like, they identify it accurately: There it is! We should avoid the term *prophecy*. A person knows something and then communicates it. The living poem responds to the needs of the times, and I could imagine no era in which poems might be superfluous. Lyric poetry is necessary. If poetry were to disappear the world would become quickly uninhabitable, even for those who know nothing about poetry. I do not talk about the "handwriting on the wall"; my poems know more than I do. Language is clairvoyant.

Photograph by Isolde Ohlbaum

Nicolas Born

Born 1937 in Duisburg

Nicolas Born, who had been originally one of the angry young antiestablishment poets, after pursuing a number of other occupations, has been working as a freelance writer and occasionally as a critic since the middle of the 1960s. He was one of the participants in an experiment conducted by Walter Höllerer: the joint authorship of the novel Das Gästehaus [The guesthouse] (1965). He is now a permanent resident of West Berlin, but spends some of his time in a country house in Northern Germany.

In addition to poetry (the first volume appeared in 1967) he has also written novels, deliberately using everyday language.

Nicolas Born was interviewed on April 15, 1975, in his apartment in Berlin. Before translation, the transcription of the tape was forwarded to him for corrections, and this resulted in a few cuts and a number of minor corrections. He reads English fluently and expressed an intense interest in my translations of his poems.

211

When I compared the poems in your volume Marktlage (Market Report) *published in 1967 with those published five years later in* Das Auge des Entdeckers (The Eye of the Discoverer) *I was struck by the tremendous changes in your style, your use of metaphors and symbols. Why such a great change in only five years?*

The poems in *Marktlage* were written between 1965 and the end of 1966, possibly early 1967. At that time it seemed to me that the poetic concepts which I had overcome had become highly questionable as far as I was concerned. This included the entire gamut of possible metaphors, of metric poems, of symbols, and the tendency toward excessive use of metaphors. Such carriers of meaning had been included in poems of mine that remain unpublished. These could no longer be our meanings; they were the established meanings, and we first of all had to do away with them. This need for change was in line with another process, a private "clearing of the thicket" *(Kahlschlag)* which I wanted to accomplish at that time. The original "clearing of the thicket," which became well known in literature after World War II, used as its basis the assumption that there was in existence a discredited vocabulary which had been made unuseable by the Third Reich and which could no longer be employed in literature. The most significant manifestation of this was in the work of Celan who (even though he did not actively participate in the "thicket clearing" program), voluntarily limited his vocabulary and used a private, biblically mythical vocabulary in his lyric poetry. This is not to mention the first postwar poems of Günther Eich and Wolfgang Weyrauch which were directly the products of the "thicket clearing" gospel. (I am mentioning just these two because I cannot remember any others offhand.)

Later I realized that my private "clearing of the thicket" did not enable me to escape from the meaning of words. I learned that these words did retain a marvelously good potential, that words cannot be classified or expelled, but rather that there is a whole spectrum of meanings, secondary meanings, submeanings, and even split-off meanings and fluctuating meanings within words and word combinations, that certain meanings are precipitated and certain new meanings are absorbed. In the last few years I have observed a contrary development from that which I had once expected: a purification of all meanings by virtue of common usage. Language is subjected daily to such a not necessarily fruitful acid test (although it has become highly flexible and rich in America, when I think of the many idioms that have sprung up in the melting pot of New York and in the ghettos). I see in the campaigns of the advertisers and the manipulators, whether they sit in the government or try to peddle a product in the markets, a constant attack upon language which is an attack upon culture which is consequently an attack upon mankind per se, an attack upon man's very being, an attempt to occupy individuals—as a conqueror occupies a country—and which, in the final analysis, is designed to disenfranchise individuals and make them easier to manipulate. Language is more and more a mere imperative and a mere vehicle for commands and information.

The tool of the poet is his language. As a sculptor might work in marble the poet creates with words. In Marktlage *you wrote:*

Da steht man und zeigt
nur noch sich selbst die Zähne.
Wenn sich die Lippen schließen
sind Bruder und Schwester tot.

There we stand and snarl
at one another.
When our lips are closed
our brothers and sisters are dead.

I seem to notice a sense of impotence in these words, and I would like to know what their message is regarding a poet's ability to influence society.

You are right. All activity is directed toward oneself and accomplishes nothing outside. The aggression which is directed toward the outside touches its originator. The snarl, this animal-like gesture, is the symbol for this.

With respect to the effectiveness, the social effectiveness of literature and especially of poetry and even more especially the socially or sociologically critical poem, I am afraid that I can no longer concede its functionalism or its efficiency, as one might have expected it and as it would perhaps even be desirable. I must say that I am not unhappy about this. If you want to change or attack an undesirable social condition, you should not necessarily use poems for that purpose. This can be done by means of letters of protest, by petitions, political speeches, polemic letters, letters to the editor, etc. There are so many possibilities for expression. I do not believe that this should primarily be done via the poem. OK, here I am generalizing! There certainly are good examples of the contrary in history, especially in the history of literature, from times when the medium of literature had far broader validity, when there was no radio, no television, no other medium—in those days literatures naturally had many additional functions. But in view of the possibilities existing today for coping with social and sociological problems, or for not coping with them, this process would surely not be made easier or more difficult by the use of poetry. I consider it absurd to create a poem with the intention of stemming any abuses. This is no longer important. Let me clarify: Such remedies are very necessary, but not the poem as a vehicle, because I have no faith in its effectiveness, because other activities can accomplish far more.

There is, however, effectiveness in the poem, not in the sense of glib, hasty pedagogy or enlightenment, but in submerged and very fine impulses which, in turn, might give the reader the impulse to clarify his identity, to remind him of his emotional life—this, after all, is inherent in language and conserved by language. Among these are the many meanings contained in a single word, the many implications and sound-values which it contains. Our memories are basically contained in words. If these are given up voluntarily, as in advertising copy for the sake of functionalism, the true character of language is betrayed. Then language can really be used only for messages on matchbooks or on packages or to address letters or to issue military orders. I mean here that language has a function of reaching people via a membrane that is not used for other purposes, not even when reading a newspaper, singing in a choir, listening to music, or contemplating a work of the visual arts. To summarize briefly: I do believe that literature and especially poetry is effective, but that this is not a clearly delineated, provable social sense when it comes to the positive evolution of society as a whole. I rather believe that the fantasy of language which is expressed in literature, and the imagination which is manifested there, contains both a constructive and a destructive nucleus. I am happy about the ambivalence and the dialectic possibility inherent in literature.

For whom do you write?

I used to have the idea that I had to reach the suppressed, the deprived, the underprivileged, etc. Now my opinion has changed.

Is literature the appropriate means for liberating people from their dependence or, to say it briefly, is literature per se a weapon in the class struggle? I believe that literature is first of all a weapon against intellectual and cultural rigidity, that literature must keep language in motion, must widen horizons, activate the imagination, so that none of these potentials are lost and that an industrialized ready-made and functional language may not be used to obliterate everything. I see this danger—which I mentioned earlier when I referred to the attacks upon culture that are taking place here and in all industrialized countries. This peril, of course, is the other extreme when compared to the unified and limited idiom that existed in a land region in the nineteenth century. Then there was still a language loaded with meaning and intact, even though it may have been limited and bore witness to a lack of culture—there was a cultural sphere, underdeveloped but an entity. Today conditions have changed. Industrialization, the standardization of the cultures of industrialized nations, these have produced a more and more unified language, a functional language. If one could assign a clear-cut mission to literature it would have to be the reactivation of fantasy, of imagination, of speculation about other ways of life—this, in essence, is the task of literature. Likewise the recognition about the character of language, which is the carrier of our communications, to recognize what all there is to language, that language is a cosmos in its own right, not created merely to facilitate the identification of objects, to make survival possible with the aid of this means of communication.

In the concluding remarks to Das Auge des Entdeckers *you said that the poet, because of his function as a habitual critic, becomes a "critical partner of power." Does this make him a part of the establishment?*

A few years ago we had and we still have a few poets who are always out to see and critically react to the mistakes of the establishment or the government. There were people who, to overstate it a bit, were listening to the morning news in their pajamas, and if there was any annoying report—whether it be about Vietnam or some rich man beating his wife—immediately wrote a poem and sent it to a publisher. This was really quite ludicrous. I do not mean to do away with the criticism of gross wrongs, but I am objecting, in the sphere of poetry and literature, to shooting from the hip—often with cannons at sparrows. Although I once used to do this myself it no longer appeals to me. I do not think it accomplishes anything; I do believe in serving a useful function in the general tug of powers and counterpowers within the social system. But I am even more inclined to believe that an author should and must operate outside of the "game," and that he can thus avoid having the rules of his game dictated to him by the people who manufacture reality in our society.

Would you then take the position that the author, the poet, should deal with the situational model, which in essence has happened several times and may happen frequently again, rather than with a specific matter of transitory interest or momentary value?

Again, I would not want to generalize. But for the sake of clarity I would like to give an affirmative answer to the last part of your question. An author *should* not get involved in subject matters that are too topical; but I do not want to say that he may never do so since a situation might arise which I cannot foresee now and which I would not want to prejudge. Everything which I have said is speculative or dependent upon developments (*tendenziell*—and I consider this to be a better term in this connection). I certainly do not want to assert that a situation could not arise where I would use the language that is at my command to react to something in a manner different from my normal reactions. I just do not know, if the state were to attack me or to attack a person with whom I identify, or groups for which I feel solidarity, how I might act out of outrage.

But when I think calmly and deliberately and ask myself: What is literature, why does literature exist, which values and human potentials should it defend? Then I must always get back to the power of imagination without which there would be no change, no real change, to fantasy without which there likewise would be no change. And thus literature acts as a constant correcting factor in its relation to reality. But I would not even want to lock myself into that definition. I would like to leave the concept of "literature" open—for me too—and I do not want to say categorically that literature is *this* and literature is *that*. I have only said that my notions of literature are thus and so. I would not want to say: Once and forever, (with respect to my position) as I used to erroneously, that literature has these and those responsibilities and nothing more. That would be a mistake. Living literature is, after all, incalculable and creates unfathomable perspectives, unexpected perspectives, surprises in every respect, creates new needs, new linguistic possibilities, new possibilities for the imagination by use of language, and repercussions upon the language resulting from imaginary processes. Both language and literature are far too much alive to permit finalized definitions.

No one who knows your work has the slightest doubt about your being an engaged poet. How would you define the parameters of your engagement?

A description? I have recently noticed that we here (in Germany) make a sharp distinction between the rational and the emotional. Thus a subjective sensitivity of the self [*Selbstempfinden*] plays far too small a part in German literary history, even during the Romantic movement, I think. Likewise the irrational has only surfaced in catastrophic eruptions, such as in the Third Reich. But that the irrational is the obvious reverse of the rational and that it is a daily, physical, individual part of the human personality and of every life, this we obviously did not understand or always tried to suppress. This is perhaps why the irrational can only surface in large doses. It is significant that dadaism did not have a chance to survive here. But when I think of American or English literature, there are far more manifestations of nonsense, neo-Dadaism and neo-Surrealism in evidence than here. Even when it was not in vogue at the time, we have always placed great value upon realism, upon realistic descriptions even in lyric poetry. This plays a significant part in my poetic concepts: I occasionally emphasize excessively, as if I were using a pointer, to the crazy presence of absurdity—no, not of absurdity but of the irrational, of that which is insane. Sometimes I start out with what appears to be a philosophical fragment and then augment it with a crazy matching thought. This has irritated a lot of people, especially in my later poems.

I consider it to be a part of my engagement to bring back both physical and spiritual possibilities that have been pushed aside, and to include them within the framework of my poems. And that everything need not be pointing toward an intellectual precept nor be solely in the form of intellectual dross. It is necessary to cope also with banalities and trivialities, to understand life in its ridiculousness, its comicality, and its tragicomedy. Its lack of alternatives must be seen with the greatest skepticism imaginable, its crazy eruptions with the greatest optimism imaginable. For both life and for poetry I consider this to be a utopian balance between life and poetry. All of these elements should be present, and this describes my engagement, which, to be sure, has now progressed beyond narrow-minded, direct, merely socially critical details, and has become much broader. But I must say again that I do not want to exclude totally the possibility that I may some day again want to talk very precisely about some specific subject.

My most recent poetry volume *Das Auge des Entdeckers* contains examples of my open-ended engagement in such poems as "Das Verschwinden aller im Tod eines einzelnen" ["The Vanishing of All Through the Death of One Individual"]:

> Mache ich mich mit zu großer Hand?
> lebe ich zu sehr aus der überfüllten Luft
> und brauche ich zu viele andere
> und schneide ich das Wort ab dem
>   der es braucht
> und lasse ich es hell und dunkel werden
>   in die eigene Tasche?
> Ich weiß nicht wie weit die Zukunft
>   mir voraus ist
> und wie weit ich mir voraus bin.
> Ich stehe in der Erde und wann immer ich abhebe
>   schlage ich hart wieder auf.
> Hier ist mein Fuß der seine eigene
> Wirklichkeit hat und seine eigene
>   Ewigkeit
> Fuß du wirst mich verlieren
> du wirst bekümmert auftreten
>   und dann stehenbleiben wie ein Schuh.
> Gestern hatten wir eine Tagesschau voll
>   von Toten
> und ein Amerikanisch/Deutsch-Wörterbuch lag
>   aufgeschlagen auf dem Tisch
> und ich lag zugeklappt auf der Couch
> während ein verbrecherischer Kommentar
>   mich segnete
> und meine Verbrecherohren spitzte.
> Sie packten die Toten bei den Fußgelenken
>   und schleiften sie zu einem Sammelplatz
> die Befehle hatten die Körper verlassen
>   und es ging auf dreiundzwanzig Uhr.
> Ich trank Kaffee und war noch derselbe
>   ich war nicht mehr derselbe.
> Ja vorgestern muß ich auf dir gelegen haben
> als jeder andere persönlich starb
>   aus der Welt fiel durch die Welt hindurch

mit nur noch einem Gefühl einem Wort
einem ganz gewöhnlichen Bild
　　das sich auflöste
und mit uns allen verschwand.

Am I too self-seeking?
do I live on too large a scale
and do I use too many others
do I cut someone short
　　who needs to be heard
do I feather only
　　my own nest?
I do not know how far the future
　　is ahead of me
and how far I am ahead of myself.
I am rooted in the earth and whenever I lift off
　　I land again with a thud.
Here is my foot which has
its own reality and its own
　　eternity
foot you will lose me
you will step forth anxiously
　　and then stand still like a shoe.
Yesterday the TV news was full
　　of the dead
and an American–German dictionary lay
　　open on my desk
and I lay slammed shut upon the couch
while a criminal commentary
　　blessed me
and my villainous ears listened attentively.
They grabbed the dead by their ankles
　　and dragged them to a collecting point
their orders had deserted these bodies
　　and it was almost twenty-three hours.
I was drinking coffee and was still the same
　　I was no longer the same.
Yes the day before yesterday I must have lain on you
as each of the others personally died
　　fell from the world and through the world
with only one more feeling one word
one quite ordinary image
　　which dissolved itself
and vanished with us all.

This is, for example, a poem in which such a complex is addressed,
also a complex such as the Vietnam War and the role of the United

States—concomitantly the role of the *Bundesrepublik* [Federal Republic of Germany]—in this war, although I essentially use the complex Vietnam merely as a metaphor for the violence used among differing interest groups, and then comment upon this problem. I imagine here that the individual not only condemns the imperialist who sticks his nose into the business of other countries, but that he also notices that he himself is a part of this imperialism-machine, that his own physical interests are caught up in it. That is what this poem is all about—not just that America is guilty of what happens in Vietnam. The poem merely states:

> Yesterday the TV news was full
> > of the dead
> and an American–German dictionary lay
> > open on my desk
> and I lay slammed shut upon the couch
> while a criminal commentary
> > blessed me
> and my villainous ears listened attentively.

This means that I identify with the situation. I know what is happening and I am a part of it. I do not assume the role of the critic who says from an outside perspective, "You bastards, you are making war and you are destroying life!" When I talk about bastards, I am one of them: I know what my share of the overall responsibility is, that I am a part of this whole business. You see, I want to avoid the kind of simplification where my poems would point to the aggressor and say: The Soviet Union has marched into Prague! Where they could be unequivocally pointed at the Soviet Union and at no one else, I never do that—at least I try to avoid it. Whether I never do it, of that I cannot be sure. I try to avoid oversimplifications. I am of the opinion that a line such as "their orders had deserted these bodies" is far more important. These are the bodies of the dead of whom I speak. For all practical purposes their orders had been like their souls. At the moment of their death these orders left their bodies. Their orders had been what set them into motion.

One does not have to use a poem to show this process in more detail, such as that Germany had a fascist terrorist regime during World War II. That is well known. And if it has to be said again there is no need to use a poem for that purpose. Likewise the evaluation by people here, such as myself, of the American role in Vietnam need no longer be formulated as an accusation in a poem. I must see to it, as a citizen of this federal republic—but I am going too far now. I am getting into politics. This is getting too caustic . . .

I have the crazy, always present vision—this sort of thing usually happens to me when I write poems—where death plays a part and where disappearance plays a part, so that I have to keep telling myself: Whenever the least among us, when anyone dies, a whole world ceases to exist by this death. This is the reason for the title: "The Vanishing of All Through the Death of One Individual." A whole cosmos is extinguished through the death of one person. The world as an exterior cosmos, as well as the interior cosmos of his body. It is a total extinction. And this happens with every single death. Such are the identification models that occur over and over again in my poems.

I would like to cite a few lines from another poem which we will not discuss in detail:

> auf dem Rücken summender Webstühle
> erreichen wir den   großen Widerspruch:
> das Erscheinen eines jeden in der Menge . . . .

> on the backs of humming weaver's looms
> we arrive at the   great contradiction:
> the appearance of each individual in the multitude . . . .

This is essentially an insane image. There is a line by Ezra Pound: "The apparition of these faces in the crowd; / Petals on a wet, black bough."[1] What I wrote is a variation on this theme. "The appearance of each individual" is a utopian image. It simply is not realistically possible for each individual to stand out in a multitude. This implies that there are only "larger individualities" which can be distinguished in a multitude. But that each single person in a multitude is in clear focus, is a mathematical improbability. Thus this is a utopian picture, an orientation buoy, which will perhaps never be reached and can never be reached, and which is nothing but a metaphor for something else, for the significance of each individual human being, perhaps ultimately a kind of humanism in this connection, or a new alienated image of humanism.

Another branch of this engagement—to get back to what we talked about earlier, this irrationality, this dada and nonsense ele-

[1] Ezra Pound, *Collected Shorter Poems* (London: Faber and Faber, 1968). p. 119.

ment, is perhaps best expressed in "Naturgedicht" ["Nature Poem"]:

Welcher Schmerz zu fließen
welche Kälte mit dem Feind allein zu sein
welch eine Aufgabe Stickstoff in die Wälder zu blasen!
    Das stille Wirken des Blattgrüns im grünen Salat
    das lärmende Wirken des grünen Salats in uns.
Ist der Löwenzahn aus unserem Leben verschwunden
    der Huflattich die Grasharfe?
Was verspricht das angelegte Ohr des Pferdes
was bedeuten die Schmerzen in den Armen der Putzfrau
    deren Welt seit zwanzig Jahren im Eimer liegt?
Warum ist die Nelke eine so dumme Blume
    so zackig gehäkelt
und warum fang ich an zu tropfen wenn ich Tulpen sehe?
Was sagt mir die Schwalbe im Tiefflug?
Wer beißt wenn der Hund des Nachbarn knurrt
    er oder ich oder der Nachbar?
Was bedeutet es wenn ich von einem Unbekannten
    einen Tip bekomme und eilig das Haus verlasse?
Wenn die Brauen meines Vaters über Nacht zusammenwachsen
und die Gesichtsnarbe des Abonnentenwerbers rot wird
wenn der Taxifahrer so lange in den Spiegel schaut
    bis der Fahrgast verdächtig ist
und der Dachdecker dem Lehrling einen Tritt geben will
    doch zu spät bemerkt daß er ins Leere tritt
wenn die Teenager im Teenagerclub die Augen verdrehen
    nach der fünften Cola
wenn der Starfighter-Pilot in der Flugpause
    einen langen Roman anfängt
wenn der Großaktionär in der Jägersuppe
    einen Pferdefuß findet
und der Kassierer der Commerzbank
    mit dem Haushaltsgeld seiner Frau verschwindet
    nachdem er ›Viva Zapata‹ gesehen hat?
Die Ruhe vor dem Sturm
der Dorn im Auge
der Balken im Zimmermann
die heiße Liebe mit Siebzehn
die Schwurhand des Vermögensverwalters
Ebbe und Flut
Mini und Maxi
und der Beamte auf dem Sozialamt
der mit Handtuch und Seife das Büro verläßt
    wenn dreißig Leute warten?
Das Montagsauto der umgekippte See
die ungewöhnliche Art in der sich in der Hand

des Arbeitnehmers Vermögen bildet
die da oben
die da unten
die Talsohle
die Gratwanderung?

Wenn ich dich liebe schneit es auf der Erde
und wenn du mich mit meinem besten Freund verläßt
    dann ist es Frühling
und wenn du völlig mittellos zurückkehrst
    ist es Herbst.
Wenn mir keiner etwas umsonst gibt
    habe ich dann Geld?
Und welchen Sinn hat es als Toter ein Buch über Archäologie
    unterm Kopfkissen zu haben?
Wenn es wahr ist daß Kriege sein müssen
    ist es dann noch wichtig daran teilzunehmen?
Ist es realistisch wenn Mann und Frau
    nach der Hochzeit beschließen zusammenzuleben?
Wenn sie ihm ein Jahr später ihre Aussteuer
an den Kopf wirft und er ihr
    seinen Wortschatz
und wenn der Fensterputzer oben am IBM–Hochhaus
in den Bann der Lochkarten gerät
aber doch seinem Selbsterhaltungstrieb folgt
    und im letzten Augenblick abspringt?
Was bedeutet es daß ich Gedichte mache
    und daß du lauter Geschichten machst?

How painful it is to flow like everything
how cold it is to be alone with the enemy
what a task to blow nitrogen into the woods!
    The silent effect of chlorophyl in the lettuce
    the noisy effect of lettuce within us.
Has the dandelion disappeared from our lives
    the coltsfoot the grassharp?
What does it augur when a horse lays his ears back
what is the meaning of the pains in the arms of the charwoman
    whose world lay for twenty years in a pail?
Why is the carnation such a stupid flower
    so jaggedly barbed
and why do I begin to cry when I see tulips?
What does a slow-flying swallow tell me?
Who bites when the neighbor's dog growls
    he or I or the neighbor?
What does it mean when I receive a tip
    from a stranger and hurriedly leave home?

223

When my father's brows grow together overnight
and the scar in the face of the subscription salesman turns red
when the taxi driver looks into the rearview mirror
    until the passenger becomes suspicious
and the roofer wants to kick his apprentice in the pants
    but notices too late that he is stepping into space
when teenagers in a teenager club roll their eyes
    after the fifth coke
when a Starfighter pilot starts reading a long novel
    between missions
when the majority stockholder finds a horse's foot
    in the game soup
and the cashier of the commercial bank
    disappears with his wife's household money
    after he has seen "Viva Zapata"?
The lull before the storm
the thorn in the eye
the beam in the carpenter
the passionate love at age seventeen
the hand of the executor raised to swear
ebb tide and flood tide
mini and maxi
and the welfare worker
who leaves the office to wash up
    while thirty people are waiting in line?
The Monday-car the overturned lake
the peculiar manner in which
    an employee acquires riches
those up there
those down there
the valley floor
the hike along a precipice?

When I love you snow falls upon the earth
and when you leave me with my best friend
    then it is spring
and when you return destitute
    it is fall.
If no one gives me something for nothing
    do I then have money?
Why should a corpse have a book about archaeology
    beneath his pillow?
If it is true that there have to be wars
    does it remain important to participate?
Is it realistic when a husband and wife
    decide to live together after their marriage?
If she one year later throws her trousseau
at his head and he his

224

> vocabulary at hers
> and if a window washer high up on the IBM skyscraper
> becomes mesmerized by the punchcards
> but follows his survival instinct
>> and jumps off at the last moment?
> What does it mean that I write poems
>> and you constantly fuss?

This probably has no direct connection with political and social criticism. It contains dadaistic ricochets. It is also a phase of my engagement. I consider it very important. I believe Aristotle said that the human drives which one chases out of the window, which one chases out of the door, come in again through the window. One cannot get rid of them; one must strive to be able to cope with them, to work at them. But they cannot be totally exorcised. They are basic human drives, an inseparable part of the human species, but they must be sublimated. This may be a little profound as an aid to interpretation. It might be better if I say that in this poem I want to show the reader how dangerous any one single thing, even a word, is. It ticks like a time bomb, and it is only harmless and useable for a limited period of time. Permit me to say programmatically with deliberate exaggeration what I expect from poems: unfathomability, a wild and ruthless mobility, dangerous sharpness, a beauty which is not pleasurable but painful, which does not lull to sleep but needles to awareness. Poems are only interesting if they do not contain the slightest agreement.

Photograph by Jörg Burkhard

Jürgen Theobaldy
Born 1944 in Strasbourg, France

Jürgen Theobaldy grew up in Mannheim, was an apprentice commercial clerk (kaufmännische Lehre), *and, after holding several jobs, began his studies of literature and political science at the universities of Heidelberg and Cologne. Since 1974 he has been a student at the Free University of Berlin. He has been active in the student movement.*

His first poetry volume (1973) attracted attention in literary circles. Since then he has published two additional volumes of poetry (one in 1976) and translations from the English language. He was included in this book at the recommendation of several leading German literary personalities who consider him to be one of the brightest young German poets.

Jürgen Theobaldy was interviewed on May 3, 1975, in the room he rents in West Berlin. The entire interview was taped and he made minor corrections on the German original transcription.

When reading your two volumes of poetry, published in 1973 and 1974, it is obvious that your engagement transcends the borders of the Federal Repub-

*lic of Germany. You are a relatively young poet and it would thus be
especially interesting to hear the reasons for this worldwide engagement.*

I believe there is one primary reason, the student movement, the
extraparliamentary opposition in which I participated, in which I
was actively involved. From its very beginning this student movement was international in scope. From its very beginning the impetus resulting from international solidarity in the student movement was very important for both agitation and enlightenment, so
that one can almost assert that the student movement owes its
existence to the pursuit of problems of international politics. Back
then, in 1966 and 1967, it was above all the Vietnam War and, in
conjunction, the discovery—and with respect to West Germany this
was a discovery indeed—of that which theorists call imperialism:
the discovery that there is such a thing as exploitation of Third
World countries; and together with that, the discovery that this can
be opposed effectively. Among students, and therefore also in my
case, there was a great need to acquire political and economic facts
and theories, making up for past neglect of these areas. From that
moment on there developed a great interest in the struggles in the
Third World, not only in Vietnam but also, to give you a particularly
cogent example, in South America. This was the time when people
like "Che" Guevara first became known to students.

The poems which I wrote before that period were quite traditional. Then, however, I became primarily interested in political
problems, especially the struggle in the Third World, and this especially because it seemed at first as though it would be very difficult to
get a handle on the problem of enlightening anyone in the Federal
Republic regarding the capitalist system. No one in the Federal
Republic seemed capable of grasping concretely or intellectually
what exploitation means. It was simpler to demonstrate the nature
of oppression by means of the wars of liberation and the situation in
the Third World. Starting with the time when I wrote the poems in
these two volumes, I was no longer just preoccupied with my
personal and private concerns, but also with the events in the
countries of the Third World. This is the reason why I wrote several
poems that did not concern themselves with problems in the Federal
Republic, but with those of the countries of the Third World.

*An example of this engagement—and you have already mentioned his
name—would be your poem: "Auf ein Foto des toten ⟩Che⟨ Guevara" ("To a*

*Photo of the Dead 'Che' Guevara"). This poem is not difficult to under-
stand, but I would still appreciate your comments.*

I always write poems in the hope that they are easy to understand. I
am convinced that conditions around us are so complicated that
even a clearly conceived poem will remain difficult enough. Perhaps
in contrast to the previous generation of lyric poets I try to write
communicative poems, poems that are not intended to be
monologues but that seek to establish direct communication with
the reader.

"Auf ein Foto des toten ⟩Che⟨ Guevara" is one of my earliest
poems:

> Sieben Männer stehen um den Toten rum
> wie komponiert;
> vertikal die Oberkörper, ein Gewehr:
> Linien, die durchbrochen werden
> vom rechten Arm des Offiziers, den Zeigefinger
> auf die Brust von ⟩Che⟨ gedrückt,
> auf die Stelle, wo die Kugel einschlug,
> die ihn mordete.
> Der Einschuß ist verdeckt.
> Ein andrer Offizier hält seine Hand
> im Haar von ⟩Che⟨.
> (Touristen knipst man so, aufgestellt
> um einen Leichnam,
> die Trophäe, erjagt auf der Safari
> für das Fotoalbum, die freie Stelle über dem Kamin.)
> Der Tote liegt wie unverletzt;
> die Hose, um den Leib gekrempelt,
> verdeckt sechs andere Wunden.
> Die Augen offen,
> mitten unter Offizieren und Agenten,
> liegt ⟩Che⟨ unverletzt.
>
>
> Seven men stand around the corpse
> as though they were posing;
> vertical their torsos, a rifle:
> lines which are broken
> by the right arm of the officer, his index finger
> pressed upon the breast of "Che"
> upon the place where the bullet struck
> which murdered him.
> The point of entrance is covered.
> Another officer has placed his hand

in "Che's" hair.
(Tourists are snapped like this, posing
around a body,
the trophy, hunted down on a safari
for the scrapbook, the empty spot over the fireplace.)
The corpse lies there as though unhurt,
his trousers, twisted around his abdomen,
hide six other wounds.
His eyes open,
amidst officers and agents,
"Che" lies there as though unhurt.

I assume that I wrote this poem in 1968—I am not sure about this anymore—while, as the title implies, looking at a photograph of the dead "Che" Guevara, a photo which had appeared in many newspapers and which has been reprinted several times since. The first thing that struck me was that "Che" Guevara did not appear at all dead, which I tried to express in the lines:

His eyes open,
amidst officers and agents,
"Che" lies there as though unhurt.

This seemed to be symptomatic for the status of the liberation movements: they will not founder just because an important leader is killed in this struggle. I suppose I wanted to exhibit in this poem that this picture, even though it depicted a dead liberation fighter, contained a perspective of the future as far as I was concerned. And this is why I consider the poem itself to be optimistic. Perhaps it contains something of the optimism which characterized the beginnings of the student movement.

Your poem "Bilder aus Amerika" ("American Images"), which is printed here for the first time, discusses your attitude toward a country which you have never seen but which has concerned you since your youth.

Weil mich, kaum geboren
in den letzten Wochen des Weltkriegs,
beinah ein Soldat mitgenommen hätte,
hinüber nach Amerika, träumte ich
oft davon, in Amerika aufzuwachen
mit Jeans und Tennisschuhen,
den Baseballschläger unter dem Arm.
Ich träumte vom frischen Rasen

229

vor der High-School, von rosa Zahnpasta
und Ananas aus der Dose. Amerikanisch
hätte ich sicher sehr breit gesprochen,
und später wäre ich, so träumte mir,
im Cadillac vors Bürohochhaus gefahren.
Aber später war ich immer noch
hier in Mannheim und fuhr jeden Morgen
auf einem Fahrrad ohne Gangschaltung
in den Hafen zur Exportabteilung.
Und noch später sah ich junge
Amerikaner, so alt wie ich,
abgeführt werden, weil sie ihre
Einberufungsbefehle verbrannt hatten.
Ich sah die qualmenden Häuser
in den Gettos der Schwarzen, und ich sah
die Nationalgarde im Kampfanzug
gegen barfüßige Studenten, sah die
Schlagstöcke der Polizisten, die lang
wie Baseballschläger sind.
Jetzt träume ich kaum noch
von Amerika, nicht einmal Schlechtes.
Aber ich frage mich oft, wie das Land
sein mag, von dem sich die Bilder
so verändert haben, so schnell
und so gründlich.

Because I, barely born
in the last weeks of World War Two,
was almost taken along by a soldier
over there to America, I dreamed
often about growing up in America
with jeans and tennis shoes,
a baseball bat under my arm.
I dreamed of a green lawn
in front of the high school, of pink toothpaste
and pineapple out of a can. I surely would have
spoken with a broad American accent,
and later on I would, so I dreamed,
drive to my office in a Cadillac.
But, later, I still remained
here in Mannheim and rode each morning
on a simple bike without gears
to the export department in the port.
And still later I saw
young Americans, as old as I,
arrested because they had
burned their draft cards.

I saw the smoking houses
in the ghettos of the blacks, and I saw
the National Guard in battle dress
encounter barefoot students, saw the
riot clubs of policemen, clubs
as long as baseball bats.
Now I hardly ever dream
about America, not even bad dreams.
But I often ask myself, how this country
might really be, this country whose
image has changed so quickly
and so thoroughly.

I believe that my image of America is shared by my generation. It was shaped by what I was taught and by the mass media, the press and television. This is why I consider this poem to be representative of the attitude of many members of my generation. I do not write from the perspective of an outsider, a poet, who writes in splendid isolation or disdaining the masses, which was the attitude that still prevailed rather widely before World War II. On the contrary, I write because I assume that others share my problems—from this conviction I derive the courage to write.

My poem contains perhaps certain subtle shades of difference which separate it from the image of America held by others of my generation because it is in part autobiographical. My mother has often told me that shortly after my birth an American soldier, probably an officer, wanted to take me with him, but that she, as she put it, tore me in the last moment from his arms. Because of this I often thought as a child how it might have been if I had grown up in America, because America was *the* country for us children during the early fifties. Newspapers and magazines called it time and again the "country of unlimited possibilities." I remember very clearly how it was when American soldiers came to the county fair in Mannheim and walked from booth to booth in search of a good time. They were always followed by a queue of German children who literally were begging for money and who thought all Americans to be rich, a people with more money and more freedom than our parents. I have never forgotten this image of America. It contributed to my notions of what America was all about.

This image of America was then shaken by the Vietnam War. In the beginning the newspapers reported very little about this war and about the American involvement in Vietnam. It took the efforts of leftist university students to effect a change in the image which other students had of both this war and of American society. From that point on, the left wing of the student body, which had grown greatly in number, especially in 1968 and 1969, took a great interest in changes that were occurring in America, including developments in American internal politics. After all, the greatest number of the West German newspapers continued to paint a positive picture of the American involvement in Vietnam and called it a struggle for freedom and democracy, thus echoing the official American line. This is why it was so difficult even at the universities to penetrate this interpretation of the war which was being disseminated by the mass media. But after a breakthrough in this regard had been achieved, at least in part, students, and consequently also my friends and acquaintances, became more and more interested in internal American politics. We started to look hard for information, and information was made available to us by dissidents in the United States. As a result of these data the image of America was newly formed, decisively changed, not only for my generation of students but also in the eyes of German youth in general. America was and is no longer the country offering unlimited possibilities. It is for us a country of violence, characterized by oppression, a land which without any pangs of conscience unleashes the juggernaut of war in order to prevent the peoples of the Third World from achieving their political and, above all, their economic independence. This, roughly, is what was on my mind when I wrote "American Images" in 1974.

The German student movement became well known throughout the world. And if a young poet from this era achieves recognition one must obviously ask: What did this movement mean to you personally, to your development as a human being and as a poet?

The student movement was, by the way, never limited to just the universities, but it also included other segments of the population, at least in West Germany, such as apprentices and high school students. This was especially during the struggle against the *Notstandsgesetze* (emergency laws, passed in 1968 by the German parliament, which would suspend parliament and replace it by a governmental commission during times of war and imprecisely defined national catastrophes). Here the student movement did more than just resist. It tried to combat the misinformation that was

232

being spread by the established press. The student movement tried to anticipate future needs, such as that for solidarity. Within the student movement there no longer existed the individual detachment that had previously been prevalent at the universities. The total isolation and the individual student's selfish focus upon examinations were abolished. All those who participated in the student movement discovered for themselves what solidarity can mean, how much it can intensify their lives.

This experience was tremendously important for me. Only in poetry, in poems of the American Beat Generation and of Pablo Neruda, for example, have I had similar experiences. My personal development during those years was probably influenced most significantly by two experiences: that poetry must not only be read divorced from all social circumstances and conditions, but that it also can contain anticipatory facets similar to those evident in the student movement. If I understand myself correctly, this is why, aside from poetry and perhaps at times even more strongly than poetry, the student movement awakened in me the hope that there is for the individual in this West German industrialized nation the possibility for living under conditions other than the mere struggle for economic survival.

You mentioned anticipatory elements in the student movement and that poetry is—or can be—anticipatory. From this I conclude that you would agree with Wolfgang Weyrauch's dictum, enunciated in 1950, twenty-five years ago, that writers are physicians and what they write is the handwriting on the wall.

I do not know whether writers are physicians. They may be physicians if we take into account that even bourgeois medicine now recognizes that illnesses can also be induced by social conditions. For this reason, there might be certain therapeutic effectiveness in the writing and reading of poetry. This is probably true in the case of the poet, though it surely is not the only reason why he writes, and the same may well be true of the reader.

"What they write is the handwriting on the wall!" There have always been attempts by writers to penetrate their isolation and to reach people who, because of their social environment, have never had the opportunity of developing a relationship with books, i.e., to use books as something of practical value. On the other hand, the pronouncement regarding the "handwriting on the wall" seems a bit euphoric. It may develop one day that poets may write their poems on walls without the police coming by, having been sent by the Department of Public Order, to remove these writings. But for now we still produce at our desks, in loneliness (if you please), and we have virtually no influence on the dissemination of that which we write, and this naturally has its damaging effects upon poems. When we write our poems on walls they will probably look different. They will be written in capital letters, poems which everyone can read.

This leads to a very interesting problem which lyric poetry has always had: wide dissemination. Of all genres poetry is probably the one with the smallest, formerly perhaps even the most exclusive reading public. How can the engaged poet hope to exert his influence through this most expressive medium which has sometimes been scorned as being too exclusive?

Exclusiveness is not necessarily innate in the poem, but rather imposed upon it by extraliterary influences, such as I said earlier, social processes, a social selection which has as its effect that only a small segment of a given age group is exposed to poetry. I do not know whether this has always been the case. At least in West Germany there used to be a larger reading public for poetry. But even if it always was like this, this does not mean that it has to remain so. There are examples of poetry readings in the Soviet Union which took place before crowds numbering into the thousands. I also know from Pablo Neruda's biography that he often read his poems in football stadiums. Thus it is not that poetry per se is only accessible to small numbers—it depends upon the social conditions in which poetry is disseminated. And it undoubtedly also depends on the poets themselves, whether they make a virtue of a necessity and consider themselves and their work to be exclusive, or whether they try to ensure that what they write is within the grasp of everyone, though it might not have been expressed in that form by everyone, as I attempt to write.

I remember a story that was told about Paul Celan. One day he was asked why he writes such difficult poems, poems which the baker at the corner could not understand. If I remember correctly, Celan is supposed to have answered that this question constituted an underestimation of the baker at the corner, for why should this baker at the corner have a less acute consciousness than any other person interested in literature? The problem now is at the very least that the baker at the corner cannot use language to master his realm of experiences. But that does not imply that he is by nature unable to understand poetry. It merely means that social conditions are such that they do not permit the baker at the corner to understand certain poems even though they are, strictly speaking, also his poems.

If I understand you correctly this means that you feel that the times for symbolic or symbolist poetry are over, that the modern poet should not use mystifying ciphers but, as Martin Luther once put it so beautifully, should look into the mouth of the common man if he wants to write a poem which can exert some influence.

I can only speak for myself. I would not want to prescribe to another poet how he has to write, or that he should forget about his symbolism and his metaphors. For me enciphered poetry is an impossibility, but I could well imagine a society where the baker at the corner will be able to understand these metaphors to the same degree to which he is now prevented from doing so.

How then can the engaged writer—in our case the engaged poet, since we are concerned with lyric poetry—avoid writing poems which, because they have been inspired by current events, appear so tendentious that they lose their impact very quickly, soon are no longer understandable and therefore no longer worth reading?

I would like to bring up a fundamental point regarding the concept of engagement, as I understand it. In my opinion, all poets who do not merely attempt to reform literature for its own sake are engaged. There is no poem, no good poem which does not contain a part of the poet. I believe that this is even true of concrete poetry. If one reads, for example, the works of various authors who consider themselves to be concrete poets one quickly recognizes how many subjective elements are contained in even these poems. I believe that a poet's engagement consists of the vitality and the determination with which he involves himself with language or delivers himself to the forces of language. Only in this manner can he accomplish extra literary goals. There are no taboos. I for one do not believe that there are any words which one should not use in poetry because they are too political in character, because they release associations which are too political, perhaps even too hackneyed. It is then the task of the poet to write his poem in such a manner that these worn-out associations are charged with new meanings.

235

There is an early essay by Peter Handke—I do not know whether it represents his current views, I could imagine that it does not—where he differentiates between an engaged writer and an engaged human being. I do not believe that this differentiation is tenable at all. As I understand it, this is as officious a differentiation as an attempt to distinguish between a human being at work and a human being after work. The latter is always the same person, and the poet is likewise the same person. The engaged poet and the engaged person are one and the same.

For me, this means that I write about the problems which touch me. Diverse problems do touch me, such as relationships with other individuals, political news and political events. I do not for the life of me see why I should in any way separate these and reject one of them as political and thus artistically inferior, while accepting the other as unpolitical and thus artistically valuable. There are no such distinctions as far as I am concerned. I am the same individual when I participate in a demonstration, when I drink a cup of coffee after that demonstration, and when I meet a girlfriend in the evening. If, however, the events at the demonstration have effected a change in me then I am also a changed person when I meet my friend in the evening. This is why I consider this distinction between engaged writers and those who are not engaged invalid. I believe that this distinction is ideological in character and that, looking at it historically, it was surely devised to find an excuse to banish those lyric poets who are politically engaged in the narrow sense of that term from the sphere of the reading public interested in poetry, and to deprive them in this manner of a part of their effectiveness.

On the other hand, I do subscribe to a differentiation between engagement and tendentiousness. I would describe poetry that aims at concrete and direct effects, that from its inception wants to fulfill only one specific function as tendentious. To cite an example: the recision of paragraph 218 in West Germany which is currently under discussion. This paragraph deals with the legality of interruption of pregnancies. I would call a poem that demands the legalizing of pregnancy interruptions "tendentious," because it would be a poem written for only one specific purpose. And this kind of poetry—and the same is also true of plays: there were especially in the nineteenth century many plays that one would have to label as tendentious—naturally loses its impact once the demanded changes have been effected. After that it has merely documentary value.

Engaged literature, as I understand it, fulfills several functions. I do not consider myself qualified to describe all of these functions, but I do believe that the political function is only one of them. This function will obviously play a part if the poem is well written.

In recent years in the Federal Republic the usefulness of literature and especially of lyric poetry has been discussed time and again. Brecht formulated the concept of "the poem as a utilitarian object" [Gebrauchsgegenstand], and this was used as a criterion for the evaluation of poetry. In other words, the question whether a poem is useful or beneficial for the reader. While I consider this an important question from which one can and should approach a poem, it does not answer the question of what the utility of a poem consists. I do indeed believe that poetry serves a purpose. And I would prove this pragmatically by the fact that poetry is still being read, though perhaps by a rather limited group of people. But poems are being read and I would simply say: as long as they are being read they fulfill functions, for they would not be read by anyone if this were not the case. Early in the seventies, even prior to that during the extraparliamentary opposition and the student movement, the slogan of the "new sensitiveness" was coined, which maintained that poetry (and literature in general) enables the reader, as well as the one who writes it, to gain a more sensitive and thus a more aware relationship to that which happens around him, and through him. For this reason, I believe that poetry (and literature in general) does help its audience to lead a more aware life. This too is a political process. He who lives more aware is less susceptible to manipulation by the mass media and by politicians than someone who does not do this. Just as this may sound vague I also have to describe the functions of literature vaguely. They lead to greater sensitivity on the part of the reader and the writer, and this is not necessarily in the interest of the ruling classes. Naturally this sensitization is dependent on the content that is being conveyed. It goes without saying that there is also sensitization toward nothingness, sensitization as a luxury, as a matter of prestige; it is thus by no means self-evident that sensitization will create a new political awareness in the right direction. There is among Germans the concept of a "bel esprit" [Schöngeist]. This describes someone who enjoys an intimate relationship with literature but is nevertheless unable to translate this relationship into anything practical, to make it a force in his life. I would like to write poems that are not useable to these "bel esprits."

237

I would like to write poems which, when they are completed, have not only changed me but will also change those who read them, poems which keep alive the presentiment of a better life, which communicate that there is the possibility of a life removed from competition, lies, suppression, and deception. This life to come is, of course, not completely divorced from what happens today— which means that the poems I write today discuss the injuries which mankind now endures. This is the reason for the title of my second book, *Blaue Flecken* [*Black and Blue*]. My poems are not supposed to depict sterile utopic counterimages, but they are poems in which the possibility of a better life rises resplendently in the midst of the traumata of the life, the damaged life, which we now live.

I believe that the poem "Ein Bier, bitte" ["A Beer, Please"] is a suitable example for this present condition.

> Ich könnte mich daran gewöhnen, wie ein gepflegter
> Mensch zu sein. Hier geht ein lautloser Tag zuende
> den ganzen Tag stand das Telefon still, und lautlos platzt
> der Wäschekorb unter dem Waschbecken.
> Auf dem Bildschirm platzt ein Haus vor dem erstaunten
> Gesicht des Sprechers. Oh the fucking news!
> sagte Mehdi gestern abend und betrank sich.
>
> Vor allem will ich Liebe. Ich will nicht
> auf die Marke meiner Unterhosen achten, meiner Strümpfe
> die ich zu Weihnachten geschenkt kriege, zum Geburtstag
> zu Ostern und zum Sterbetag. Als Kind habe ich mir
> eine Eisenbahn gewünscht und ein Oberhemd bekommen
> was Praktisches in Cellophan, mit tausend Nadeln drin.
> Dieses Gedicht ist praktisch nichts. Bedenk doch:
> Wie soll untergehen, was wir nicht stürzen, außer der Seife
> im Badewasser. Ich mache wieder Witze, obwohl mir
> nicht danach ist. Muß ich wirklich
> die Haare waschen, bevor du kommst? Haare waschen
> ist eine schreckliche Erinnerung . . .
>
> Und dann liebe ich alle Verwandten, besonders meine Frau
> die nicht mit mir verwandt ist. Wie bitte? Ich habe nichts gesagt.
> Die Tagesschau ist zuende, die Schau des Tages, the fucking
> news. Heute gab es gute Nachrichten. Das Amerika-Haus
> wurde besetzt, ich sag nicht wo. Der Film beginnt
> und meine Haare sind noch nicht gewaschen!
> Du bist nicht meine Frau. Ich liebe dich. Beschütze mich
> denn ich rauche zuviel! Man wird nervös in dieser Wohnung
> nach 1933 und nach 1945. Hörst du überhaupt zu?

THEOBALDY

Plötzlich bin ich in einer Kneipe mit viel Trara
am Tresen. Dieses Gedicht steckt voller Möglichkeiten
wie unser Leben. Natürlich vergeht kein Tag
ohne Alkohol. Oh Alkohol, ich fühl mich wohl.
Mehdi sitzt da, endgültig betrunken. Du bist auch da, schon
eine Weile, und du hast Gründe, nicht mit mir zu reden.
Laute Nacht, die Musik ist laut. Ich bestelle einen Klaren
für meinen klaren Kopf. Ein Bier, bitte. Was immer
du von mir hältst, es ist mir wichtig zu sagen: auch du
hast dieses Gedicht geschrieben. Es war keine Kunst; es war
mit dem Rücken zum Fenster.

I could get used to being a well-groomed
person. A silent day ends now
all day long the phone was quiet, and silently
the laundry basket explodes under the washbasin.
On the TV screen a house explodes before the astonished
eyes of the announcer. "Oh the fucking news!"
said Mehdi last night and got drunk.

Above all I want love. I do not want
to pay attention to the label of my shorts, of the socks
I receive for Christmas, for my birthday
for Easter, or my funeral. As a child I
wished for a train and got a shirt
something practical in cellophane, with a thousand pins in it.
This poem is practically nothing. Consider:
How will anything perish if we don't destroy it, except for the soap
in the bath water. I am joking again, even though
I am not in the mood. Must I really
wash my hair before you come? Washing my hair
awakens terrible memories . . .

And then I love all my relatives, especially my wife
who is not related to me. How is that? I said nothing.
The daily news is over, the news of the day, the fucking
news. Today there was good news. The America House
was occupied, I won't tell you where. The film is beginning
and I still have not washed my hair!
You are not my wife. I love you. Protect me
for I am smoking too much! One gets nervous in this apartment
after 1933 and after 1945. Are you listening at all?

Suddenly I am in a dive with much hoopla
at the bar. This poem is full of possibilities
like our lives. Naturally not a day passes
without alcohol. Oh alcohol, you make me whole.

Mehdi is sitting there, totally drunk. You have also been there
a while, and you have reasons not to talk to me.
A loud evening, the music is loud. I order a clear whiskey
to clear my head. A beer, please. Whatever
you think of me, it is important that I tell you: you too
wrote this poem. It wasn't a feat; I wrote it
with my back to the window.

appendix

Although it will be the chief purpose of my interview with you to discuss your poetry and your attitude regarding the problems inherent in social and political engagement, I would like to submit the following possible discussion topics to you. If you should wish to take a position regarding some of these topics, it would be helpful because it would provide a certain amount of common material and thus help to unify the interviews in my book. Besides, two poets asked that I send them some questions prior to the actual interviews.

1. How do you react to the following statements?

a. "Real literature . . . by means of criticism wants to conjure up that utopian state of affairs which sophisticated language can proclaim."

b. "The more West German society became stabilized, the more urgently it demanded social criticism in literature; the less successful the *engagement* on the part of writers became, the louder became the clamor for it. This mechanism secured for literature an undisputed place in society, but it also led to self-deceptions which appear grotesque today."

c. "Literature . . . intends to act and to agitate, but all it really does is react."

d. "It is particularly disturbing that the future as a topos seems to have been leased by the authors of the GDR, while the lyric poets of the West evidently do not recognize hope as a principle and, at best contribute dire predictions and prophecies of doom when they ought to be discussing that which should happen tomorrow."

e. "The poet as a leader tries to approach an ideal step by step and attempts to bring this ideal to reality through his own person. The *engaged* poet disrupts the concentration upon himself, looks toward his fellow man and investigates the prerequisites and tools for action. . . ."

f. "Because I discovered that I could change myself by means of literature, that I could live more consciously only with the aid of literature, I am convinced that I can change others by my literature."

g. "The words *Hitler, Auschwitz, Lübke, Berlin, Johnson, napalm bombs* have become too charged with meanings, too political, and I can thus no longer use them as words unconstrainedly."

h. "There is no such thing as an *engaged* literature. The concept is a contradiction in terms. There are *engaged* people, but no engaged writers. The concept *engagement* is political. It can at best be used with respect to political 'writers' who are not writers in the sense in which we employ the term, but who are politicians who write what they want to *say*."

i. "Poems exist for the purpose of being used as model situations."

j. "It seems difficult for West German lyric poets to become involved at all in the

241

social process. Their verses follow prescribed courses, schools and doctrines. The real voice of the poet is sorely lacking."

k. "Poets are physicians and what they write is the handwriting on the wall."

2. Can we afford the luxury of creating new beautiful works of literature unless we first call the attention of mankind to the dangers extant in our present-day society?

3. Must "tendentious" be synonymous with "inferior"?

4. Culture has often been described as the privilege of the elite. Lyric poets are primarily read by educated people, a relatively small and exclusive reading public. Under those conditions, how can they exert as broad an influence as possible? (Perhaps because their exclusive reading public occupies key positions and is consequently able to manipulate the masses?)

5. What do you consider to be the greatest problem of literature, especially poetry, with respect to its effectiveness as a means of mass communication?

6. Do you agree with the thesis that literature has both an aesthetic and a social function?

7. Can literature, and especially poetry, influence the formation of opinions regarding new problems, where opinions and positions have not yet crystallized? Should it?

8. Are the electronic information systems, which will soon be available to each member of "civilized" society going to replace literature as an important factor in the use of leisure time by educated people?

9. When a poet has acquired a reputation, probably initially in the educated upper classes of society, and if he is also conscious of his social obligations, should he then consciously write for the masses in order to be able to fulfill his social function as widely as possible?

10. P. O. Chotjewitz comments on the currently popular utilitarianism as follows: "Two of the worst inheritances from bourgeois society . . . are the constraint to have to justify each thought and each action, and really not to be permitted to do anything that isn't of some utilitarian value."

11. Does the poet have a public responsibility? His work is designed to be disseminated. What he writes reaches thousands of readers. If he expresses an opinion on television, he may reach millions. If he takes advantage of his rights as a citizen in this manner, the publicity which he had previously gained as a poet will act as a multiplier of his public effectiveness. Does not the fact that his profession gives him access to a larger audience impose a special public responsibility upon him?

12. Can literature, especially poetry, change reality?

selected bibliography

Adorno, Theodor W. "Engagement." In *Noten zur Literature III*. Frankfurt a.M.: Suhrkamp, 1965.
———. "Rede über Lyrik und Gesellschaft." In *Noten zur Literatur I*. Frankfurt a. M.: Suhrkamp, 1963.
Arnold, Heinz Ludwig, ed. *Text und Kritik. Zeitschrift für Literatur*. 9/9a. *Politische Lyrik*. Munich: Richard Boorberg, 1973.
Bender, Hans. *Aufzeichnungen einiger Tage*. Berlin: Literarisches Colloquium, 1971.
———, ed. *Deutsche Lyrik seit 1945. Widerspiel*. Munich: Carl Hanser, 1962.
———. *Die halbe Sonne*. Baden-Baden: Hans Frevert, 1968.
———. "Die Weisheit der unausgesprochenen Worte," *Merkur* 15 (1961), 178–90.
———, ed. *Junge Lyrik 1957. Eine Auslese*. Munich: Carl Hanser, 1958.
———, ed. *Mein Gedicht ist mein Messer. Lyriker zu ihren Gedichten*. Heidelberg: Wolfgang Rothe, 1955.
———. "Über politische Gedichte." In *Jahresring 68/69. Beiträge zur deutschen Literatur und Kunst der Gegenwart*. Stuttgart: Deutsche Verlags-Anstalt, 1968.
———. *Worte, Bilder, Menschen. Geschichten, Roman, Berichte, Aufsätze*. Munich: Carl Hanser, 1969.
Bienek, Horst. "Politische Augenblicke." *Frankfurter Allgemeine Zeitung* 13 (July 1963), 51.
Born, Nicolas. *Das Auge des Entdeckers. Gedichte*. dnb 21. Hamburg: Rowohlt, 1972.
———. *Marktlage. Gedichte*. Cologne and Berlin: Kiepenheuer and Witsch, 1967.
———, F. C. Delius and Volker von Törne. *Rezepte für Friedenszeiten. Gedichte*. Berlin and Weimar: Aufbau, 1973.
Braun, Karlheinz, ed. *Materialien zu Peter Weiss' "Marat/Sade."* Frankfurt a.M.: Suhrkamp, 1967.
Demetz, Peter. "Literary Scholarship: Past and Future." *Comparative Literature Studies* (Urbana) 10 (1973), 364–73.
Domin, Hilde. "Das politische Gedicht und die Öffentlichkeit." *Schweizer Monatsheft* 48 (1968–69), 623–33.
———. *Doppelinterpretationen*. Frankfurt a.M. and Bonn: Athenäum, 1966.
———. *Ich will Dich. Gedichte*. Munich: R. Piper, 1970.
———, ed. *Nachkrieg und Unfrieden. Gedichte als Index 1945–1970*. Neuwied and Berlin: Luchterhand, 1970.
———. *Nur eine Rose als Stütze*. Frankfurt a.M.: S. Fischer, 1959.
———. *Rückkehr der Schiffe*. Frankfurt a.M.: S. Fischer, 1962.
———. *Von der Natur nicht vorgesehen. Autobiographisches*. Munich: R. Piper, 1974.
———. *Wozu Lyrik heute. Dichtung und Leser in der gesteuerten Gesellschaft*. Munich: R.

Piper, 1968.

Fritz, Walter Helmut. *Aus der Nähe*. Hamburg: Hoffmann and Campe, 1972.

―――. *Die Zuverlässigkeit der Unruhe. Neue Gedichte*. Hamburg: Hoffmann and Campe, 1966.

―――, ed. *Über Karl Krolow*. Frankfurt a.M.: Suhrkamp, 1972.

―――. *Veränderte Jahre*. Stuttgart: Deutsche Verlags-Anstalt, 1963.

―――. *Zwischenbemerkungen*. Stuttgart: Deutsche Verlags-Anstalt, 1964.

Fügen, Hans Norbert, ed. *Wege der Literatursoziologie*. Soziologische Texte 46. Neuwied and Berlin: Luchterhand, 1968.

Geiger, Theodor. *Aufgaben und Stellung der Intelligenz in der Gesellschaft*. Stuttgart: Ferdinand Enke, 1949.

Grass, Günter. *Ausgefragt. Gedichte und Zeichnungen*. Neuwied and Berlin: Luchterhand, 1967.

―――. *Dich singe ich Demokratie*. Neuwied and Berlin: Luchterhand, 1965.

―――. *Die Vorzüge der Windhühner*. Neuwied and Berlin: Luchterhand, 1956.

―――. *Gesammelte Gedichte*. Sammlung Luchterhand 34. Neuwied and Berlin: Luchterhand, 1971.

―――. *Gleisdreieck*. Neuwied and Berlin: Luchterhand, 1960.

―――. *Porträt und Poesie*. Neuwied and Berlin: Luchterhand, 1968.

―――. *Über das Selbstverständliche. Politische Schriften*. Neuwied and Berlin: Luchterhand, 1969.

Hädecke, Wolfgang and Ulf Miehe, eds. *Panorama moderner Lyrik Deutsch-sprechender Länder*. Gütersloh: Sigbert Mohn, 1965.

Handke, Peter. *Prosa Gedichte Theaterstücke Hörspiel Aufsätze*. Frankfurt a.M: Suhrkamp, 1969.

Hasselblatt, Dieter. *Lyrik Heute. Kritische Abenteuer mit Gedichten*. Gütersloh: Signum, 1963.

Heise, Hans-Jürgen. *Besitzungen in Untersee. Gedichte*. Hamburg and Düsseldorf: Claassen, 1973.

―――. *Ein bewohnbares Haus. Gedichte*. Frankfurt a.M.: S. Fischer, 1968.

―――. *Uhrenvergleich. Gedichte*. Hamburg and Düsseldorf: Claassen, 1971.

―――. *Vom Landurlaub zurück*. Düsseldorf: Claassen, 1975.

―――. *Vorboten einer neuen Steppe*. Dichtung unserer Zeit 16. Wiesbaden: Limes, 1961.

――― and Annemarie Zornack. *Die zwei Flüsse von Granada. Reisen durch Spanien, Nordafrika und Maderia*. Düsseldorf: Claassen, 1976.

Helms, Hans G. "Zur Phänomenologie gegenwärtiger Prosa." *Alternative* 7, 38/39 (1964), 107–12.

Heselhaus, Clemens. *Deutsche Lyrik der Moderne von Nietzsche bis Yvan Goll*. Düsseldorf: August Bagel, 1961.

Höllerer, Walter. *Der andere Gast*. Munich: Carl Hanser, 1952.

―――. *Gedichte. Wie entsteht ein Gedicht*. Frankfurt a.M.: Suhrkamp, 1964.

―――. *Systeme. Neue Gedichte*. Berlin: Literarisches Colloquium, 1969.

Holthusen, Hans Egon. *Plädoyer für den Einzelnen*. Munich: R. Piper, 1967.

Horst, Karl August. "Der Schriftsteller und seine Öffentlichkeit." *Studium Generale* 23 (1970), 698–709.

Jokostra, Peter. *Die gewendete Haut. Neue Gedichte*. Hamburg: Claassen, 1967.

―――. *Feuerzonen*. Munich: Delp, 1976.

―――. *Hinab zu den Sternen*. Neuwied and Berlin: Luchterhand, 1961.

Jünger, Friedrich Georg. *Der Ring der Jahre*. Frankfurt a.M.: Vittorio Klostermann, 1954.

―――. *Der Taurus*. Hamburg: Hanseatische Verlagsanstalt, 1937/1943.

―――. *Gedichte*. Frankfurt a.M.: Vittorio Klostermann, 1949.

―――. *Schwarzer Fluß und windweißer Wald*. Frankfurt a.M.: Vittorio Klostermann, 1955.

Keller, Hans Peter. *Auch Gold rostet. Gedichte*. Wiesbaden: Limes, 1962.

———. *Die nackten Fenster. Neue Gedichte*. Wiesbaden: Limes, 1960.
———. *Die wankende Stunde*. Wiesbaden: Limes, 1958.
———. *Extrakt um 18 Uhr. Verse Bruchstücke Prosa Spiegelungen*. Wiesbaden: Limes, 1975.
———. *Grundwasser. Gedichte*. Wiesbaden: Limes, 1965.
———. *Herbstauge. Gedichte 1960–61*. Wiesbaden: Limes, 1961.
———. *Kauderwelsch*. Wiesbaden: Limes, 1971.
———. *Panoptikum aus dem Augenwinkel*. Wiesbaden: Limes, 1966.
———. *Stichwörter Flickwörter*. Wiesbaden: Limes, 1969.
Krolow, Karl. *Alltägliche Gedichte*. Frankfurt a.M.: Suhrkamp, 1968.
———. *Aspekte zeitgenössischer deutscher Lyrik*. Gütersloh: Gerd Mohn, 1961.
———. *Ausgewählte Gedichte*. Frankfurt a.M: Suhrkamp, 1962.
———. "Das politische als das öffentliche Gedicht." *Anstösse* 1/2 (Feb. 1962), 1–19.
———. *Das Problem des langen und kurzen Gedichts-heute*. Mainz: Verlag der Akademie der Wissenschaften und der Literatur, 1966.
———. *Die Zeichen der Welt*. Stuttgart: Deutsche Verlags-Anstalt, 1952.
———. *Ein Gedicht entsteht*. Frankfurt a.M.: Suhrkamp, 1973.
———. *Fremde Körper*. Frankfurt a.M.: Suhrkamp, 1959.
———. *Gesammelte Gedichte*. Frankfurt a.M.: Suhrkamp, 1965.
———. "Manche mögen es lang." In *Unter uns Lesern*. Darmstadt: Gesellschaft Hessischer Literaturfreunde, 1967.
———. *Nichts weiter als Leben*. Frankfurt a.M.: Suhrkamp, 1970.
———. *Unsichtbare Hände*. Frankfurt a.M.: Suhrkamp, 1962.
———. *Wind und Zeit*. Stuttgart: Deutsche Verlags-Anstalt, 1954.
———. *Zeitvergehen*. Frankfurt a.M.: Suhrkamp, 1972.
Kuttenkeuler, Wolfgang, ed. *Poesie und Politik. Zur Situation der Literatur in Deutschland*. Stuttgart: W. Kohlhammer, 1973.
Leonhard, Kurt. *Moderne Lyrik. Monolog und Manifest. Ein Leitfaden*. Bremen: Carl Schünemann. 1963.
Losehütz, Gert. *Von Buch zu Buch—Günter Grass in der Kritik. Eine Dokumentation*. Neuwied and Berlin: Luchterhand, 1968.
Meckel, Christoph. *Bei Lebzeiten zu singen. Gedichte*. Berlin: Klaus Wagenbach, 1967.
———. *Der glückliche Magier*. Baden-Baden: Hans Frevert, 1967.
———. *Die Balladen des Thomas Balkan*. Berlin: Dieter Stollenwerk, 1969.
———. *Lyrik Prosa Graphik aus zehn Jahren*. Munich: Wilhelm Unverhau, 1965.
———. *Nebelhörner. Gedichte*. Stuttgart: Deutsche Verlags-Anstalt, 1959.
———. *Verschiedene Tätigkeiten. Geschichten, Bilder und Gedichte*. Stuttgart: Philipp Reclam, jr., 1972.
———. *Wen es angeht*. Düsseldorf: Eremiten-Presse, 1974.
———. *Werkauswahl. Lyrik. Prosa. Hörspiel*. Munich: Nymphenburg, 1971.
———. *Wildnisse. Gedichte*. Frankfurt a.M.: S. Fischer, 1962.
Meister, Ernst. *Die Formel und die Stätte. Gedichte*. Wiesbaden: Limes, 1960.
———. *Es kam die Nachricht. Gedichte*. Neuwied and Berlin: Luchterhand, 1970.
———. *Flut und Stein*. Neuwied and Berlin: Luchterhand, 1961.
———. *Gedichte 1932–64*. Neuwied and Berlin: Luchterhand, 1964.
———. *Sage vom Ganzen den Satz*. Neuwied and Berlin: Luchterhand, 1972.
———. *Zahlen und Figuren. Gedichte*. Wiesbaden: Limes, 1958.
———. *Zeichen um Zeichen. Gedichte*. Neuwied and Berlin: Luchterhand, 1968.
Morawietz, Kurt, ed. *Deutsche Teilung. Ein Lyrik-Lesebuch*. Wiesbaden: Limes, 1966.
Nonnenmann, Klaus, ed. *Schriftsteller der Gegenwart*. Olten and Freiburg i.B.: Walter, 1963.
Pfeifer, Martin, "Unsagbarkeit-Erlebbarkeit." *Blätter für den Deutschlehrer* 12 (1968), 14–16.
Prutz, Robert C. *Die Politische Poesie der Deutschen*. Leipzig: Otto Wigand, 1845.

Riha, Karl. *Moritat Song. Bänkelsang. Zur Geschichte der modernen Ballade.* Göttingen: Sachse and Pohl, 1965.
Rudolph, Ekkehart, ed. *Protokoll zur Person. Autoren über sich und ihr Werk.* Munich: Paul List, 1971.
Rychner, Max. *Zwischen Mitte und Rand. Aufsätze zur Literatur.* Zurich: Manesse, 1964.
Salis, Richard, ed. *Motive.* Tübingen and Basel: Horst Erdmann, 1971.
Schnurre, Wolfdietrich. *Abendländer.* Munich: George Müller, 1957.
————. *Ich frag ja bloß.* Munich: Paul List, 1973.
————. *Kassiber.* Frankfurt a.M.: Suhrkamp, 1956.
————. *Kassiber / Neue Gedichte / Formel und Dechiffrierung.* Frankfurt a.M.: Suhrkamp, 1964.
————. *Schreibtisch unter freiem Himmel.* Olten and Freiburg i.B.: Walter, 1964.
Schöne, Albrecht. *Über politische Lyrik im 20. Jahrhundert.* Göttingen: Vandenhoeck and Rupprecht, 1965.
Schwerte, Hans. "Die deutsche Lyrik nach 1945." *Der Deutschunterricht* 14/3 (1962), 47–59.
Steinitz, Wolfgang. *Deutsche Volkslieder demokratischen Charakters aus sechs Jahrhunderten.* Vol. 2. Berlin: Akademie Verlag, 1962.
Suhrkamp, Peter. "Die Aufgabe der Literatur." *Welt und Wort* 15 (1960), 175–76.
Theobaldy, Jürgen. *Blaue Flecken. Gedichte.* Reinbeck bei Hamburg: Rowohlt, 1974.
————. *Sperrsitz. Gedichte.* Cologne: Palmenpresse, 1973.
————. *Zweiter Klasse. Gedichte.* Berlin: Rotbuch, 1976.
Walser, Martin. "Engagement als Pflichtfach für Schriftsteller." In *Heimatkunde. Aufsätze und Reden.* Frankfurt a.M.: Suhrkamp, 1968.
Wellershoff, Dieter. *Literatur und Veränderung. Versuche zu einer Metakritik der Literatur.* Cologne and Berlin: Kiepenheuer and Witsch, 1969.
Weyrauch, Wolfgang. *An die Wand geschrieben.* Hamburg: Rowohlt, 1950.
————. *Bitte meiner älteren Tochter.* Vienna, Linz, Munich: Gurlitt, 1952.
————. *Das erste Haus hieß Frieden. Die SOS-Kinderdörfer Hermann Gmeiners.* Munich: Kindler, 1966.
————. *Die Spur. Neue Gedichte.* Olten and Freiburg i.B.: Walter, 1963.
————. *Etwas geschieht.* Olten and Freiburg i.B.: Walter, 1966.
————, ed. *Expeditionen. Deutsche Lyrik seit 1945.* Munich: Paul List, 1959.
————. *Gesang um nicht zu sterben. Neue Gedichte.* Hamburg: Rowohlt, 1956.
————. *Mit dem Kopf durch die Wand, Geschichten, Gedichte, Essays und ein Hörspiel.* Darmstadt and Neuwied: Luchterhand, 1972.
————, ed. *Neue Expeditionen. Deutsche Lyrik von 1960–1975.* Munich: Paul List, 1975.
————. "Was mir an mir mißfällt." *Welt und Wort* 15 (1960), 79–90.
Wiese, Benno von. *Politische Dichtung Deutschlands.* Berlin: Junker and Dünnhaupt, 1931.
Wolf, Gerhard. "Besprechungen." *Neue deutsche Literatur* 16/9 (1968), 158–70.

246

index

Karl H. Van D'Elden is professor of German at Hamline University in St. Paul, Minnesota. He holds degrees from Pennsylvania State University (B.A., 1947), Harvard University (M.A., 1948), Case-Western Reserve University (Ph.D., 1950), and William Mitchell College of Law (J.D., 1979). Van D'Elden is a frequent contributor of articles and translations to scholarly journals and is the co-author of a German reader.

The manuscript was edited by Jean Spang. The book was designed by Don Ross. The typeface for the text is Palatino, designed by Hermann Zapf about 1950. The display face is Friz Quadrata.

The text is printed on P. H. Glatfelter's Offset paper. The book is bound in Joanna Mills' Linson cloth over binder's boards. Manufactured in the United States of America.